LAND, LAW AND ENVIRONMENT

Anthropology, Culture and Society

Series Editors:
Dr Richard A. Wilson, University of Sussex
Professor Thomas Hylland Eriksen, University of Oslo

LAND, LAW AND ENVIRONMENT
Mythical Land, Legal Boundaries

Edited by
ALLEN ABRAMSON AND DIMITRIOS THEODOSSOPOULOS

Pluto Press
LONDON • STERLING, VIRGINIA

First published 2000
by PLUTO PRESS
345 Archway Road, London N6 5AA
and 22883 Quicksilver Drive,
Sterling, VA 20166–2012, USA

www.plutobooks.com

British Library Cataloguing in Publication Data
A catalogue record for this book is available from
the British Library

ISBN 0 7453 1575 5 hbk
ISBN 0 7453 1570 4 pbk

Library of Congress Cataloging in Publication Data
Land, law, and environment : mythical land, legal boundaries / edited by
Allen Abramson and Dimitrios Theodossopoulos.
    p. cm.— (Anthropology, culture, and society)
    ISBN 0–7453–1575–5 (hardback)
    1. Human geography. 2. Landscape assessment. 3. Landscape changes.
4. Land settlement patterns. 5. Land tenure—Law and legislation. I.
Abramson, Allen. II.
  Theodossopoulos, Dimitrios. II. Title. IV. Series.
  GF50.L33 2000
  304.2'3—dc21
                                                          00–009107

        09   08   07   06   05   04   03   02   01   00
        10   9   8   7   6   5   4   3   2   1

Designed and produced for Pluto Press by
Chase Publishing Services
Typeset from disk by Stanford DTP Services, Northampton
Printed in the European Union by TJ International, Padstow

CONTENTS

1 MYTHICAL LAND, LEGAL BOUNDARIES: WONDERING ABOUT LANDSCAPE AND OTHER TRACTS[1]

Allen Abramson

The treaty divided the valley between France and Spain through the centre of the plain ... But the 1660 treaty failed to define the exact territorial location of the Spanish-French boundary. Only the Treaties of Bayonne in 1866–1868 formally delimited the political boundary, as France and Spain placed border stones along an imaginary line demarcating their respective national territories ...

[However] The Treaties of Bayonne have left no trace in the memory of the Cerdans: the boundary itself – the border stones – are attributed to the earlier accord. (Sahlins 1989: XV, 294)

Traditionally, anthropologists and other social scientists have set about the analysis of land as though it were a mere setting for other things. Recently though, interdisciplinary research in the humanities has shoved land centre-stage by making the symbolisation of space central to the understanding of land relations. In texts like *Landscape: Politics and Perspectives* (Bender 1993b), *Reading Landscape* (Pugh 1990), *A Phenomenology of Landscape* (Tilley 1994), *The Anthropology of Landscape* (Hirsch and O' Hanlon 1995), *Landscape and Memory* (Sharma 1995) and, most recently, in *Archaeologies of Landscape* (Ashmore and Knapp 1999), land now begins to appear in the humanities as a resonant expanse of distinctive representations, meanings and experiences and as an important area to revisit theoretically.

Looks, maps, narratives, experiences, contestations and memories: all these features of human land relations come into sharper focus with the theoretical promotion of land as landscape. As Strang says of the Australian landscape (in this volume), landscape embeds 'history, spiritual being, aesthetic meaning, social relations and concepts of nature ...'. These studies highlight the embedded histories of the land and its populations: the ruins, traces and imprints, encrypted legacies – palimpsests (Hoskins 1985; Bender 1998: 6) – of successive and overlapping periods of meaningful habitation. How do we deal with this symbolic aspect of land relations? De we subsume it to the comparative study of landscape? Or, rather, post landscape itself as a singular land relation amongst others? This question needs to be answered unambiguously if a strong basis for comparison is to be found.

Anthropologies and archaeologies of landscape base comparison upon the variation of a human function. The latter is normally cognitive or experiential. For example, following Heidegger (1972) and Merleau-Ponty (1962), Tilley (1994) establishes the phenomenon of landscape universally out of the human experience of significant place and as a product of the phenomenological mediation of place and identity. For Hirsch (1995), by contrast, the primary basis for the establishment of a universal landscape is cognitive. For every social setting, the symbolic construction of enveloping space juxtaposes a hinterland of ancestral origins and structural possibilities with a foreground of actual forms. The cultural parameters of this juxtaposition delivers the sense of a landscape.

Linking landscape to primary human processes helps theoretically defend the symbolic study of land from utilitarian excess. However, there are reasons for caution. In the first place, landscape has to be protected not just from resource-oriented excess but also from crasser deconstructions which match landscapes to actors willy-nilly, deriving as many meaningful landscapes as actors can be found to imagine and inhabit them. Such spurious fragmentation is the theoretical effect of wishfully planting the human actor beyond the realm of *structure*. Lost on these deconstructors, is the constructed appropriateness of land as a material signifier of cultural difference in a limited range of situations.

Second, when conceptualised as the realisation of a primary human function, landscape may be too strongly opposed to features of land economy and tenure. In this theoretical juxtaposition, landscape tends to emerge as 'ideal land' with property and economy interfering as 'historical realities'. The danger here, comparatively speaking, is of conceptualising land tenure and land economy primarily as spoilers whose only significant effects are as intrusions in the Garden of Eden. In this volume, contributors have been invited to focus on property relations analytically whilst not losing sight of the different regimes of meaning in which patterns of property in land crystallise.

And, third, in rooting landscape in the cognitive and experiential mediation of place and space, there is a danger of underestimating the peculiarity of *land* and its several cosmic relations where land emerges as a cult or symbolic obsession. After all, it is not any old space which sensibly qualifies as Landscape. The constricted interior of a prisoner's cell; the entire universe of surrounding space suggested by any cosmology (i.e. Space); or the cellular view through a microscope – all these spaces are only landscapes to us in a figurative or metaphorical sense.

In this volume *land* itself has been selected for investigation not on the strength of its cognitive or experiential importance alone, but precisely because, in all of its human settings, land appears both as an object with use-value and as a symbol with meaning. Dualised land; land, 'economic and

symbolic, scarce and unlimited' (Besson, in this volume) forms the focus of
this collection. In the process, 'landscape' is adopted in its historically
restrictive rather than in its universal human sense. As such, it reappears as
the product of a quite singular relationship between a certain structure of
property and a peculiar myth of personified land.

What, then, can the comparative project be which incorporates landscape
but subsumes it, which deals the landscape card as part of a larger hand?
Mythical Lands, Legal Boundaries tackles this question by exploring the
relation between myths of land relatedness and regimes of property in land.

THE BIRTH OF LANDSCAPE

Freedom

Historical landscape emerged in the modern West in the 16th century as a
terrestrial realm of desirably invasive sights, sounds and smells, and as a
movement whose members sought to give aesthetic and moral expression
to these sensory forms. From its inception, two opposite themes lent shape
and meaning to this realm: on the one hand, a feeling of unconfined and
sublime freedom but, on the other hand, a feeling of alienation and palpable
loss. The result was then, and remains today, the discovery of a land relation,
beautifully suffused with nostalgia.

As freedom, it is clear that landscape first worked for a subject, nurtured
in confinement. Bemoaning their isolation from it, one early radical
observed: 'The English Spinner Slave has no enjoyment of the open
atmosphere and breezes of heaven' (*Black Dwarf*, 30 Sept. 1818 quoted in
Hill 1980: 14). Similarly, the industrial subjects in L.S. Lowry's paintings of
northern English cityscapes appear still imprisoned by their narrow streets
and forbidding factories even as they walk outside, stiff, bowed and blind to
the beckoning horizon of hills, which only the viewer sees.[2] Landscape's
freedom is for 'virtually a new kind of human being', wrote the utopian
socialist Robert Owen (quoted in Hill 1980: 14), a kind which negatively
learns to recognise itself by its constraints. 'We are accustomed to being
boxed up, trussed up, nailed down by the limits of our limbs (where) ... The
reach seldom exceeds the grasp' (Neve 1990: 99). Consequently, in the
landscape, 'we find a humanising influence even in the wastes where our
grandfathers could see nothing but what repelled them as savage and
ferocious' (Henry Salt, in Hill 1980: 15).

It comes as no surprise to find therefore that the arts of walking, touring,
climbing, skiing and simply being 'in the countryside' mushroomed therefore
as a passion for unconfined space itself. Viewpoints, mountain-tops and
towers were marked and enshrined, both for what they revealed of this
rambling unconfinement and for the zenith of expansive freedom their own
physical inaccessibility seemed to symbolise.[3] Where before, mountains had

loomed large as a diabolical hinterland of dangerously encircling forces, now they marvellously transformed as a sublime backdrop to free lives, seeking further freedom in the sheer, the icy and the craggy. The devils and monsters evacuated this space leaving only their names and purported traces as landmarks on the emergent landscape.

This same freedom also underscores a certain conception of the body. When medieval communities peopled the mountains with predatory monsters, they feared the margins as a tract that would colonise their bodies or consume them (Sharma 1995). These terrors were but extreme manifestations of the normal view: namely, that land, house and body formed a tangible unity and that existence was tolerable as long as the bond between tame land, house and person was strong (Gurevich 1985/1972). Landless anti-socials (such as Jews, Gypsies and outlaws) were morally suspect precisely because they were physically rootless. Normal and semi-divine bodies were rooted in strips of land or estates which formed the basis for ordered and regular lives. Houses, moreover, had to be consecrated not to prevent them falling down but to stop them becoming the very ghostly bodies of the souls who had previously occupied them.

The Renaissance, too, made a virtue out of this historic detachment and a science out of disenchanted and de-personalised things. Inside Nature still, but loftily raised to its pinnacle by the powers of Culture and Reason, human subjects found new insights – found *objectivity* – in theoretically premised transcendence. In Society, this transcendent objectivity would help deliver knowledge philosophically as freedom. On the Landscape, this same freedom would be expended, explored and aesthetically materialised.

Loss

Obversely, science and freedom were won at the expense of sensory banishment. Set in the defining context of rural enclosure, uprootedness and urbanisation, the freedom which was beautified on the historical landscape was also shaped by the subjective split in the modern subject. Consequently, the gaze directed over the landscape revelled in the freedom of the eye to roam, but it also bathed in the nostalgia of human phenomena, lost. This is why iconic landscapes in their respective national cultures have always tended to inspire wistful feelings as well as feelings of exhilaration or national pride. Salisbury cathedral, in one of Gainsborough's famous paintings of the English countryside, for example, is beautiful for being tinged by 'the magic of distance', as the French poet Baudelaire put it (cited in Pugh 1990: 4), as well as for the graceful shape of its spire. Other effective landscapes trap their arcadian subjects in an obviously mythical time. Subjects appear alongside tombs, ruins and marble gods, entangled in enveloping undergrowth which seems to wilfully absorb these contemporary figures in the primordial past. Then again, in Turner's impressionist art, the startling light captivates the onlooker not only for what it illuminates of its subjects but also for what its glare and haziness shrouds and half-conceals. Such famous light is the light of aeons as well as the light of seasons and the time of day. Elsewhere, the landscape is depicted as the appropriate place for jilted lovers to discover poetic solace (as, for instance, in Schubert's *Winterreise* cycle of songs). Similarly, having transferred much of his own power to his vengeful monster, the scientist Frankenstein finds himself condemned to a search for his lost alter ego on the harsh coldness of Alpine glaciers and the vastness of the polar ice (Shelley 1818). The beautiful but inhospitable bleakness of these fictional landscapes invites the literary invocation of extreme rupture, loss and exile.[4]

Reacting to this generic human loss, landscape subtends a strategic series of ephemeral returns to the land. These returns appear as so many temporary repairs to fractured essence, all of them as much medical as recreational and aesthetic. (In fact, the medical and the recreational fuse on the landscape with the elite invention of the Grand Tour and, after that, with the development of popular trips and holidays.) On these landscapes, the eye 'takes in' the panorama. The view 'takes away' the breath. The mouth 'drinks' or 'gulps in' the fresh air. The body 'takes to' the spa waters. Art critic Neve remarks that: 'It is as if the spirit renewed, feels itself part of everything else' (Neve 1990: 100). Moreover, even re-confined within the city, the Subject embraces a flow of 'whole foods', 'natural medicines' and 'earth religions' from the country: in fact, an entire homeopathia of curative relics, all of them apparently able to cure by returning to body and soul what has been putatively lost somewhere, somehow (Coward 1989).

Consequently, the discourse on landscape is always open to lapsarian suggestion and semi-religious awe. Indeed, landscapes seem to offer themselves up as appropriate spaces for the retrieval of religious, historic and personal memories, not so much because their earthy tangibility helps trigger memories which we have culturally archived there (Sharma 1995), but because landscape embeds in symbols mainly that which has been lost and, consequently, that which can only be retrieved precisely as recollection and memory.

Property

Historical landscape coheres around the civilisational dialectic of modernity: around freedom, pursued and won only at the expense of roots and foundations. However, the modern passion for landscape is more than just culture. Landscape also entails a definite history of property relations in which both the physical reality and collective recollection of rural dispossession lends backbone to the aesthetic and philosophical sensibility of loss.

Indeed, as an artistic movement of painting and gardening, the passion for landscape first developed in the two European countries which experienced the fastest urban development and the greatest number of exiles from the countryside: i.e. Holland and England (Colley 1996: 68). And, it was in the 16th-century Netherlands that, semantically speaking, '*landschap*' was invented (Hirsch 1995: 2). As the seaborne empires evolved, so the Dutch and English towns quickly grew (Colley 1996). The need for rural surpluses grew, land became more valuable, and so bourgeois property relations in rural land hardened and became more exclusionary. In Britain, where they were not broken up by revolutionary forces, the large estates were rationalised and enclosed. The people's rights to common land around them was violently abrogated (a situation well described for England and Scotland by Karl Marx in volume 3 of *Capital*). In the 18th century, the revolutionisation of agricultural technology led to the further displacement of the rural labour force in the direction of the towns and cities.

It was in the context of this changed structure of property relations and this polarisation of population that the new image of land cohered, and that it cohered primarily as a cultural act of urban imagining (Williams 1973). Indeed, in direct proportion to its rate of capitalisation, land on its way to becoming landscape, expanded as a site of cultural memory for those exiled and self-exiled in the towns. Landscape, in effect, was:

Fostered by instincts of an urbanised population, torn increasingly from its ancient roots in the soil by the industrial revolution ... (Theirs was) an urban existence that pushes the primeval background out of sight, that makes it remote and unavailable, that deprives people of intimate contact with it ... (Footpaths and Access to the Countryside Report, UK, 1947, quoted in Hill 1980: 13)

Similarly, in the spacious ex-colonies[5] like Australia, where the drift into the towns has proceeded more recently, landscape becomes progressively definitive of Australianness (Strang, in this volume) the more the large urban communities find themselves cut off from rural ownership, possession and occupation. 'Ironically', writes Strang, 'the romanticisation of the outback ... was generated by a greater distance between (white) people and the land.'

Moreover, to the extent that it manufactured images and experiences of the factory worker's alienation alongside the conveyor-belt of goods – recall Charlie Chaplin being sucked up by the machine in the film *Modern Times* – the memory of rural dispossession and the romanticisation of severed land is also reproduced by urban capitalist process. Indeed, wherever urban capitalism, depicted as an anti-human process seems itself to induce fractured bodies and the theft of labour power, it appears not just as a system of profits but also as the continuation and the deepening of the urban social body's estrangement from the land.

In sum, historical landscape emerged in the modern West as a palliative mediation of the dialectic of freedom and loss. Its main characteristics are not universal. Elsewhere, the articulation of different types of property relation and different mythologies of land and person prompts different visions of land and entirely different mediations. The next section explores the terms by way of which these differences may be thought.

MYTHICAL LANDS

Identity and Property: the Meaning of The Cherry Orchard

Chekhov's play *The Cherry Orchard* (Chekhov 1904) is set somewhere in Russia at the end of the 19th century, some time after the freeing of the serfs. The ageing Madame Ranevska finds that her estate no longer makes enough money to pay for its economic reproduction nor for the ludicrously anachronistic lifestyle of her family. Lopakhin, wealthy son of an ex-serf of the estate, greets the family with the news that the subdivision of the bulk of the estate into developable lots will raise enough revenue to pay off debts and preserve the place of the family in the neighbourhood. However, Madame Ranevska cannot contemplate the dismemberment of her family estate. Born there herself, her own young son is buried on the estate along with his family forebears. In fact, for all of the family, the organic bond that connects the estate, the family and its lineage seems to emanate from one special place: the cherry orchard. In it, the beautiful cycle of blossom and fruit has come to symbolise the family's nobility, rootedness and continuity. The end of the play sees Lopakhin marry one of the daughters, and take over the new property development whilst the older generation simply leaves the scene. The cherry orchard is about to be chopped down. The very oldest servant, an ex-serf, lies down, apparently to die.

As the lights fade on this scene, the audience is saddened at this picture, but not wholly so since the estate had already been reduced to a mere economy of memories. The youngest daughter is ambivalent anyway. For her, the cherry orchard is haunted by the souls of the feudal labourers who worked unfreely there. 'Throw away the keys', her young free-thinking tutor commands her, observing that she will become free of the ties which bind her to these morbid local memories. Like the serfs who have been freed before her, the free young generation will henceforth come to stand before the landscape of Mother Russia herself.

Chekhov's narrative aesthetically juxtaposes two kinds of land relation. On the one hand, it outlines the demise of a strong *relation of identity*, one which affectively bonds Madame Ranevska to her ancestors through the memories invoked by the cherry orchard. On the other hand, it focuses upon the *property relation* which Lopakhin lusts after, and which will give him the power to appropriate and subject the estate. Both of these land relations – the one finding strong moral and emotional identity with the estate, the other commercially objectifying it from a subjective distance – are culturally imagined and practically instituted. Both relations incorporate specific understandings of land, time and person, but in starkly contrasting ways.

However, the relation of identity is linked to *mythical* contexts of continuity, in which the past is inevitably embedded in the land as an inviolable substance. The property relation, by contrast, is linked to the *jural* context under whose jurisdiction the strength of each unit of property, no matter what its history, rests upon the legitimacy of contemporary mediations rather than the authority of the past. In the next section, formal properties of both of these type of land relation are further defined and explored.

Mythical Land Relations: Axes of Identity and Belonging

Modern Western landscape and the Ranevskas' cherry orchard are examples of mythically embedded lands. Both are traversed by property relations and both are subjected to use. However, in spite of this objectification, these tracts of land are brought into being as somatic and spiritual facets of the persons who associate and belong with them. Embedded links between land, people and their combined pasts create this association as a distinctive cultural fact.

Such mythical land relations may be defined ideal-typically using four criteria which seem to logically presuppose one another. These criteria are (1) relations of participation, identity and belonging; (2) the inevitable pathology of fractures; (3) the ritual reproduction of normal connections; and (4) the possession of sacred centres and diffuse or absent boundaries.

These four elements may not always be present together. And, as with the formulation of all ideal-types in social analysis, the bundling of criteria is designed not to capture the essence of a phenomenon (which is a familiar empiricist utopia), but to help guide analysis towards the discovery of credible and significant connections. As such, ideal-types are theoretical models which realise their value as much in the location of discrepancy, exception and deviation as in self-affirmation through 'the real'.

Relations of participation, identity and belonging
People associate with mythical land not as owners or citizens but as organic or spiritual components of the soil and its inner powers. As Veronica Strang says of aboriginal Australians generally: 'As hunter-gatherers, their lives were wholly bound up with the land ... their entire social and spiritual existence was mediated by the land and the ancestral beings embedded in it, whose lives they were spiritually directed to emulate.' Of the Australian Yolngu people of Northeast Arnhem Land specifically, Williams notes that their souls 'exist at focal sites on the land; they enter a foetus to animate it; they depart at death ... to a site on clan land to be able to animate another Yolngu foetus' (Williams 1986: 30). Aboriginal Australians, like many others, are thus not only descended from their land. They are reincarnated through it. 'All the generations of dead are successively transformed into country ... (and) it is through ... the country with its stores of ancestral power, that the human subject is brought into being' (Munn 1970: 148). Conse-

quently, for these autochthonous peoples and others, mythical land and its stewardship forms a critical part of their physiognomy and destiny.

Generally, where land is mythically inherited and resecured, both being and behaviour is imaginatively structured by this felt unity of land, person and ancestors. The Western Apache (in North America) inhabit a landscape which they also depict as fully inhabiting them; so that the two phenomena become 'virtually one' (Basso 1988: 122, quoted in Eves 1997: 176). Bakhtin's 'lower bodily stratum' – the late medieval lower social classes – were as rudely shaped and dispositioned as the teeming earth which was their allotted estate (Bakhtin 1966). Munn reports a Pitjantjatjara woman (in Australia) saying that 'a marking upon a particular ancestral rock at her birthplace was also on her body. The rock was the transformed body of the ancestor lying down and the marking was originally his hair' (Munn 1970: 146).

Usually, too, this mythical unity is symbolised emblematically. Besson (this volume) reports that, living in London, some Jamaican migrants pack small amounts of soil into sacks and place them in their English houses. This is Jamaican soil which is taken from the house-yards in which the family dead are buried. Subsequently, baggaged and domesticated, this soil reproduces the felt connection between expatriate life and the active ancestral spirit world which has only notionally been left behind. Fijian clansfolk observe that their male ancestral *vu* (terrestrial spirits) simultane-ously colonise their lands and their genitals (Abramson, in this volume). Additionally, the umbilical cord of every male Fijian infant is buried in the earth inside of a growing coconut, thus reproducing, against the biology of mothers, the patrilineal connection between the land of masculine ancestors and all Fijian men.

Often, indeed, it seems that, with this organic intimacy, mythical 'land owns its people' (de Coppet 1981; Williams 1986) rather than vice versa, and that these same people work very hard to ensure that their subsumption to the land and its ancestors, and their stewardship of the connections between them, holds firm against the official objectifications of law and property. As Theodossopoulos (in this volume) describes the situation for the Vassilikiots of the Greek island of Zakynthos, legal ownership may actually seem to flow more naturally and more justly from the ancestral blood, sweat and tears – the *agona* (struggle) – embodied by the land, than from jural recognition transmitted through the state.

Pathological fractures

Ruptures, fractures, uprootings, alienations: these are the root causes of the malaises precipitated by economic and political dislocations of the mythical land relation. In effect, when the ties are sundered, people weaken and land suffers. The thread connecting land, inner ancestry and externalised descendants has to remain unbroken if the collectivity is to prosper.

The urgency of this connection is politically central in nationalist cultures where, typically, a volkish 'return to the land' is a precondition of collective strength and redemption. In Europe in the 1930s, for example, Nazi ideologues equated German national decline with colonisation by landless foreign bodies: especially by Jews and Gypsies. Ideologically, and with familiar consequences, leaders of the Third Reich attempted to restore a mythical communion of Land, Blood and Nation via the sacrificial destruction of these landless bodies (Mosse 1964: 22). Paradoxically, the Jewish (though not the Gypsy) response was to reconstitute the historical potency of its own decimated nation by re-rooting the people in their putatively original land. In Israel, with the eponymous *sabra* (or prickly pear cactus) as their totem, the historic rebirth of the nation imaginarily proceeded in direct proportion to the re-colonisation and blooming of the desert.

In Indonesia, displaced from the inner forest to live by the main road running through it, and subject to the depredations of landlessness, some Sakai people have elected to return to their original land. Their declared purpose: to build a shrine to one of their shamans who would subsequently help them reinstate communication with the spirits of their ancient territory (Porath, in this volume). For these Sakai, it is the possibility of spiritual communication with the ancestors rather than ancestral embodiment (as in Fiji), that makes the possession and repossession of ancestral land important. Of displaced Gumai, another relocated Sumatran people, Minako Sakai writes:

In order to maintain their affiliation with the ancestral place, the *Jurai Tue* brings a handful of soil and the trunk of an areca nut tree (*pinang*), both of which are planted in the centre of the new village ...

Failure to maintain ties is believed to infuriate the ancestral spirits and will cause misfortune amongst their descendants. (Sakai 1997: 50, 60–1)

Cases like these indicate the anthropological possibility of a comprehensive medical economy of broken land relations.

The ritual reproduction of original connections
As Kusum Gopal points out (in this volume) mythical land relations are predominantly influenced by subjective, cyclical readings of time. These lands exist for people who inhabit worlds with recurring origins in which, as Eliade famously put it, life, time and space is constituted and regenerated about a myth of an eternal return (Eliade 1974/1949). This return is most powerfully secured in ritual practice: which is to say, formally, in performative recuperations of the power of origins. However, as Bourdieu has famously shown for the Kabyle in the Atlas mountains, it is not only these rites but also the myriad symbolic encrustations of quotidien practices associated with them (especially productive routines), which ground descendants in the soil of their ancestral origins. For the *kisans* of precolonial Uttar Pradesh in northern India,

the renewal and regeneration of the earth (and all forms of life on earth) could only be possible by submitting the body and the mind to the cues offered by nature. The *kisans* were moving among the surroundings, not as trespassers, but as participants in a steadily directed life which was theirs by habitual right: a life which went forward, day after day, allowing them to partake in its process of renewal ... (Gopal, in this volume).

Typically, therefore, the relationship which descendants have with their mythical land seems more determined by the durability of the powers and figures who originally established the relationship than with new motives and interests. Besson shows (in this volume) how ex-slaves of the Leeward Maroon polity in Jamaica reproduce the communal status of their village lands by annually cementing their common genealogical relationship to ancestors who inhabit the forest. All the key relationships are activated in a pilgrimage into the forest, which wends its way past tombs of the old warriors who fought the successful wars against plantation slavery. In this local context, therefore, it is apparent that the treatied entitlements to the Maroon commune firm up the ritual redefinition and reproduction of ancestral ties as well as merely establishing land rights.

By implication, such land rites are also person rites and, as such, frequently transform the relations between persons by ritually invoking and symbolically 'foregrounding' (Hirsch 1995: 4) their respective relations to land. It is useful to recall how in Nuerland, the one who ritually prevents or dissipates homicidal vengeance is commonly known as the leopard-skin chief but also as the earth-priest. Evans-Pritchard noted that the earth-priest would prevent fights by 'running between the two lines of combattants and hoeing up the earth here and there' (1940: 173). Furthermore, the many blood-sacrifices of livestock which the earth-priest is called upon to make in the prevention of homicidal feud are always directed at 'lower divinities of the earth' (Hutchinson 1996: 306).

Sacred centres, absent boundaries
A crucial quality of mythical land is the fuzziness or absence of boundaries. Manifest boundaries are often symbolically dissolved in the latent reversals of ritual time. Consequently, even where mythically imagined lands are legally delineated on paper, their boundaries and borders will tend to be weak. How, then, are mythical lands geometrically ascertained?

Principally, by way of their sacred centres. Centres may be stopping places on migration tracks (e.g. Munn 1970; Layton 1995: 218), sites of important past events, places of recurrent ritual practice, historical monuments. At their centres, mythical lands are precise, strong and uncontestable whereas beyond, definition wanes (Strang 1997: 257–8). In fact, like ripples working their way centrifugally from the spot where a pebble has been thrown into water, the extremities of mythical land are physically indeterminate. Consequently, on the margins, land claims tend to be vociferously pursued in direct proportion to the impossibility of substantiating them. Hence, the ubiquity and intractability of border disputes which, though they may actually appear to spring from weaknesses in the law, are much more likely to emanate from the intrinsic unboundedness of mythically underlying lands.

Stonehenge, to give one topical British example, is one of the sacred centres of the British landscape, functioning as a site of intensive national as well as druidic worship (Bender 1993a: 245–79, 1998). As the sacred centre of lands past as well as lands present, it is the centre of a mythically cumulative landscape whose margins are undefinable. Of which land is and was Stonehenge the sacred ritual centre? Wessex? England? Britain? Europe? The World (representatives of whose far-flung reaches constantly make the pilgrimage to the stones and the Heritage Centre)? We can never be perfectly sure. Who should own Stonehenge and its surrounding lands? Tourists? Druids? National Heritage? The British Army? We cannot convincingly say. There seem to be as many landscapes with Stonehenge at their centre as there are groups who define a British or English landscape for themselves (including UNESCO's World Heritage committee). We may want to theorise this pluralism as an expression of human difference, or as the cultural extension of 'power-filled' social space (Massey 1995, cited in Bender 1998: 38). However, it may also useful to locate such prismatic fragmentation in the *shared* notion of Stonehenge being the centre of a mythical landscape with indeterminate provenance and unempirical boundaries.

In not disclosing boundaries, Stonehenge is similar to the old villages and clan lands in contemporary Fijian chiefdoms (Abramson, in this volume). Additionally, championed by the Green organisations described by Burnham, Durman, Strang and Theodossopoulos in this volume, the environment also forms an expanse which is regularly centred by spectacularly demonstrative protests but which has no clear boundaries itself: only a dense matrix of ecosystemic connections. On the Malay-Indonesian border, displaced Sakai set up a sacred shamanic centre on land in the forest which they hope to reclaim as property but whose actual shamanic parameters stretch outwards beyond their plot to an indeterminate circumference, deep within the old Sakai forest. Jamaican expatriates in London carry their native land over its legal national boundaries in sacks, whilst their Rastafarian countrymen find both baggaged Jamaica in London and jural Jamaica in The Caribbean to be fallen provinces of the greater Land of Babylon (Besson, this volume). Finally, Louise Perrotta shows how, still tied to the sacred centres of Ukrainian Sovietism, bureaucratic managers are only able to institute the legal shell of private property in land in the Ukrainian countryside. Even where Ukrainian farmers are provided with clear certification of their individual property rights, they are not equipped with the means of bounding any particular area within the collective farms of which they remain members. This private property is then quintessentially mythical.

JURAL LANDS

Property can, of course, be defined *naturally*: in which case, it is defined to coincide with the universal fact of possession. It can also be defined *practically* as being primarily a social relation between persons with respect to objects. In this volume property – and property in land, in particular – is *culturally* defined. Following Weber (1922), Humphreys (1985) and Hann (1998), property is defined here primarily as a jural element of formal legal codes, but also as a localised notion arising out of 'the institutional and cultural contexts within which such codes operate' (Hann 1998: 5). This option enables the social theorist to mark and highlight the strongest differences – where they are thought to exist – between uncodified land relations of a mythical type, and land relations officially codified initially to register and strengthen possession. The aim is not to pose a universal dichotomy in fact, but to find adequate concepts for investigating the articulation of land relations of identity and relations of property in different contemporary settings.

Given this starting point, it is useful to define jural land ideal-typically, according to a model in four parts. These parts are: (1) the imagined split between owner and owned; (2) the latent transferability of property in land; (3) reproduction of rights through the irreversibility of jural outcome; and (4) the definitive nature of legal boundaries. Once again, defined theoretically as an ideal-type, the model of a jurally defined property relation in land guides analysis pragmatically towards the elucidation of possible and likely connections rather than towards the confirmation of human or historic inevitabilities.

Owner and Owned: Law and the Subject/Object Split

As a relation of ownership, the property relation implies a hierarchical relation of subjects *over* objects and, before that, logically, the physiognomic separation of owner and owned. Culturally speaking, therefore, ownership presumes disenchanted, disembodied land.

Precisely because the culture of property implies and shapes a dissociative relation, a property only really comes into being with the effective exclusion of other persons. Louise Perrotta (in this volume) offers a case in point. On collective farms in the contemporary Ukraine, individual families are granted certificates proving private ownership of land. To the extent, though, that the Ukrainian state forbids the leasing or sale of these lands, and makes the demarcation and repressive protection of private plots impossible, it is evident that the state seeks neither to exclude itself nor other citizens from participating in the control of this property. Private property will never be established in the Ukrainain countryside until the state creates structures which guarantee exclusion as well as jural attachment.

Generally speaking, for property to exist, it has to exist as an exclusive relation of control over an object which others could just as well possess precisely because, relationally, there is nothing intrinsically personal between a property and its current owner.

Transferability

When land speculators, for example, identify with land, they identify not with the substantive nature or history of the land but with its transferability. Indeed, land ownership for speculators finds its epiphany in the transformation of the tangible land into the paper tokens which legally certify its ownership and which economically express its worth. More generally, where land jurally appears as propertied wealth, it tends to yield its commercial or political value irrespective of its ownership. This is in stark contrast to the performance and valorisation of mythical land, whose qualities are usually strongly dependent upon the definite identity of the owner and upon the integrity of the organic or spiritual bond connecting land, ancestor and descendant.

Because of this independence, propertied land may be safely alienated. The land will continue to perform for its new owner, whilst the old owner is unlikely to suffer adverse consequences. By contrast, where strongly ancestral land is transferred to non-descendants, the danger of mystical come-back is ever-present and transfers tend to be reversible and temporary. Annette Weiner showed that one of the major motifs of Trobriand funerals is the return of widely distributed affinal usufruct rights to the dead man's matriclan (Weiner 1976: 137–68).

Law and Linear Time: the Irreversibility of Property Rights

Mythical land relations are ritually reproduced in the course of reversible time. Consequently, current boundedness is ambiguous and unstable. By contrast, jurally instituted, property relations in land are embedded in the stream of linear time, as the outcome of irreversible legal events and processes. In particular, previous ownerships no longer play a role in determining the behaviour of their propertied successors or antecedents. Each change of ownership takes place as an event, disconnected from all others.

Moreover, even where, jurisprudentially speaking, property rights in land are enunciated as divine reward for improvements made to God's earthly estate (see Durman and Burnham in this volume), this property is defended jurally in God's name not through God's jural reincarnation. In general, the gods of law are gods of linear time. Moreover, even where the law recognises and underwrites 'traditional' tenure, the law codifies 'tradition' framed as a system of customary property rights rather than as an affective relation of belonging (Abramson, Burnham, Strang, in this volume). The jural codification of 'tradition' therefore sets up the possibility of future transfers in ownership even where protecting vulnerable communities from wholesale land alienation is the initial motive. In fact, recourses to history and tradition in court are radically different to the evocation of the past in ritual. Whereas in ritual, the past is invoked to summon up ancestral powers in the interests of providing a continuous line of mediation with the present, the jural past is always invoked either as precedent to better illuminate the present, or as genealogy to establish the disconnections inherent in any particular current claim to ownership.

Indeed, illumination, clarification and decidability are of the essence in matters of law and property. Thus, land law, in effect, ideally transcends ambiguity, supplying principles which wave aside the undecideable. Indeed, law, generally, may be defined as an idealistically unambiguous and coherent body of rules which are enforced to sustain the totality of values and principles, pertaining to society as a whole. The essentially ambiguous quality of mythical boundaries consequently cuts no ice with the law. And, as Gopal (in this volume) puts it in relation to Indian caste relations, whereas in precolonial times caste and village land relations were not immutably tied together, colonially, caste as the fundamental principal for defining identity and relations of individuals within society, was fixed and bound by a tightly structured matrix of significations. This bears out Merry's observation that customary law was transformed through the colonial impact from being 'a subtle, adaptable, and situational code to a system of fixed and formal rules ... abstracted and disembodied ... ' (Merry 1992: 365, quoted in Harris 1996: 3). Is it possible that the repeatedly noted flexible character of 'customary land law' is due to custom's own cultural embeddedness in lands with mythically fluid or absent boundaries?

Jural Lands, Boundaries and Measurable Area

Property not only presupposes the ontological separation of present from past, owner and owned. It also entails the separation of tracts of land from one another. Separated by boundaries, propertied tracts are mapped, measured and, if not physically, then at least conceptually, enclosed. As a consequence, these tracts come to possess definite area. In fact, jurally, propertied lands must possess precisely defined boundaries and area.

Fixed and effective boundaries do not rely upon maps for their practical existence. The former can be marked out concretely on the ground with the help of posts, ditches, hedges and fences. However, the converse is not true. Maps mark out the relative size and position of bounded areas in space. And, for this representation to be possible, places and spaces must be representable in terms of intrinsic boundaries and stable extremities. In which case, it is clear that maps used for the purposes of navigation and survey come into being culturally, once propertied land relations begin to prevail over mythical relations and when, consequently, spatial boundaries are no longer thought of as fluid epiphenomena, in ritual time and space. In effect, maps capture boundaries once boundaries freeze in linear time, and once sacred centres become less definitive of a given tract than the identity of its current boundaries and owners. Indeed, Bender (1998: 108) stresses the importance of 'a changing technology of power' not only to 'refinements in surveying and mapping' in the modern West but also, strikingly, to 'the redefinition of property'. Olweg (1996) concludes that this new technology of power:

created geometrical, divisible, and hence saleable space by making parcels of property out of lands that had been previously been defined according to rights of custom and demarcated by landmarks and topographic features. (Olwig 1996, in Bender 1998: 108)

A new technology of power, a redefinition of property and a market: but, just as crucially, the subjective disembedding of human being from the land and its transformation into an object of mathematical scrutiny.

THE ARTICULATION OF JURAL AND MYTHICAL LANDS

The aesthetic poignancy of *The Cherry Orchard* springs from the fact that summer villas (property) are wholly to replace the cherry orchard (myth) in a linear sequence which completely juxtaposes these contrasting relations. Separated by the passage of time, the paired opposition of land relations becomes metaphorically pegged to the process of human ageing and to the juxtaposed succession of generations. And, in using 'history' in this deliberately ambiguous way, the play wilfully aims at art rather than history. Consequently, what Chekhov says about the juxtaposition of land relations is, from the standpoint of lived history, an appropriate aesthetic distortion.

However, as Louise Perrotta reminds us in her contribution to this volume, working with binaries to mirror true history is unhelpful. In most real-life situations, land relations are built up out of a combination of jural and mythical factors, so transcending the ideal-typical purity imagined for them in certain forms of text. Do these polarities exist at all then? They do, but not in any simple sense. Thus, in probably every social setting, the lived hybridity of 'the real' is paralleled by purposively disaggregated mental scenarios which, in their abstraction, are good for thinking the real (Lévi-Strauss 1970). In mythical narratives, legal codes, aesthetic forms (like *The Cherry Orchard*), political ideologies and discursive theorisings (like parts of this Introduction), lands of myth and lands of property may be brought into opposition with each other in their purest forms. As they do so, these idealisations pass powerful comment upon 'the real', ensuring that actual complexity – 'lived' as opposed to 'thought' reality – is experienced as an articulation and reduction of ideal-types rather than as a random entanglement of historical factors.

Given the worldwide spread of international law in the 20th century, this palpable hybridity of the lived is now germane. Indeed, it can be safely said that (1) there is no contemporary tract of land, sea or space which is not jurally subsumed and/or legally owned in some way (except perhaps for no-man's-land which is unowned but jurally subsumed); and that (2) there is no adult human actor on the contemporary planet who does not have a mythical relation with some tract of land or other. Unlike the forms of thought reality therefore, lived reality exhibits partial combinations of land myth and land law, variable articulations of land rites and land rights, and singular interpenetratations of property and identity.

In this volume four sorts of articulation are explored. These are (1) the jural dominance over mythical lands; (2) the mythical embeddedness of legal boundaries; (3) the dominion of mythical systems over jural realms; and (4) the mythical embeddedness of jural practices. These hybrid conditions are summarised below.

The Jural Dominance over Mythical Lands

Jural dominance over mythical lands occurs where the reproduction of mythical land relations, such as they remain, occurs primarily through the courts and in legal terms. Jural dominance eats into the integrity of organic land-bound identities, making them vestigial. A good case of jural dominance *not* being achieved (which helps elucidate the point) was in colonial Fiji where, though bureaucratically defined and managed from above, the new colonial culture of land law never developed grassroots. Instead, ritualised relations with the embodied ancestors, rather than relations with the disembodied bureaucracy, continue to this day to dominate and frame local understandings of land distribution and ownership.

Gopal, by contrast, intimates that the colonial transformation of mythical land relations in Uttar Pradesh in northern India was complete, and that affective participations with the spiritual substance of the village lands culturally fell away. Why was this? It was because the colonial invention of land ownership by caste led to the rigidification of caste membership in social and religious life. The freezing of the old spiritual channels deprived a large proportion of the untouchable *kisan* population of access to land with which they would previously have had direct spiritual access. This condemned them to low caste status, and to dependence upon the political and legal systems for redress. Fighting for land rights in and out of the courts (with the law against the law) became a local necessity, and it was this enforced legalism which guaranteed the generalised dominance of a culture of property in matters related to land. For different reasons, but with the same result, Sakai people of Sumatra rendered themselves landless by selling their legal entitlements to land to would-be farmers so that they might enter the money economy and cloak themselves with the purchasable trappings of 'development' (Porath, in this volume). In doing so, most Sakai ruptured their lines of communication with their forest-bound ancestors, opted out of the ritualised 'flow of life' in the forest (Fox 1980) and became dependent upon the law for any access to land, wealth or redress.

In contemporary Australia aboriginal groups are *obliged* to approach the courts to establish land rights. Establishing these is important both in order to win back a degree of economic control over their territories and to inspire recognition of their primordial primacy on the national landscape. The dominance of the courts in matters relating to the ratification of land-relatedness means that, often with anthropological aid, clansfolk are both able and obliged to translate mythical categories into legal terms. Ancestral tracks and ritual sites become the basis for drawing up boundaries, whilst spiritual guardianship transposes as legal ownership. As Strang points out, though this jural subordination is oppressive, the liberal dominance of the contemporary courts does in fact begin to reverse the primitivist logic as well as the brute facts of Australian colonialism. However, unlike in Uttar Pradesh, the jural *mis*representation of true aboriginal land relations still bequeaths the ancestral dreaming strong local authority. Amongst closely inter-marrying clans, for example, legal terms of ownership by clan may well be heavily compromised by mythically embedded tenets of reciprocity and co-guardianship.

In fact, like a blanket thrown on a fire, true jural dominance starves ritualised land relations of their mythic oxygen, reducing them to mere ethnic markers. This normally happens, as we have just seen, where, for whatever reason, local groups themselves contract into the jural process in search not only of legal title but also of practical guarantees (i.e. policeable property relations). This far down the road, cultural bridges are crossed. By contrast, where the dominance of jural processes is reflected at the local level mainly in modern idiom, the ritual reproduction of the land relation continues beneath the legal umbrella.

The Mythical Embeddedness of Legal Boundaries

Where land law bears down heavily, the landscape assumes a characteristically broken appearance. Enclosures proliferate. Boundary posts, fences, stone-walls, wires, hedgerows, dikes and ditches physically close off separate areas as properties. However, just how strong property 'on the ground' is depends upon the cultural embeddedness of these boundaries.

Displaced Sakai and lower-caste *kisans* (Gopal, Porath, in this volume) experience intense exclusion because they themselves have embraced axioms of the national legal culture to which they were forcibly subordinated. In different settings though, legal boundaries are more porous, more disputable and, often, more rescindable than their bounded inhabitants suggest. Ownership rights over patriclan land in the Fijian forest, for example, are never as exclusive as they are either officially inscribed or locally recounted. Requests for reciprocal access always override protestations of trespass. This occurs because, in much-repeated oral history and ritual practice, the primordial unity of all clans with their land (as 'the flesh of the land') categorically overrides the indigenous and jural differentiation of land and village by clanship.

Theodossopoulos in his contribution to this volume shows how the jural definition of landownership on the Greek island of Zakynthos is less central in legitimating and reproducing land rights than local narratives, the latter historically underpinned by threats of local force. This is in large part because landownership not only promises economic gain in Zakynthos, it also passionately subtends the desire to preserve the civil autonomy, which was locally won by farmers' grandparents in their land battles against post-feudal patrons. Both the memory of this bitter struggle and the autonomy won by their grandfathers is enshrined by this soil and transmitted along with it. Of course, the liberal Greek state does constitutionally offer to protect both land and liberty through law, but only in exchange for the normal concessions on local sovereignty demanded by the nation-state. However, because they tie their land rights primarily to their defining story of human land and freedom rather than the grand narrative of the Greek state, Vassilikiot farmers reject the state's Green defence of the turtles which happen to breed on their beaches! For Vassilikiot farmers, land law is but an official seal on their family stories of agony and justice. Similarly, writing of the Jamaican Maroon's attitude towards their legal rights to the commune and its forest hinterland, Besson (in this volume) observes: 'From the colonial viewpoint, the treaty ceded land rights to a marginal wilderness reservation designed to confine the rebel slaves. However, from the maroon perspective this legal document became a sacred charter of corporate identity reflected in the commons.'

In these situations legal boundaries persist but, because they are culturally embedded in mythical realms, they remain practically vestigial. And, it is precisely in these situations that top-down jural efforts to change land tenure nearly always fail (also see Burnham and Perrotta in this volume).

The Dominion of Mythic Systems over Jural Lands

The previous section briefly examined the fate of legal boundaries which are sown on mythical soil. Sometimes, though, the force of mythical conceptions is actively brought to bear upon propertied reality. In these circumstances, the boundaries to latent properties may never actually appear.

Thus, Louise Perrotta (in this volume) observes how, in the Ukraine today, the initiation of private property in land lags far behind its appearance on the statute books, as bureaucratic power is both unable and unwilling to foster real transition (see also Verdery 1998). Rural collectivism still materially prevails in the Ukraine and, consequently, private property in land remains a jural ideal. Perrotta shows that the helmsmen of this transition fear the 'fragmentation' of land and the decentralisation which will write them off as a class. They cling to an image of bureaucratic holism, beyond or outside of which, they can see only chaos and decline. Perhaps, too, beyond the retention of raw power, bureaucratic holism and historically collectivised land also derives its durability from an imagined debt to the collectivising ancestors of Marx, Engels, Lenin, Stalin and the heroic military dead of the Nation. In the rural Ukraine, consequently, the legislative realm unfolds within a mytho-administrative bubble, haunted by the collapsing, creaking unity of ancestral memories and presences. (To be fair to her, I must note that Perrotta only hints at this level of cultural embededdness; for post-1991 Russia and Hungary, Hann [1998: 18] is much more explicit.) Durman (in this volume) also draws our attention to an entirely different setting wherein newly constructed properties (e.g. roads; airport runways) are invaded and boundary-lines refused, all in the name of a relatively recent mythical land: the environment. The nature of this important land is discussed in the last section.

The Mythical Embeddedness of Jural Practices

There is a second sense in which jural land relations may be mythically embedded, at source so to speak, in the philosophical grounding and heroic foundation of legal codes and systems.

   Thus, to be authoritative, all law requires philosophical grounding or an heroic charter (or both), furnishing practicionners with both the inspiration to practice and with 'last instance' authority. Springing from God, Nature, temporal law-givers (such as Hamurabi) or from the Romans, the authority of origins tends to lodge symbolically in key institutions – in courts, law schools and centres of jurisprudence – where legal activity takes place under the sculpted and monumental gaze of in-house founders and heroes. These are sites indeed where the re-sanctification of jural authority occurs through the repeated scholarly invocation of the legal gift-givers and the philosophic ancestors. In this context, too, normally conducted in special garb and in extraordinary language, the perennial recourse to discursive ancestors sustains the essential ability of law to cut through knots of intractability and to disambiguate the ill-defined. All in all, the mythical embeddedness of its discourse and the ritualised invocation of its origins are necessary supports to the specifically jural project of promoting normative order through discursive disambiguation – and force!

   In this volume several authors (Burnham, Durman, Strang, Abramson) have highlighted the colonial construction of 'waste' lands (Australia) and 'vacant' lands (Fiji), lands which, to colonial thinking, were essentially deemed to be unowned because they were seen to be unbounded. Strang (in this volume) quotes one white colonist in Australia in 1781 who opined of the aboriginal hunter-gather mode: 'In this vagrant life men have scarce any connection with land more than ... the air they breathed or the water they drank ... '. Such 'waste' and 'vacant' territory was surveyed, codified, transmuted into Crown or state land and redistributed to settlers as property to 'develop'. Why, or how, was this dispossession morally sustained? There was, of course, the political rationale of administrative expediency. However, the comforting proximity of influential philosophy also served to render this expediency morally defensible to its executors. Thus, Durman in his contribution to this volume emphasises the importance of John Locke's *Treatise on Property* in supplying an enlightened basis upon which the as-yet uncolonised margins might be morally appropriated in the cause of empire and development. For Locke, 'development' meant the productive improvement of pristine Nature according to God's will on this earth. Consequently, so long as it was predicated upon the systematic investment of productive labour, the human urge to acquire property rights in land and enclose it emerged as an extension of God's purpose. Property in land was thus humanly just. In this way, embedded in Locke's myth and without precedent to rely upon, colonial land law found against native relations of economic intimacy and spiritual belonging in favour of settler enclosure, technical dominion and appropriation. (Similar thinking to Locke's crassly resurfaces every time a Scottish estate owner habitually defends the enclosure of the grouse moors in terms of stewardship and protection.)

Having said all this, it has to be stressed that, heroic charters notwithstanding, the ideal certainties of law are just that: viz. ideals. In his book *The Mythology of Modern Law*, Fitzpatrick (1992) brilliantly shows how modern law is never transcendent but always jostled, contradicted, compromised and forced back on the interpretative flexibility of its own discourses. This happens because of the interpolation of law within a 'real' world which, the counter-evidence of legal practice shows, is actually untranscendable and, in the final analysis ambiguous.

THE DEATH OF THE LANDSCAPE?

But what happens, structurally speaking, with a change in the mythical premise? What happens to the culture of land-based property, and to property in land itself, once the technical transformation of land ceases to be underpinned by a divine mission or by human proclivities? These questions are of fundamental topical importance in the modern West.

From Sovereignty to Survival

States, NGOs, media, conservationist lobby groups (such as the Worldwide Fund for Nature), pressure groups (such as Greenpeace) and a host of other ideological organs at the heart of 'global civil society' have all, to vastly differing extents, begun to address the ecological impact of policy and practice. Implementing best practice or avoiding having to do so, political states now release a stream of Green rhetoric for public consumption which, sincere or not, still succeeds in fuelling cultural change generally, and even in lending encouragement to the activist margins.

The most common response of the centralised polities is legalistic. Their characteristic response is to impose laws, quotas and regulatory bodies from above. Such top-down legalism is often as politically expedient as it is structurally ineffectual, side-stepping as it usually does, the question of popular consent. There is a sense, too, in which, exported to alien contexts, the utopian quality of some Green thinking blinds policy-makers to emergent indigenous possibilities. In this volume, Burnham shows how, in modern Cameroon, naïvely romantic notions of primary rainforest and traditional livelihoods hopelessly underestimate the historical and structural complexity of indigenous systems of property and land use. Neither the old colonial legacy of a legally homogeneous body of forest 'traditions', nor new conservationist mythologisations of primordial links between people and forest, properly tune in to realities which are readily detectable by the ethnographer. In a revealing case study, Theodossopoulos (in this volume) also shows how, in addressing the plight of the rare loggerhead turtle, the Greek state fails through the force of law to brush aside the established land rights of Vassilikot farmers. Nourished by their distinctive mythology of the origin of their land rights, farmers resist Green enforcement by pre-emptively building touristic structures, near the turtles' breeding sites.

By contrast, for all its *illegality*, Green activism, directed against the technological despoliation of local Western ecosystems, seems to make striking inroads into the popular Western imagination (see Durman, in this volume). In spite of its apparent failure to stop a majority of projects from going ahead, the strong imagery and histrionic tactics of militant ecopolitics provides a highly resonant and effective ideological politics of symbolic practice. There is no symbolic magic here, of course, but something tangible to work with right from the outset: namely, a civil society, ambiguously positioned in relation to science, technology and Nature, and unknowingly caught halfway between the waning authority of power/knowledge and the rapid rise of media power.

What exactly is the nature of the environment which stars in this political theatre? What new land relations does the latter begin to imply? Three coordinates seem to fix the environment's cultural position, also helping explain its rapid cultural and political rise in the West. First, though impressively effective locally and in the short term, most modern technologies are nonetheless perceived to be heavily unpredictable globally in the longer term. Mythologically expressed, the possibility of a high-tech order is countenanced in which nuclear power and other technologies take a Frankensteinian turn and are ready to wreak havoc on the environment. Once upon a time, new technology seemed to produce sharp, localised impact. Now, by contrast, technological interventions seem diffuse in their impact, seem to ramify uncontrollably, and, worst of all, seem to vengefully rebound on their beneficiaries (as with the much-cited Gaia effect: Lovelock 1979).

In the second place, the powerful authority delivered to scientific knowledge by philosophy since the Enlightenment has declined. The efficacy of power/knowledge is waning and the very relationship between knowledge and things, subject and objects, knowledge and worldly action has become culturally problematic. In particular, the idea that knowledge brings control over Nature is cast into serious doubt. Popularly, positive totalising knowledge begins to be culturally replaced by surplus flows of information and useful bits of communication.

In the third place, a new humanism has begun to cohere on the grounds of the new dialectic. In response to the widespread feeling that the effects of high technology are unknowable and uncertain, and that science cannot be positive, systematic postmodernism prompts human subjects to refuse the emasculations of representation by voicing intrinsic 'difference'. On the other hand, opposing – or maybe complementing – the near-religious worship of human difference, Green thinking insists on 'One planet, one ozone layer, one global ecosystem!', so making the survival of the planet and its species a prior condition for the reproduction of human cultural difference.

Green consciousness is, thus, of crucial cultural importance in the West because of the way in which it tempers the celebration of autonomy and difference with the discovery of a common human vulnerability to dangerous Nature. This is the context in which new land relations of identity and newly conceptualised relations of property in land are emergent. What are these new relations? Where is Landscape amongst them?

Mythical Land Relations and Legal Boundaries in the World of High Technology

A three-way cultural contrast between *historical* landscape and *historical* environment helps answer these questions. Thus:

Contrast 1   Landscape cohered as a passion for land and space, as land became increasingly distant and as human nature felt increasingly fractured. Green consciousness, by contrast, arrives to re-position human being inside Nature as a united and integral species. Whereas enlightened humanity saw itself as having rationally transcended the instinctual unreason of other species, Green humanity anthropologically defines itself with these species, interacting organically with them for the benefit of the whole environment. Moreover, where Landscape staged these species as part of an essentially moral tableau for a watching human audience, environment incorporates human beings as *dramatis personae*. In effect, the environment draws other species out as it pulls humans in, creating a re-valued, interactive middle-ground in the process. This environment is new mythical land.

Contrast 2   Historical Landscape belongs to the epoch of subjective detachment and the positive knowledge of Nature and its object-world. By contrast, Green consciousness espouses knowledge as a fallible and provisional activity for which the only true certainties seem to be the eternally problematic nature of truth, progress and survival. Consequently, in the environment the power of human agency to control history and Nature seems drastically reduced. In effect, appearing as a well-positioned receiver of messages and relayer of signals, Green agency unravels as Nature's intelligently reflexive self-consciousness, discharging its responsibilities as those of ecological *stewardship* rather than cultural *governance*. In the land of the environment the large-scale technological transformation of Nature still proceeds, though now nearly always greeted by the well-publicised opposition of eco-militants, Green radicals, NGOs and relevant government ministries. In some Green philosophy, enslaved Nature herself seems to join this Luddite rebellion.

Contrast 3   As a sensory phenomenon, the Landscape is to be 'taken in', its lost wholeness fleetingly and nostalgically recaptured over a range of strategic practices. Landscape is, in these senses, the other half of ruptured modern being, its signified expansiveness being clearly the appropriate place narcissistically to seek out lost selves, past histories and repressed memories. In order to address the problem of human survival, by contrast, Green consciousness aims at a broader altruism.

Thus, dietary systems have altered to register a moral transition. Moral vegetarianism mushrooms and meat-eating whitens. Organic methods flourish in a symbolisation of both the moral symbiosis of species and a serious distaste for continuing physico-chemical intrusions into the 'natural' ecosystem. Key species, hugely loaded with anthropomorphic symbols (e.g. whales) disappear from the killable-eatable register. Expressions of kinship and affinity with, or courtship of, other species is proscribed. Alliance, too, as in the recent case of a supermarket brand of roast ham that bore the slogan: 'Animal Welfare through Partnership' (the labelling carried out, of course, by the senior living partner.)

Nowadays, too, many travellers make pilgrimages to see whales, rainforests, turtles and other rare species in their wild habitats. These pilgrimages passionately demonstrate newly emergent quasi-kinship relations with animals and also begin to exercise the benign calling of a compassionate stewardship. Swimming with dolphins (and, in one notable case in the north-east of England, entering into presidential relations with them), recently formed the basis for popular eco-pilgrimages off the UK coastline. In the Red Sea, in Israel, such swims are managed and are actually termed 'interactions'. And, not just visiting rainforests, but joining conservationist projects to protect them, has become a normal holiday activity. Saving seals from hunters and oil-splattered seabirds makes for high-profile newscasting. Whilst, in the new age, North American hunter-gatherers and Tibetan lamas have both become exemplary Green icons, the former offering a primitive model of reciprocity with hunted animals, the latter a design for modern living which includes the refusal to kill even the tiniest of creature. In effect, these ingestions, trips, courtships and ethnic borrowings represent so many altruistic extensions of a new human morality to non-human creatures and a virtual zoologisation of the residual human subject.

These new ethical practices place human beings on the inside of Nature's moral sphere as interactive species rather than transcendent beings. Consequently, symbolic expressions of exteriority and dominance are persistently attacked. This, for example, is the case with fox-hunting in the UK which has become politically central not only because the fox is ritually humiliated but because the hunt blasts out a celebration of the squirearchical traditions of lordship and dominance over dogs, horses, fox and lowly people: in fact, over the interactive elements of all of Nature. In effect, the traditional hunt in the UK feudalises Nature at the same time as Green thinking has begun radically to democratise it. In the process, the fox is symbolically reprieved from the unkind corpus of previous mythology, to be coopted as a hero of the new Green politics. It is interesting and perhaps not altogether accidental that all the while this symbolic rectification of Reynard has been proceeding, townsfolk have been buying up places in the country whilst the fox has moved into town!

Protesters against the building of a new runway at Manchester Airport totemised intimate relations with other species by nicknaming themselves after the natural forms they defend (Durman, this volume). More widely amongst UK Ecowarriors, Swampy and Muppet Dave (the Muppets, of course, being cuddly TV animals) and others palpably adopt the grain and texture of the Environment in their bodily politics, tacking themselves onto the ecosystem in ways that symbolically exaggerate, as they aptly express, the emergent land relation. Protesters take to tree-houses, chain themselves to trees, tunnel deep inside the earth, making techniques of identification with the Environment double-up as tactics in its defence. Moreover, non-violent themselves, these protestors provocatively make their own removal conditional upon official acts of violence and, in this theatrical way, make their own politics mimic the predicament of the vulnerable species which are physically embraced by the protest. In the world of the Green land relation moreover, Durman argues, technology itself has to be functionally redefined from being the external instrument of domination *over* Nature to being an organ of Nature itself. Technology has to work in, with and as an organic extension of Nature, no longer merely as reified *techne*. Moreover, in this political theatre of protest, the organisation of the Manchester Airport runway protest was run on strictly libertarian grounds, mirroring inside the protesting human group, the reciprocal relations ideally to be instituted between humans and other species. In other words, element by element, this theatre of protest unfolds as a symbolic microcosm of the new mythical land relation.

CONCLUSION

The image of a new Green land relation works itself diffusely into Green consciousness, discourse and protest. Its genesis corresponds with the growing
urbanisation of the Western countryside (Williams) and with the contem-
poraneous shrivelling of modern alienation. Urban capitalist experience in
the West, indeed, is no longer necessarily chartered by a history of land dispossession, rural exile and self-estrangement. Instead, rather than being seen
as an epochal destination, the high-tech town is reframed an historic starting
point: indeed, as a base-camp for launching expeditions from the uncertain
world into which Westerners find themselves 'thrown'. (This is, perhaps, the
most basic meaning which we can sensibly attribute to the term
'postmodern'.) More particularly, the historic redefinition of the countryside
from being the womb of the town to being its green-field overspill marks the
key context in which Landscape begins to mutate categorically into
Environment.

Thus, Environment is not a place to which we return (since we now feel
that we have never left it), which we need not 'take in' (since we are already
inside it), and which does not really symbolically articulate and spatially
extend our freedom (since it is not our freedom but our and other species'
survival which is at issue). So then, in the wake of the death of its Subject
(Foucault 1970), is Landscape actually dead, killed off by Environment? Not
in any literal sense, of course. The aesthetic need for wild and open space,
and the cultural fascination with spatially objectified history, memory and
identity, endures. However, these phenomena become progressively
subsumed as specialised planes of mythical Environment. Whilst still aesthetically compelling, iconic landscapes come to focus less upon receding
horizons (evocative of our nostalgia), and more upon those receding habitats
and dwindling species whose arresting demise compounds our senses of
anxiety, urgency and will to protect. This anxiety does not rule out beauty
though, since, as one of the American astronauts recently put it: 'My
experience on Apollo 8 helped me to see how isolated and fragile our earth
really is. It was also beautiful' (Frank Borman quoted from the *Guardian
Weekend*, February 5 2000). The beauty of this mythical land lies in the
poignancy of its fragility.

More to the point, the mythical transition begins to alter existing
investments in legal boundaries. In particular, the once popular understanding that owning land meant a divine right freely to exploit the land and
to exclude others from possessing a say in its future, is receding. Increasingly,
the neoliberal affirmation of the interconnectedness of ecosystems and the
requirements of supralocal stewardship seems justifiably to subvert the local
autonomy of the landowner (and, hence the problems suffered by
Cameroonian forest-dwellers and Vassilikiot farmers). Why is this?

For one thing, the historical love of landscape first went hand in hand with a resigned acceptance of property, enclosure and exclusion, and with only a defining nostalgia for lost primordial unity.[6] Indeed, the imagined community of the 19th- and 20th-century nation creatively took shape on the basis of this signified rupture, usually transferring to the nation-state, the people and the national landscape, the mission to restore *spiritually* the *bodily* unity hitherto thought to be imparted by autochthonous relations with the land. Moreover, because the historic Landscape came into being not as an essential tract 'in and for itself' but, self-consciously, only as the partial perception of definite viewpoints, there could only be a plurality and overlapping fragmentation of significant landscapes. Consequently, short of disbarring access,[7] no property in land would ever impinge upon all local unravellings of landscape. In sum, broken up by legitimate boundaries but also fragmented by viewpoints, the articulation of property and landscape proved historically accommodating.

By contrast, aesthetic, moral and personified (i.e. mythical) land relations of environment tend to clash with relations of property. In the first instance, this is because high-tech productive investments in land-based property now ramify, inordinately and uncertainly, exporting more effects beyond legal boundaries than discharging them within them. There is precious little scope left, therefore, for either the theological or the enlightened moralisation of private property in land on the strength of improvement. (This is quite apart from the fact that landowners are now increasingly likely to be global food corporations or mining conglomerates rather than latter-day Robinson Crusoes: Hann 1998: 2.)

In the second place, where the basic definition of Landscape as a fragmentation of viewpoints and subjectivities seems theoretically to invite a relatively dispassionate phenomenology of the landscaping subject, the environment, defined as densely packed space of interconnections and precarious balances, seems to engender an urgent demand for consensus: viz. a neo-realism of the environmental object. This means that a contradiction between the inflexibility of property relations in land and the urgency of stewarding the boundless Environment emerges as one of the defining tensions of modern Western culture. This dialectic is marked by a persistent sense of crisis and by the constant regulation of property in land from the centre and at the grassroots.

By conceptualising land relations of identity and property, rites and rights, myth and law in terms of their possible articulations, it becomes possible to think of contemporary land relations as a combination of meaning and control or, in other cases, of meaning and loss of control. Using these concepts, both Landscape and environment can be put in their rightful historical places whilst, elsewhere, and in other times, the tensions arising out of the articulations of very different kinds of land relation can be productively traced and explored.

NOTES

I should like to acknowledge the helpful support and criticism of Drs Eric Hirsch, Mark Jamieson, Dimitris Theodossopoulos and Richard Wilson who all helped shape this chapter through their comments. Early partial versions were also patiently received and helpfully considered by participants of Anthropology seminars in the Universities of Oxford and Hull, and the University of Wales Lampeter.

1. I am indebted to Paul Durman (in this volume) for the way he resonantly uses the term 'tract'.
2. Lowry is thus a landscape painter by default, an artist who conjures up for the mind's eye the wide Bruegelian space which is obviously negated in his depictions.
3. Switzerland – as Helvetia – became the European symbol of a national freedom, running deep into Western Europe's highest mountains. The same is true for the Scottish Highlands for the memory they seem to store of Robert the Bruce, William Wallace and the Jacobites, all of whose rebelliousness seem to remain engraved onto the granite majesty of the Highlands. The importance of the Highland tradition to Scottish nationalism lies in its enduring ability to ground contemporary feelings of difference and longings for autonomy in a real tradition of rebellion.
4. Tilley (1994: 12), arguing from a phenomenological viewpoint, derives the experience of separation from the human condition.

    > Being-in-the-world resides in a process of objectification in which people objectify the world by setting themselves apart from it. This results in the creation of a gap, a distance in space. To be human is both to create this distance between the self and that which is beyond and to attempt to bridge this distance through a variety of means ...

    This humanism inevitably confers upon landscape the status of a *universal* rather than an historical space of loss and restitution.
5. The appropriateness of this argument is well exemplified by the symbolism of the great frontier landscapes of the New World. These apparently virginal landscapes are always striking for the great spaces they seem to offer the best expenditure of our freedom. However, whilst this may well be true, the American landscape is also compelling for the fact that we know that it remains apparently uncolonised because it is so starkly resistant to our manicured and civilised habits, and that, unlike the American Indian, we have lost our roots in this land because we have lost the habits needed to cope with it.
6. The investment of memory inhering in modern Western landscape is symptomatic of only one of the two modern cultural responses to bourgeois enclosure and urban exile. The other response is, or at least, was explicitly political. Over the centuries there have been occupations of capitalised land in Britain, most notably, by returning soldiers, unemployed and unrecognised, after the end of the Second World War. It is the Diggers, though, who keep alive the memory of the early opposition to expropriation and who continue to transmit the tradition. The Diggers continue, albeit with little political impact, the ideological struggle to reverse the original bourgeois appropriation of common land in favour of the people's Commonwealth.
7. Barbara Bender's accounts of the Druidic occupation of Stonehenge shows how the concern of the New Agers is not with ownership of the sacred stone circle but with direct access to its sacred centre. In fact, the latter-day druids seem to 'out' symbolically what is implicit for others who inhabit 'these sceptred isles': namely, that collective historical memory continues to somehow 'live' in the land as a live organ of both its geography and our national anatomy.

REFERENCES

Ashmore, W. and Knapp, A.B. 1999. *Archaeologies of Landscape*. Malden, MA: Blackwell Publishers.
Bakhtin, M. 1966. *Rabelais and His World*. Cambridge, MA: MIT Press.
Basso, K.H. 1988. 'Speaking with names: language and landscape among the Western Apache', *Current Anthropology* 3(1):16–20.
Bender, B. 1993a. 'Stonehenge – Contested Landscapes (Medieval to Present-Day)', in B. Bender (ed.) *Landscape: Politics and Perspectives*. Oxford: Berg.
—— (ed.) 1993b. *Landscape: Politics and Perspectives*. Oxford: Berg.
—— 1998. *Stonehenge: Making Space*. Oxford: Berg.
Chekhov, A. 1904. *The Cherry Orchard*. New York: Dover, 1991.
Colley, L. 1996. *Britons. Forging the Nation, 1707–1837*, 3rd edn. London: Vintage.
de Coppet, D. 1981. 'The life-giving death', in A. Humphreys and H. King (eds) *Mortality and Immortality in the Anthropology and Archaeology of Death*. London: Academic Press.
Coward, R. 1989. *The Whole Truth: The Myth of Alternative Health*. London: Faber & Faber.
Eliade, M. 1974 (1949). *The Myth of the Eternal Return*. Princeton, NJ: Princeton University Press.
Evans-Pritchard, E. 1940. *The Nuer: A Description of the Modes of Livelihood and Political Institutions of a Nilotic People*. Oxford: Clarendon Press.
Eves, R. 1997. 'Seating the place: tropes of body, movement and space for the people of Lelet Plateau, New Ireland (Papua New Guinea)', in J. Fox (ed.) *The Poetic Power of Place: Comparative Perspectives on Austronesian Ideas of Locality*. Canberra: Australian National University.
Fitzpatrick, P. 1992. *The Mythology of Modern Law*. London: Routledge.
Foucault, M. 1970. *The Order of Things: An Archaeology of the Human Sciences*. London: Tavistock (first published Paris: Editions Gallimard in 1966).
Fox, J.J. 1980. *The Flow of Life: Essays on Eastern Indonesia*. Cambridge, MA: Harvard University Press.
—— (ed.) 1997. *The Poetic Power of Place: Comparative Perspectives on Austronesian Ideas of Locality*. Canberra: Australian National University.
Gurevich, A.J. 1985 (1972). *Categories of Medieval Culture*. London: Routledge & Kegan Paul.
Hann, C. M. 1998. 'Introduction: the embeddedness of property', in C. Hann (ed.) *Property Relations: Renewing the Anthropological Tradition*. Cambridge: Cambridge University Press.
Harris, O. (ed.) 1996. *Inside and Outside the Law: Anthropological Studies of Authority and Ambiguity*. London: Routledge.
Heidegger, M. 1972. 'Building dwelling thinking', in D. Krell (ed.) *Martin Heidegger, Basic Writings*. London: Routledge.
Hill, H. 1980. *Freedom to Roam: The Struggle for Access to Britain's Moors and Mountains*. Ashbourne: Moorland Publishing.
Hirsch, E. 1995. 'Introduction: landscape: between place and space', in E. Hirsch and M. O'Hanlon (eds) *The Anthropology of Landscape: Perspectives on Place and Space*. Oxford: Clarendon Press.
Hirsch, E. and O'Hanlon, M. (eds) 1995. *The Anthropology of Landscape: Perspectives on Place and Space*. Oxford: Clarendon Press.
Hoskins, W.G. 1985 (1955). *The Making of the English Landscape*. Harmondsworth: Penguin.
Humphreys, S. 1985. 'Introduction: law, anthropology and history. Law as discourse', *History and Anthropology* 1(2): 241–65.
Hutchinson, S.E. 1996. *Nuer Dilemmas: Coping with Money, War and the State*. Berkeley: University of California Press.

Layton, R. 1995. 'Relating to the country in the Western Desert', in E. Hirsch and M. O'Hanlon (eds) *The Anthropology of Landscape: Perspectives on Place and Space.* Oxford: Clarendon Press.

Lévi-Strauss, C. 1970. *The Raw and the Cooked: Introduction to a Science of Mythology.* London: Jonathan Cape.

Lovelock, J. 1979. *Gaia, a New Look at Life on Earth.* New York: Oxford University Press.

Massey, D. 1991. 'Flexible sexism', *Environment and Planning D: Society and Space* 9:31–57.

—— 'Thinking radical democracy spatially', *Environment and Planning D: Society and Space* 13: 283–8.

Merleau-Ponty, M. 1962. *The Phenomenology of Perception.* London: Routledge.

Merry, S.E. 1992. 'Anthropology, law and transnational processes', *Annual Review of Anthropology* 21: 357–79.

Mosse, G. 1964. *The Crisis in German Ideology: Intellectual Origins of the Third Reich.* London: Weidenfeld and Nicolson.

Munn, N. 1970. 'The transformation of subjects into objects in Walbiri and Pitjantjatjara myth', in R.M. Berndt (ed.) *Australian Aboriginal Anthropology: Modern Studies in the Social Anthropology of the Australian Aborigines.* Nedlands: University of Western Australia Press.

Neve, C. 1990. *Unquiet Landscape: Places and Ideas in 20th-Century English Painting.* London: Faber & Faber.

Olwig, K. 1996. 'Recovering the substantive nature of landscape', *Annals of the Association of American Geographers* 86: 630–53.

Pugh, S. 1990. 'Introduction: stepping out into the open', in S. Pugh (ed.) *Reading Landscape: Country – City – Capital.* Manchester: Manchester University Press.

Sahlins, P. 1989. *Boundaries: The Making of France and Spain in the Pyrenees.* Berkeley: University of California Press.

Sakai, M. 1997. 'Remembering origins: ancestors and places in the Gumai society of south Sumatra', in J.J. Fox (ed.) *The Poetic Power of Place: Comparative Perspectives on Austronesian Ideas of Locality.* Canberra: Australian National University.

Sharma, S. 1995. *Landscape and Memory.* London: Fontana.

Shelley, M. 1818. *Frankenstein, or the Modern Prometheus.* Harmondsworth: Penguin (1994).

Strang, V. 1997. *Uncommon Ground: Cultural Landscapes and Environmental Values.* Oxford: Berg.

Tilley, C. 1994. *A Phenomenology of Landscape: Places, Paths and Monuments.* Oxford: Berg.

Verdery, K. 1998. 'Property and power in Transylvania's collectivisation', in C. Hann (ed.) *Property Relations: Renewing the Anthropological Tradition.* Cambridge: Cambridge University Press.

Weber, M. 1922 (1978). *Wirtschaft und Gesellschaft* (translated as *Economy and Society*). Berkeley: University of California Press.

Weiner, A. 1976. *Women of Value, Men of Renown.* Austin: University of Texas Press.

Williams, N.M. 1986. *The Yolngu and their Land: A System of Land Tenure and the Fight for its Recognition.* Stanford: Stanford University Press.

Williams, R. 1973. *The Country and the City.* New York: Oxford University Press.

2 WHOSE FOREST? WHOSE MYTH? CONCEPTUALISATIONS OF COMMUNITY FORESTS IN CAMEROON

Philip Burnham

This chapter examines the operation of several myths and legal fictions, both ancient and modern, in the context of current international efforts to promote biodiversity conservation and sustainable forest management through 'community forestry' in the humid forest zone of Cameroon.[1] This is an issue which is fraught with conceptual contradictions. On the one hand, we have the underlying principle of colonial land tenure law in Cameroon which argued that the great majority of land, including the vast tracts of rainforest in the southern part of the country, was 'vacant and without master' at the time of the colonial conquest and could therefore legitimately be considered as state land. This concept still remains valid, in the postcolonial state's eyes, today. Moreover, this statist conception of Cameroon's timber-rich forests as the 'permanent forest domain of the state' has become even more accentuated over the past two decades as a result of the increasing importance of forestry for Cameroon's economy, as well as the growth of donor aid available for this sector.

On the other hand, over the past decade, the future of Cameroon's rainforests has attracted much concern among Northern 'Green' non-governmental organisations (NGOs), the international scientific community, international and bilateral aid agencies, and other institutions with an interest in biodiversity conservation and 'sustainable' development. In the context of these external pressures, and in particular the environmental and neoliberal conditionalities of the World Bank's structural adjustment programme, the Cameroon state has been induced to enact a new forestry law, clauses of which now permit local people to lay claim to 'their' forests. Donor-government aid programmes, and their overseas and local NGO allies, are enthusiastically seeking to promote community forestry activities, judging these to be important sources of rural empowerment and a promising mode of sustainable environmental management. Regrettably, a closer inspection of current efforts to promote 'community-based' conservation and forest management in Cameroon raises serious questions concerning the conceptual basis of such activities, which derive an

31

essentially mythic sanction from prevalent Western notions of 'pristine rainforests' inhabited by 'indigenous peoples'. Reliance on externally imposed and socially unrealistic policy prescriptions, which relate more to funding conditionalities affecting Western donors and NGOs than to social and environmental conditions in African countries such as Cameroon, offers little hope either for effective environmental management or for environmentally sensitive development.

CAMEROON'S FORESTS – A VALUABLE AND CONTESTED DOMAIN

The humid forest zone of Cameroon is conventionally said to comprise some 20 million hectares of forest[2] – the second largest forest estate among African countries after the Congo (former Zaire). The flora and the fauna of the rainforests of Cameroon are exceptionally rich and diverse, with numerous endemic species (Gartlan 1989). The human population of the forest zone (excluding the major cities) can be estimated at some 3–3.5 million persons, the majority of whom are farmers who utilise shifting cultivation methods to produce a diverse range of crops both for subsistence and market sale. Aside from the urban and peri-uban areas, most of Cameroon's humid forest zone is characterised by low to medium population densities (in the range from 5 to 25 persons per square km), and agricultural land is generally not scarce.

As mentioned above, the forests of Cameroon are the focus of a major timber industry. Since its inception before the First World War, Cameroon's timber industry has been dominated by expatriate firms, and this situation shows no signs of changing today. Foreigners own 90 per cent of the companies in the logging sector; the majority of these are European firms but in the last few years, Asian companies have substantially increased their activities (ITTO 1998). As of 1995, Cameroon sent 78 per cent of its timber exports to Europe (Fondo n.d.; see also Tchomba 1992).

For more than a decade, Cameroon has been in economic crisis, largely due to imprudent government spending, and since the late 1980s it has been subject to a World Bank structural adjustment programme aimed at promoting more effective fiscal management and the repayment of foreign debts. With Cameroon's petroleum exports in decline and several of its major export crops suffering from low prices on world markets, the country's timber industry has had to take on an even more central role in generating export earnings. Throughout the 1990s, Cameroon has been expanding its timber exports, which is very much in keeping with the announced priorities of the Cameroon government, in its National Forestry Action Plan (Ministry of Environment and Forestry, Cameroon 1995). According to the most recent figures from the International Tropical Timber Organisation (ITTO 1998), Cameroon is now the second largest exporter of tropical hardwood logs in Africa and the fourth largest exporter in the world.

Historically, commercial logging in Cameroon has been a sector rife with mismanagement and corruption. Despite the high levels of activity in Cameroonian commercial forestry in recent years, fiscal returns from the forestry sector to the Cameroon government's coffers have been notoriously lower than they should be. In 1993, this situation was the subject of one of the rare debates in the Cameroonian National Assembly (which normally rubber-stamps government budget proposals and other legislation) and also received substantial negative comment in the independent press.

Given the limited institutional capacity of the Cameroon government and the political characteristics of the present regime, forestry is too lucrative a domain for effective controls. Indeed, so important is the forestry sector as a source of political perquisites that, from time to time, the allocation of timber concessions has been carried out at the level of the Prime Minister's Office or the Presidency, without reference to the statutory inter-ministerial technical committee which is supposed to control such licensing. Also very problematic, from the point of view of sustainable forest management and administrative controls, is the practice of allocating timber concessions to favoured elites by the practices known as *gré-à-gré* and *vente de coupe*. These procedures, which do not involve competitive tendering for a logging licence, are ostensibly used to encourage the efficient exploitation of small tracts of forest falling outside the remit of normal forestry concession procedures, and to ensure that involvement in the logging industry is not totally monopolised by expatriate firms. However, in practice, these arrangements permit quite blatant uncontrolled logging and illegal exportation of timber.

At the same time, the Forestry Department suffers from inflated staff numbers in relation to its minuscule field operating budget. As a result, the provincial-level staff of the Forestry Department typically have no functioning vehicles at their disposal to monitor the vast tracts of forest under their jurisdiction, and logging companies are able to exploit their concessions with little oversight. Unsurprisingly, the Forestry Department has proved unable efficiently to collect timber taxes, and many logging companies have repeatedly been able to evade taxation. Cameroon's 1994 Forestry Law, which is discussed below, has as one of its main aims the reform of the forestry sector, with particular emphasis on administrative and fiscal procedures. However, these reforms have proved difficult to carry through (ITTO 1998) and, as of early 1999, it continues to be 'business as usual' in Cameroon's logging industry.

Despite the many fiscal and other irregularities that have dogged the sector, it is important to note that Cameroon's logging companies have contributed substantially to the infrastructural development of the regions in which they have worked. In many areas of Cameroon's humid forest zone, the major logging companies have been responsible for the construction of most of the motorable road network and have been the largest employers of salaried labour. Indeed, in the remote and lightly populated forest zones of southern and eastern Cameroon where the Cameroon government territorial administration and other services are particularly thin on the ground, it is hardly an exaggeration to say that the large timber companies act as a surrogate state in their provision of employment and infrastructure, as well as in their informal political-economic dominance.

The *de facto* dominance of timber companies in the regions where they operate has led to an ambiguous relationship with the inhabitants of these forested zones. In general, local village communities and elites are happy to have logging companies operating in their areas due to the improved facilities, as well as the salaried and informal employment that they provide. Nonetheless, disputes tend to arise over issues such as: (a) the relative proportion of locals versus outsiders employed by the timber firms, (b) the cutting of certain tree species that are important sources of non-timber forest products, and (c) perceptions that village chiefs and other elites are benefiting in a disproportionate manner from compensation, 'gifts' and other amenities given by the timber companies to local people.

INTERNATIONAL PRESSURES AND THE RISE OF FOREST
CONSERVATION CONSCIOUSNESS IN CAMEROON

Over the past decade or so, Cameroon, in common with many other tropical countries, has been the focus of a great upsurge of interest in the conservation of rainforest emanating from Northern environmentalist movements and 'global resource managers' (see Goldman 1998). The rapidity of growth and the considerable scale of these interventions have been quite remarkable. Although limited efforts at forest management and conservation had been made by Cameroon's Forestry Service during the colonial period, the overriding orientation in the forestry sector has been, from the start, extractive logging. At the start of the 1980s, Cameroon had no significant externally funded programmes relating to rainforest conservation and management. But, from the mid-1980s, forest conservation issues began to gain more attention – initially as a result of the Tropical Forestry Action Plan (TFAP), an international initiative inaugurated by the FAO, in cooperation with UNEP, the World Bank and the World Resources Institute in 1985 (FAO 1985). The aims of this programme were to raise funds for tropical forest conservation, to promote the creation of national forestry action plans in signatory countries, and to provide an international umbrella organisation to coordinate activities in the tropical forest conservation and management sector. The Cameroon government signed the TFAP convention in 1986, which led to the drafting, in 1988, of Cameroon's National Forestry Action Plan (NFAP). At the heart of Cameroon's NFAP was a shopping list of forestry projects requiring funding and, by 1989, many of the major donor governments, including Canada, France, the Netherlands and Great Britain, had agreed to support some of these projects. One of the key projects in this first tranche of NFAP funding was the development of a National Forest

Management Plan (often referred to as the *Plan de Zonage*) for the whole of Cameroon's humid forest zone, which was begun in 1988 by a subcontracting firm working on behalf of the Canadian government.

Another landmark in the development of Cameroon's institutional structures for forest conservation and management was the creation of a separate ministerial portfolio to deal with this domain. Cameroon's Ministry of Environment and Forestry (MINEF) was established in April 1992, primarily in response to donor pressure, in the run-up to the Rio 'Earth Summit' Conference (UNCED). Prior to 1992, government activities relating to Cameroon's forest estate and the natural environment more generally had been dispersed in several ministries and parastatal organisations. One indication of the Cameroon government's generally weak institutional capacity in the environmental field at this time was the fact that Cameroon's position paper for Rio was drafted largely by expatriate technical advisers in the Forestry Department and overseas NGO lobbyists in Yaounde.

Throughout the 1990s, the level of activity in Cameroon's conservation and forestry management sectors has continued to expand exponentially, with numerous externally funded projects springing up. Up through 1995, one can estimate that over US $100 million was spent in Cameroon on rainforest-related projects. Since then, with the expansion of World Bank and European Union funding in particular, it is likely that this total has more than doubled. Indeed, throughout Cameroon's present economic crisis, the rainforest sector has been one of the few areas of donor aid largesse, and numerous local NGOs have sprung up to capitalise on the funding opportunities in this domain.

THE WORLD BANK AND THE 1994 FORESTRY LAW

Increasingly, with the progressive 'greening' of its policies under international NGO pressure from the late 1980s onward, the World Bank has played a leading role in efforts to promote sustainable management and conservation of rainforests. One of the key environmental conditionalities promoted by the Bank in Cameroon was the drafting of a new national forestry law embodying fiscal and administrative reforms as well as currently popular environmentalist policies such as restrictions on log exports, the development of forest management plans, and the creation of community forests (see Ekoko 1997). The experience of the drafting of Cameroon's forestry law provides a good illustration of the regrettably all-too-frequent practice in foreign aid contexts to trust in a naïve and effectively unpoliticised conception of the capacity of law to effect social change. As Franz von Benda-Beckmann (1993: 116) has written recently:

The idea of legal engineering, of achieving social and economic change through government law, still ranks foremost in the arsenal of development techniques. Law, as 'desired situation projected into the future' is used as a magic charm. The law-maker seeks to capture desired economic or social conditions, and the practice supposed to lead to them, in normative terms, and leaves the rest to law enforcement, or expressed more generally, to the implementation of policy.

The expatriate consultants who drafted Cameroon's forestry law were treating law as another form of technical development fix. Virtually ready-written legal clauses, embodying currently popular principles, could be taken off the shelf and incorporated into the text with little attempt to adapt them to the country where they would be applied. Locked into an externally imposed project cycle, which dictated that the Canadian consultancy firm would not be paid unless the required project outputs had been achieved within the deadline, there was simply no time for the niceties of participatory consultation with the people who were expected to undertake the participatory management of community forests.

The passage of the 1994 Forestry Law was an occasion for a substantial debate in Cameroon's National Assembly. Many deputies expressed the view that the law was much too favourable to expatriate logging interests and was being rammed through by external pressure. The law was substantially amended during the debate, so that it assumed a form that was satisfactory to no one. Considerable behind-the-scenes pressure was exerted by the World Bank to expunge some of the revised text's more discordant elements prior to the passage of the law's application decree in 1995. Nonetheless, the National Assembly did manage to hold out regarding the maximum size and duration of logging concessions, having lowered them to 200,000 ha and 15 years respectively, instead of the 500,000 ha and 25 years favoured by the World Bank and expatriate conservation and logging interests. The larger and longer concession regime was said by the Bank to be more conducive to sustainable forest management but was seen by the Cameroonian legislators as increasing expatriate domination of the forestry sector. It is not my aim here to discuss all the law's various components (for a useful discussion, see Nguiffo 1994); it will suffice for my purposes simply to focus on several of the key provisions relating to resource tenure and management.

The 1994 law was grounded on the assumption that a comprehensive national forest management plan could be established and effectively administered. At present, however, this *Plan de Zonage*, produced under Canadian supervision but again with no participatory involvement of the rural population and other local stakeholders, contains obvious pitfalls. Highly favourable to commercial logging interests, the *Plan de Zonage* assigns large tracts to the 'Permanent Forest Estate' category – forests which are exclusively reserved for commercial logging despite their long-standing usage by local village populations. In the heavily forested zones, narrow corridors of secondary forest along the roads are defined as 'Non-Permanent Forest Estate' available for use both by the rural population and the timber companies. It is very much an open question as to whether this plan, in its present form, will ever be practically implementable (or, if it is implemented, whether it will not be very detrimental to forest people's interests).

Contrary to the desires of the World Bank and other donors, the 1994 law continues to authorise the granting of small forest concessions to Cameroonian nationals according to the *vente de coupe* and *gré-à-gré* procedures mentioned above. This leaves open the major loophole through which much of Cameroon's illegal logging is achieved, while retaining much scope for prominent political figures to allocate rewards to favoured clients.

While the 1994 Forestry Law reinforced the conception of the state as ultimate owner of the national forest domain (a key provision of Cameroon's 1974 Land Tenure Law which still remains in force), it also established for the first time in Cameroon the possibility for rural people to gain rights of commercial exploitation over forest resources in their neighbourhood. According to the law's conception of a community forest, a group of villagers may apply for long-term exclusive use rights over a 5,000 ha tract of forest adjacent to their village (in the 'Non-Permanent Forest Estate'), which may then be exploited and managed by them according to a management plan agreed with the Forestry Department. This more participatory theory of forest management stands in marked contrast to the authoritarian traditions of the Forestry Department, the body responsible for the law's administration. Whether or not such an approach to management will succeed in this context remains an open question, and five years after the law's passage, no such community forests have yet been legally established in Cameroon. On the other hand, several so-called 'community forests' have recently been established through the influence of external elites, who have used their influence to obtain what amounts to personal logging concessions without respect for the procedures stipulated in the new forestry law (see Milol 1998).

COMPETING CONCEPTIONS OF TENURE AND FOREST MANAGEMENT POLICY

As already mentioned, Cameroon land tenure law continues to follow the French colonial conception in which all lands considered 'vacant and without master' were defined as state land. The criteria for recognition of personal ownership of land are quite strict, so that swidden cultivation fallows, for example, do not count unless perennial cash crops such as coffee and cocoa have been planted. From this perspective, vast tracts of forest in southern Cameroon are firmly placed under state ownership.

As Fisiy (1996) has argued in a recent article which reviews the implications of concepts such as 'Crown' or 'state lands' in the colonial and postcolonial laws of Cameroon, such legal theories have the pragmatic aim of facilitating acquisition of local communities' lands through the nullification of traditional conceptions of land tenure. By stipulating a mythical 'time zero' before which precolonial societies were defined as living in a largely unsocialised environment, colonial rulers sought to institute a 'legal monolithism' that was very convenient for their purposes (Fisiy 1996: 229). We should note here, in passing, the strong contrast between French colonial land tenure law versus the legal system which obtained during the colonial period in British Cameroons. Under the British colonial system of 'indirect rule', 'vacant' lands were considered, in the last instance (following the Land and Native Rights Ordinance of 1927), to belong to local communities – in the person of colonially created 'native authorities'. There was no corresponding notion of communal or 'native' lands in the francophone area, and when the two federated territories were unified in 1972, the British-inspired conception was scrapped in favour of the French one.

Indeed, it is this statist conception of land tenure which prevails in Cameroon's still-operative 1974 Land Ordinance although, as already mentioned, the community forest clauses of the 1994 Forestry Law now give local people the possibility of establishing claims to forest resources adjacent to their villages. However, under the 1994 Forestry Law, the land itself underlying a tract of community forest is not owned by the community. Rather, it is just the rights to the utilisation and commercialisation of forest resources which are allocated to the community group for the duration of the community forest agreement. Moreover, the 1994 Forestry Law does not in fact recognise the legal existence of an entity that one might define as a 'traditional' community. In general, Cameroonian legal theory, deriving from the French tradition, is extremely wary of acknowledging the rights of traditional collectivities (see, for example, Egbe 1996), and the 'community' forest clauses of the 1994 law stipulate that, in order to apply for a community forest, a group must first legally constitute itself under modern Cameroonian law as a 'communal initiative group' (commonly abbreviated as GIC), with a written constitution specifying its rules of membership. As such, a GIC does not necessarily have to correspond to any social grouping defined by 'traditional' principles and has no obligation to include among its membership, for example, all the residents in a village or other local grouping. Thus, in several respects, there is still in Cameroon no sure legal basis for the ownership of lands or forests by 'traditional' communities – despite the current popularity of this notion within the rhetoric of development programmes.

In such conditions, it is not surprising that forest resources have been a focal point for local political mobilisation and protest in Cameroon from the early colonial period up to the present day. There are numerous well-documented cases of dispute recorded in Cameroon's National Archives that were linked with the actions of the Forestry Department in creating forest reserves, as well as in response to the activities of timber companies within their forestry concessions. During the mid-1950s, the French colonial government suspended the establishment of new forest reserves in the face of continual protests by African representatives to the (newly created) Legislative Assembly of Cameroon, about forestry and land tenure matters

– for fear of negative publicity reaching the United Nations, which had oversight of Cameroon as a mandated territory. Today, many forest reserves exist more in theory than in practice, as local people assert what they see as their rights to farm the lands adjacent to their villages and encroach on reserve boundaries. Speaking more broadly and in practical terms, the whole field of Cameroonian land law is riven with conflicts between theory and practice, and the local courts are continually clogged with cases.

Alongside such disputes over land tenure, local conflicts concerning the utilisation and conservation of forest resources have also been prevalent in recent years. Several cases from the Eastern Province of Cameroon have focused on the *moabi* tree (*Baillonella toxisperma*), a prime timber tree which yields a fruit with an oily kernel that is used as a primary source of oil for sauces. According to the resource tenure conceptions current in many Cameroonian forest societies, individuals or families may establish usufruct rights over the fruits of particular economically useful trees such as the *moabi* (see Schneemann 1994). However, despite informal commitments in some timber concessions to the contrary, logging companies habitually cut down the *moabi*, and this has led to protests and even violent confrontations between local village populations and timber company employees, and the gendarmes sent to intervene.

For some years now, many of the individuals and organisations who are concerned with the future of Africa's forests and forest peoples have become very interested in the tenurial systems operating in this zone, with marked divergences of opinion on their potential for effective resource conservation and management quite evident. On the one hand, the dominant neoliberal and neo-Malthusian position espoused by powerful institutions such as the World Bank, UNDP and many Northern donor governments has tended to favour privatisation of land and forest resource tenure, despite acknowledging that land privatisation policies have often proved problematic in Africa. At the same time, such neoliberal institutions have also attacked state ownership of farm and forest lands, motivated both by a general philosophical aversion to the state and by a practical experience of state corruption and failure in many parts of Africa. Individual ownership has been promoted by this constituency on the grounds that it provides incentives to farmers to invest in the improvement of their land and intensify their agricultural practices. Such investment, in turn, is thought to encourage the demise of slash-and-burn agriculture which, in the context of rapid population growth, is often seen by these institutions as the main cause of deforestation.

In opposition to this neoliberal position, there is the 'common property' constituency which argues, in contrast to Garrett Hardin's (1968) famously negative view of 'the tragedy of the commons', that traditional regimes of common property rights offer considerable potential for effective management of natural resources in many cases. The detailed local knowledge of traditional communities, developed over many generations of usage of forest resources, is seen by these proponents as well adapted to the task of sustainable management. In the last few years, one can note a certain impact of this argument even within neoliberal bastions such as the World Bank where, as a result of effective lobbying by Northern 'Green' NGOs, an environmentalist voice has gained a foothold. In consequence, we are now seeing a more pluralist approach to land tenure being advocated by some World Bank officials, although there is still a marked aversion to state control (see, for example, Cleaver 1992: 75–6).

Another constituency that tends to favour common property regimes of tenure is comprised of radical or populist African social scientists, who see the prevalence of nationalised systems of land tenure, such as that in Cameroon, as a perpetuation of colonial exploitation. According to this argument, African political elites in the post-independence period have simply stepped into the shoes of the former colonial powers and continue to use the conception of the state as 'guardian of all lands', combined with the idea that private ownership should be the basic concept for allocating resources, to garner large tracts of land for themselves and their clients (Fisiy 1996: 244–50; Jua 1989: 750–1). According to such commentators (see also Nguiffo 1998), it will only be in instituting an effective legal pluralism, and especially in recognising local people's customary rights in their lands, that equitable and effective resource management can be achieved.

One can easily sympathise with such protests against the long history of exploitation of the inhabitants of Cameroon's forested zone by the colonial powers and their postcolonial successors and can also agree that it is high time that the people who live in these forests should not be systematically excluded from the benefits that may accrue from their exploitation. However, there is a danger that, in attacking the colonial myth that the majority of these lands were 'vacant and without master', and thus the domain of the state, one may set another collection of myths in its place. One such pitfall lurks in the uncritical acceptance of an unhistoricised notion of 'customary law' (or related notions such as 'traditional land tenure'), which many global resource managers are presently proposing as a panacea for effective environmental management.

Just as we have seen that the colonial concepts of Crown or state lands had the effect of creating an historical initial point before which the local populations' uses for or claims to such land were denied or relegated to the category of myth, so too can the notion of 'customary law' freeze history and create socially unrealistic fictions. As Fisiy (1996: 228) has rightly observed, these effects are also outcomes of colonialism, whose gate-keeping and labelling functions created a logical space to which local conceptions of laws and customs have been forced to adjust. To cite one example, customary law as conceived of today by most inhabitants of the forested zone of anglophone Cameroon refers to the legal and customary procedures of the British colonial 'native authority' system of indirect rule. This 'customary law' is still held in fond regard by disgruntled anglophone Cameroonians, who resent the imposition of a unified national legal code – based largely on the statist legal concepts of the French system – in 1972. Customary law in the British colonial system was in fact a corpus of laws and customs codified by colonial administrators and functionalist ethnographers, who saw each tribal people as having its own particular set of customary principles that was adapted to the particular circumstances of each society. In practical terms, such a concept of customary law – frozen at the time of colonial conquest and purged of elements that were deemed unacceptable to European under-standings of justice – can hardly be taken as an accurate representation either of precolonial land tenure or of *de facto* local land tenure today.

To take another example, Mariteuw Diaw has recently produced a survey of traditional land tenure concepts in southern Cameroon and has voiced considerable optimism regarding the utility of these systems for community-based resource management. Diaw (1997: 3) writes:

> It is our contention that the superimposition of State structures and legal systems on this traditional (tenurial) structure has not fundamentally altered its functioning within the forest communities of Southern Cameroon.

Diaw (1997: 26) goes on to emphasise, toward the end of his article, the resilience of the land tenure system of the Beti and other peoples of southern Cameroon and concludes:

> The capacity to contain social change within the boundaries of a set of fundamental principles confirms the robustness of those institutions and their validity as vehicles of social reproduction. This is a critical point to remember in the light of the spirit of reform which nowadays marks out the dominant approaches to forestry conserva-tion and agricultural development in the tropical forests of Africa. As an example, the identification of the relevant institutions to which should be devolved the community forests currently being created in Cameroon, constitutes one of the major stumbling blocks in the implementation of that country's new (1994) forestry law. In the on-going discussions, there is great temptation to bypass traditional institutions in favour of 'legal entities' [i.e. the GICs I have discussed above – PB].

Now it is hardly surprising that Diaw, an anthropologist working as a Rockefeller Fellow at the International Institute of Tropical Agriculture in Cameroon, should have an evident interest, in line with the presently fashionable neoliberal thinking on common/communal property mentioned above, to portray traditional village systems as separable from the influence of the state. However, this is not a socially accurate depiction, as Diaw himself documents in passing elsewhere in his own article. For example, Diaw (1997: 16) cites approvingly the findings of Weber (1977) and Leplaideur (1985) that:

> the major drive (among southern Cameroonian farmers) to establish cocoa plantations in the 1930s . . . was originally motivated by the desire to establish tenure security within the *nda bot* [minimal lineage or local residential group – PB] and not by financial motives. It is only through permanent embodiment of labour in the resource, as in the case of houses and other similar infrastructure, that permanent exclusive use rights can be established.

Diaw (unlike Leplaideur and Weber) glosses over the colonial legal context in which these cocoa farmers were operating which specified, as we have seen, that all lands that were 'vacant and without master' were state property. In such a legal setting – which is still operative in post-independence Cameroon – the establishment of tree crop plantations is the easiest and cheapest method available to villagers to create *de facto* private ownership of land and, *pace* Diaw, this certainly represents a fundamental change in 'traditional' structure, which is unequivocally due to the influence of the state.

While it is not possible within the space of this short article to enter into the details of 'customary' land tenure practices in southern Cameroon, it is useful nonetheless to highlight some of the basic social characteristics of the Cameroonian forest societies within which such 'customary law' has developed. Historically, the societies of Cameroon's forested region uniformly lacked chiefs or other centralised forms of political authority in the precolonial period. There was a widely shared ethos that political leadership and village formation were functions of the pioneering efforts of 'big' men, who penetrated thinly inhabited tracts of forest and there gathered around them groups of kin, affines, slaves and clients via their exploits in warfare, in forest conversion, in trade and in control of magical powers. Taking the case of the Beti peoples so well documented by Laburthe-Tolra (1977, 1981, 1985) and others, their attitudes toward land and forest were closely bound up with these conceptions of political leadership and their self-image as a 'noble' people. In this context, the swidden agricultural system of the Beti, involving annual clearance of high forest for new fields, had symbolic significance as iconic of the hegemony of Beti 'nobles', who controlled sufficient wealth, in wives and prestige goods, as well as the labour and political support of lineage juniors, clients and slaves, to colonise and bring under productive cultivation 'virgin' forest zones. Although women carried out the major part of day-to-day agricultural activities, the initial work of forest clearance was accomplished by men, thus culturally validating their 'strength' – that is, their political and economic prominence. Men who cleared large fields needed many wives and daughters to cultivate them and in turn could produce substantial surpluses to participate in the competitive feasting and ceremonial gift-giving (*bilabi*) which were features of Beti big man-status (Laburthe-Tolra 1981: 360 *et passim*).

Here then we have a clear linkage in Beti ideology between bush clearance and personal power. However, according to Laburthe-Tolra (1977), Weber (1977) and Leplaideur (1985) who have studied the issue most closely, the implications of this link have changed over time. Land appropriation, in the sense of the establishment of permanent ownership, was a colonial development, and Leplaideur (1985: 366) notes that plots of land were not transmitted through inheritance in the precolonial period. With the introduction of cocoa cultivation from the 1920s, bush clearance became associated with the process of creating cocoa plantations. As already mentioned, Leplaideur (1985: 180) argues, in his major study of cocoa farming in the Cameroon forest zone, that the planting of cocoa was first aimed at establishing firm title to a plot of land in the context of colonial land law.

In the precolonial period, processes of political competition among Cameroonian forest peoples tended to generate onward movements of forest colonisation, which are particularly well-described for the Beti and related peoples (see especially Laburthe-Tolra 1977, 1981), but which are also well-attested for other groups such as the Mkako (Copet 1977; Copet-Rougier 1990) and Mpiemu (Giles-Vernick 1996). This mobility was associated with territorial expansion and competition for long-distance trade links, and occasioned considerable local-level warfare between adjacent groups. According to Weber (1977; see also Dounias 1996: 163), such group fluidity and mobility continued until after the First World War, after which colonial pacification, forced resettlement and land tenure policies stabilised village populations and encouraged the development of *de facto* forms of freehold landownership. It was during this period of colonially induced stability of settlement that a new category of rural elites emerged, whose pre-eminence rested in large measure on their status as major '*planteurs*' of cocoa (Guyer 1984). Significant changes such as these remain unacknowledged in Diaw's overview of southern Cameroonian land tenure. Although recognising that mobility and group fission were key characteristics of the peoples of the Cameroon rainforest, Diaw's account is still too marked by the static structural-functional tradition of analysing social forms as mechanistic outcomes of social structural rules, rather than seeing group formation as an accomplishment of the motivated practices of individuals operating within a political economic framework defined, at least in part, by the state.

Not only has the present tendency for Northern environmentalist NGOs and many development agencies to treat the 'community' as a self-evident 'traditional' entity tended to generate idealised, unhistoricised accounts of village-level land tenure relations, but it has also led to a failure more generally to acknowledge the social complexity of the political-economic relations impacting at the local level. On the one hand, despite repeated efforts by the colonial powers to create stable chieftaincy structures in Cameroonian forest communities, the acephalous nature of these societies is still quite evident today. The ethnography of present-day Cameroonian forest peoples continues to be dominated by discussions of the fluid and contingent character of most local groups. Rather than a model of presumptively perpetual corporate lineages, we have models that emphasise competitive redefinition of groups over time and tendencies toward local group fission linked with an ethos of egalitarianism and weak relations of authority, which are in turn associated with chronic spates of witchcraft accusation leading to social levelling and mistrust within local groups. This uncentralised character of local-level political structures remains an important conditioning factor in the relationship between these rural forest peoples and the state institutions, NGOs, and private logging firms which are involved in promoting programmes of forest management, exploitation and conservation.

On the other hand, however, it is important to recognise the key role of modern elites in the articulation of local village social relations with such external institutions. These elites function in many roles. There are the retired teachers, civil servants and other educated elites who have returned to their natal villages. There are the 'external' elites in the urban centres and the provincial and district headquarters towns, who may be organised into ethnic or elite associations and who retain an active interest in village affairs. The activities of political parties, local NGOs, churches, regional or village cooperatives, and GICs, as well as business dealings, development programmes and conservation projects, all provide occasions when modern elites are likely to become involved in village affairs and to act as formal and informal vehicles of state or other more global influences at the local level. Despite rhetoric to the contrary (cf. Nguiffo 1998), our observations in many rural Cameroonian settings in recent years reveal little sign that there really is a will, in such elite circles, to try to reinstitute 'traditional' social forms (whatever this might mean), although arguments of this type may well be mobilised when it comes to defending local interests. In view of the World Bank's present enchantment with administrative decentralisation policies, it is likely that such localising strategies will become more popular in the future.

On a related theme, the emphasis on 'traditional' communities in the present-day environmental and development discourses also often has the effect of glossing over the significant degree of ethnic pluralism in many Cameroonian rural settlements. Even in the precolonial period, it was quite usual for the population of an area to be composed of layerings of several different peoples – the politically subordinate being more or less assimilated within the politically dominant group, although sometimes retaining a degree of cultural distinctiveness in daily life (see, for example, Laburthe-Tolra 1981: 192–6, 209). In the present day, the local ethnic situation is even more complex, to which the prominent discussion, in many social contexts, of 'natives' versus 'strangers' and '*autochtones*' versus '*allogènes*' gives witness (see Sharpe 1998b: 31–2 for an example from South-West Province). The recent accentuation of ethnically phrased discourses in Cameroonian public life is a very regrettable tendency – one that can easily unleash nasty spates of ethnic violence (Burnham 1996). Development agencies seeking to appropriate such language for their own purposes would do well to take care.

Finally, it is also worth noting in passing that the all-too-common failing of conservation and development projects adequately to conceptualise the regional political economic forces that impact on rural peoples is often exacerbated by the 'participatory rural appraisal' or 'rapid rural appraisal' methods presently favoured in many development circles. Ironically, many Northern development agencies pride themselves on being attentive to vulnerable groups and yet, in practice, use methods that rarely yield an informed assessment of the local political economy that defines such vulnerability or powerlessness.

Thus, we have a situation in which numerous government and NGO planning documents, drafts of new laws, publicity statements, etc. are shot through with references to 'participatory' forest management by 'traditional communities' but little attention is being paid to how these 'communities' are constituted and defined in practice. Given that what is at issue in the case of community forests is the regeneration of hardwood timber trees, which require a minimum period of 30 to 50 years to mature (if not a great deal more), the expectation that local villagers will be prepared to make substantial labour inputs into forest management or agroforestry schemes, which will only yield financial returns to generations to come, raises fundamental questions about the social organisational continuity of local groups, their inheritance rules and land tenure conceptions. When I raised these issues with a foreign technical advisor in the Cameroonian Forestry Department who had been closely involved with the drafting of the 1994 Forestry Law, he remarked that where communities do not exist, it is up to development-oriented NGOs to create them!

INDIGENOUS PEOPLES AND PRISTINE RAINFORESTS – SOME MODERN MYTHS

The argument that I have been developing in this chapter thus far has focused on some evident problems that have emerged as globalising discourses concerning rainforest conservation, emanating from the Northern countries, have begun to engage with localised social realities in Cameroon. A rapid perusal of any of the numerous policy pronouncements that are now available on the subject of rainforest conservation and management will serve to confirm that this is a field which has more than its fair share of taken-for-granted assumptions embodied in its currently fashionable terminology – in our research, we have taken to calling them 'buzz-words'. Such buzz-words, which come in and out of style with international fashions, have significant social, political and environmental effects, as we have begun to see in the discussion of the notion of 'traditional communities' presented above. Other obvious candidates for the buzz-word list would include 'sustainable' (as in sustainable forest management), 'participatory' (as in participatory development or participatory rural appraisal) 'indigenous' peoples, and 'primary' or 'pristine' rainforests. While a great deal can be said about each of these concepts, I propose to limit myself to some remarks about the latter two – with the aim of arguing, among other points, that the functioning of these terms in international policy circles shares some interesting parallels with mythic discourse.

Indigenous Peoples

A key notion that conservationists have been increasingly drawn to, as a means of making common cause with the inhabitants of many of the forested areas that they wish to conserve, is the notion of 'indigenous peoples'. For example, in the recent book *Indigenous Peoples and Sustainability* produced by the International Union for the Conservation of Nature's Inter-Commission Task Force on Indigenous Peoples, the argument is advanced that, via respect for the distinctive socio-cultural identities and knowledge systems of indigenous peoples and their involvement in efforts to 'attain sustainability', more effective programmes of conservation and development may be achieved. According to this view, indigenous forest peoples live in harmony with the rainforest, causing little long-term damage because of their simple technologies, their intimate knowledge of their environments, and their low population densities. At the same time, however, the task of providing a clear-cut definition of indigenous peoples has proved to be a difficult one, as various authors have noted (e.g. Marsden 1994; Furze et al. 1996; Richards 1996; Sharpe 1988a). Definitions formulated by international organisations working in the conservation, development and human rights fields[3] usually make reference to their possession of distinctive cultures and languages, their long residence in a particular territory, their common ancestry with the original inhabitants of the land, and their minority status within the present-day states in which they live. Most of these definitions are also based on an assumption that indigenous peoples' minority status can be understood in relation to a history of colonialism, with some commentators arguing that the term should only be applied 'to peoples living within nation states founded and still dominated by European settler populations' (IUCN 1997: 29). Finally, many definitions take the view that '*self-identification* as indigenous or tribal shall be regarded as a fundamental (definitional) criterion' (from ILO Convention 169 on indigenous and tribal peoples, quoted in IUCN 1997: 28).

The World Bank has also been active in developing policies for dealing with indigenous peoples. Its 'Tribal Peoples Operational Directive' of 1982 was superseded in 1991 by its Operational Directive 4.20 on Indigenous Peoples, which was the result of a five-year 'implementation review' of a sample of relevant World Bank projects (Dyson 1992). A key aim of Operational Directive 4.20, which recognises the existence of conflicting views on appropriate methods of approaching indigenous peoples in the development process, was to press for the informed participation of the people themselves through direct consultation. However, as we have seen with regard to the preparation of Cameroon's 1994 Forestry Law and associated *Plan de Zonage*, this commitment has not been carried through in practice.

So, who are the indigenous forest peoples of Cameroon? Or of West and Central Africa more generally? As acknowledged by World Bank staff (Dyson 1992) at a 1991 international conference on the conservation and management of rainforest resources in West and Central Africa, the concept of indigenous peoples as used in most environmentalist discourses was developed primarily in relation to Amazonian Amerindian groups – usually small and often quite isolated populations within much larger societies of different cultural backgrounds. However, even the new World Bank Operational Directive, like those of the ILO, the IUCN and other international or non-governmental organisations, is poorly adapted to the social and political realities of African societies,[4] and such definitions of indigenous peoples can, with no need to stretch their criteria, be made to apply to a great many of the different social groups that inhabit an African country like Cameroon.

It goes without saying that recognising the majority of the rural inhabitants of an African country as indigenous is not what such international organisations have in mind and, at the World Bank conference just mentioned, the Bank's definition of indigenous forest peoples, in practice, evidently excluded all agriculturalists from the 'indigenous peoples' category, since papers were commissioned on Pygmy peoples only. By this dubious logic, all the millions of people inhabiting the forested zones of West and Central Africa (with the exception of some few tens of thousands of Pygmy hunter-gatherers) could be passed over in the planning of the environmental future of the region. However convenient this may be for World Bank planners or conservation NGOs, it is clearly not a conception that accords with on-the-ground political or cultural realities. For that matter, however distinctive the culture of groups like the Baka Pygmy hunters-gatherers of south-eastern Cameroon, and however 'untouched' they may appear in popular ethnographic films, they are as deeply enmeshed in the complex processes affecting Cameroonian rainforests as any other of the inhabitants of this zone.

Discourses about 'indigenous' status always tend to have a political character, and this is hardly a new feature in the Cameroon context. Returning to our case of the Beti mentioned earlier, their attitudes toward the forest were and continue to be closely bound up with their conceptions of themselves as a 'noble' people. Beti oral traditions relating to a period 300 or more years ago assert that they migrated from the savanna zone to the north and entered the forest zone where they encountered 'less civilised' forest peoples, such as the Baka Pygmies, the Maka, the Basa and the Njem (Laburthe-Tolra 1981: 52 ff). Thus, although political and economic status in Beti society implied successful penetration of the forest and exploitation of its resources, it is clear that the precolonial Beti did not conceive of themselves as an indigenous forest people. A Beti man might demonstrate his strength and fearlessness by his hunting exploits but, for the Beti, it was the forest groups whom the Beti found on their arrival, archetypically the Pygmies, who possessed the 'deepest' knowledge of the forest. Beti men therefore valued links with Pygmy clients, who would exchange ivory, bushmeat, etc. for agricultural produce and who could serve as scouts to identify new routes through the forest to open up new trading opportunities (see, for example, Laburthe-Tolra 1981: 155–8).

Reflecting back on these oral traditions today, Beti villagers utilise discourses about indigenous status situationally. Beti may claim, on the one hand, that as long-standing inhabitants of their region, they are the owners of their forest lands and, in the area adjacent to the town of Mbalmayo for example, Beti villagers have conducted a 50-year dispute with the Forestry Department concerning the expropriation of their 'ancestral' lands for a forest reserve. On the other hand, in contexts where they wish to emphasise their greater 'civilisation', they are likely to stress that they came originally from the savannas to the north, bringing civilisation to the backward indigenous inhabitants of the forest zone.

As is apparent from the above discussion, discourses on the 'indigenous' status of this or that ethnic group or forest people are not recent developments in West African history. However, in the context of recent debates over forest conservation, notions of 'indigenous peoples' have taken on new resonances. Just as Beti commentators may utilise the concept of 'indigenous peoples' in several contrasting ways, depending on the argument they wish to sustain, so too do the representatives of modern-day environmentalist NGOs and international organisations, according to context. On the one hand, the notion of 'indigenous peoples', along with the closely linked term 'participatory development', often figures prominently in the advertisements and campaigning literature of these organisations. (See, for example, Rainforest Foundation [1998] and compare de Maret and Trefon [1998].) At the same time, NGOs like the Worldwide Fund for Nature (WWF) have become well aware of the danger posed to their fund-raising activities in the North, not to mention their relations with the governments of the South, of appearing to care more for animals than for people. The WWF is therefore usually quite careful in its fund-raising publicity to convey an image of working in close partnership with 'indigenous peoples' and defending their interests against external threats to their forest environment. However, when it has suited their aims, WWF staff have resorted to quite different rhetoric and practical action. For example, the former Director of Korup National Park (Cameroon's only national park in the rainforest zone), in a conference paper discussing park management, attempted to legitimate plans conceived by WWF and the Cameroon government to enforce the eviction of villages located within the park boundaries on the grounds that these villages are not indigenous to the area (Allo 1991: 155):

Historically, the Korup people have moved in and out of the Korup National Park within the last 50 years. Villagers (*sic*) split up to form new ones ... It is erroneously claimed that the villagers in the park are indigenous people, and too often we refuse to acknowledge that these are 20th century people with 20th century expectations ... They have chain saws, firearms of all sports (*sic*) (including automatic weapons), and poisonous compounds. They hunt indiscriminately. They have tin-roofed houses, etc. ...

Apparently, according to the park director's reasoning, the settlement mobility of swidden agriculturalists and their possession of items of modern material culture disqualify them as indigenous persons. Moreover, political manipulation of the definitional boundaries of the 'indigenous peoples' category is evidently legitimate when it suits the WWF's purposes but is considered illegitimate when local people use this tactic for aims other than biodiversity conservation. To quote the head of WWF's programme in Cameroon (Gartlan 1997: 2):

while the concept of indigenous people has never been scientifically precise (and, in many ways, as in the case of many of today's African 'tribes', seems to have been created by former colonial powers) some of these peoples, in order to stem the tide of land expropriation and environmental destruction, and who are becoming politically aware in the process, have re-defined the concept of 'indigenousness' and are increasingly using it to assert or re-assert territorial rights. This is the case even though many of these groups are highly sophisticated politically and often far removed from traditional ways of life. On the other hand, other 'traditional groups' such as the BaAka have no rights and virtually no political voice. It is important that the concept of 'indigenous peoples' is refined scientifically and that those groups with genuine claims are separated from those whose essential goal is territorial and expansionist. Claims for land and territory are often vigorously upheld indiscriminately by social anthropologists, the human rights movement and increasingly by the orthodox conservation movement. However, recent research indicates that in the complex mix of old and new migrant populations that characterize the forest margins throughout West Africa, that narrow definitions of the category 'indigenous peoples' should be avoided.

Interestingly, and quite contrary to the environmentalist discourse on indigenous peoples that I have been discussing up to now, Gartlan goes on to say that indigenous peoples don't have the scientific knowledge to halt habitat degradation and, if they had it, it would be no guarantee against greed. I will return to such dissenting views in the conclusion of this chapter.

Pristine Tropical Rainforest

For many of the same reasons that the international agencies and NGOs involved in struggles to conserve the world's rainforests have an evident interest in supporting a very restrictive definition of 'indigenous peoples', they also prefer to portray these forests as pristine, primeval Edens, which are only now being threatened by the avaricious demands of modern society. The concept of 'primary growth forest', represented as the ultimate outcome of centuries of undisturbed existence, is much used in conservation organisations' publicity. This popular notion fits in with the so-called Clementsian conception of climax forest regeneration derived from ecological research in the temperate zone (Clements 1916). In this view, a geographical area of a particular soil type and climate will tend to develop a particular climax vegetation, which will then remain stable, barring climatic change or human disturbance. More modern theoretical conceptualisations of humid tropical forests however, are based on a conception of 'gap ecology', which views these forests as much more dynamic and heterogeneous in their processes of development and replacement, and which acknowledges that 'disturbance is particularly important to the process of regeneration in tropical rain forest' (Brown 1998: 46). Unsurprisingly, given the powerful evocativeness for Northern donor audiences of the primordial rainforest image, this current theoretical thinking does not figure prominently in the NGOs' campaign literature.

Likewise, any discussion of the role of the 'hand of man' in the production of highly biodiverse 'natural' rainforests, which seems a contradiction in terms when viewed from the perspective of conservationist rhetoric, is either avoided altogether in this discourse or, as in the case of a recent paper by Steve Gartlan (1997: 3), the head of WWF's programme in Cameroon, is adamantly rejected as a naïve and wrong-headed view perpetrated by 'fundamentalist social scientists'. And yet, there is now abundant evidence from various parts of the world that apparently 'pristine' rainforests are often 'anthropic' landscapes – that is, forest environments which demonstrably have been altered by human impacts. Among the rainforests of the world, those of Africa are considered to be particularly anthropised. As the late P.W. Richards (1973: 24), one of the foremost botanists of rainforests in the post-war years, put it: 'Even in the depth of the so-called primary forest there is often evidence of former human occupation in the form of pottery and charcoal fragments in the soil,' and he took the view that 'human influence on African forests has been so strong and so continuous that no African rainforest can be accepted as untouched or 'primary'' (Jacobs 1988: 136). In Cameroon, substantial research on this theme has recently been carried out in several parts of the forest zone by the ethnobotanist Edmond Dounias. For example, working among the Mvae, a Fang group near the Equatorial Guinea frontier, Dounias, following earlier work by Letouzey (1985) the premier forest botanist of Cameroon, has carefully documented the marked degree of 'anthropisation' of many of the forests of this zone. Judging by the prevalence of recent archaeological remains in some of these areas, as well as the age structure of key tree species, these forested zones – termed 'forests of substitution' by Letouzey, were evidently areas of extensive cultivation in the past (Dounias 1993: 32).

Returning to Gartlan's defence of the concept of pristine rainforest against the attacks of so-called 'fundamentalist social scientists' (see, for example, Denevan 1992 or Fairhead and Leach 1998), one can understand that for a conservation organisation like the WWF whose aim is to create a system of protected areas throughout Cameroon analogous to, say, the national park system of the United States, and which is seeking to fund this arrangement by appealing to large public and private Northern donors (Moye 1998), complex historical and sociological arguments concerning the relation of African societies to their forest environments are inconvenient.

Publicity phrased in terms of urgent Threat to pristine Nature is more likely to attract donations. Undeniably there is a threat, as anyone who has visited Cameroon in recent years and watched the convoys of logging trucks rolling down the road can attest. But, as the unhappy catalogue of acrimonious relations between the Korup National Park authorities and the local people of that region bears witness, for example, the tendency of conservation NGOs to ignore or misunderstand the social realities of African rainforest environments serves the interest of no one in the end.

TOWARD A CONCLUSION

This chapter has attempted to sketch in the many competing interests contesting the present and future of Cameroon's rainforest. The rapid globalisation of this debate over the past fifteen years has been remarkable – a debate which has been dominated, up to now, by Northern environmentalist interests, donor governments and international institutions such as the World Bank. The content of this rainforest conservation discourse, as we have seen above, is quite striking in its very schematic appreciation of the local realities of life in rainforest societies, despite the frequent invocation of terms such as 'indigenous peoples', 'community-based conservation', 'participatory development' and 'stakeholder analysis'. Although it is evident that the use of these terms in some institutional contexts is little more than a tactical manoeuvre, I would argue that the social and historical blind spots of environmental NGOs and development organisations should not be interpreted simply as a function of insincerity or ignorance. In my view, there are powerful and persuasive cultural logics at work in this discourse which account for the prevalence of these blind spots, some operating in the domain of policy formulation and implementation and some in a more abstract, myth-like domain.

Taking the issue of policy formulation and implementation first, observation of the practices of international agencies, donor governments and Northern NGOs working in the field of rainforest conservation and management in Cameroon over the past seven years has convinced me that, whereas many projects working on the ground are often in serious need of a more adequate conceptualisation of the complex socio-political contexts in which they are working, the formulation of rainforest policy by governments and multinational agencies is virtually never based on detailed local knowledge. In fact, in these complex institutional contexts, too much local knowledge, or too careful an examination of the premises on which policies are grounded, is likely to be viewed as a hindrance, rather than a help, to efficient disbursement and management of aid funding. Employees of the institutions responsible for policy formulation and project development are subject to numerous organisational constraints which encourage them to take major policy decisions on the basis of currently fashionable theories and generalised, taken-for-granted assumptions that serve to oil the wheels of organisational consensus. In this world of short memos, of executive summaries and of 'bulletised' points, regional, let alone local expertise, is devalued as an employment qualification, in favour of general and purportedly transferable skills such as cost-benefit analysis, 'logical framework' construction, and other project planning and appraisal methods.

As anthropologists increasingly turn their research attention to the processes of policy formulation and issues of organisational culture in such complex bureaucracies, such findings are being reported again and again. In an influential study of organisational factors in overseas aid projects in southern Africa, James Ferguson (1994: 18) has argued that:

> the thoughts and actions of 'development' bureaucrats are powerfully shaped by the world of acceptable statements and utterances within which they live; and what they do and do not do is a product not only of the interests of various nations, classes, or international agencies, but also, and at the same time, of a working out of this complex structure of knowledge.

In particular, as the title of his book *The Anti-Politics Machine* suggests, Ferguson has shown how development agencies such as the World Bank manage to define their interventions in narrowly technicist terms, thereby excluding consideration of fundamental and determinative socio-political dimensions of the societies in which they work.

From the point of view of aid programme administrators, analyses of the political factors implicated in processes of underdevelopment, or of rainforest destruction, are likely to be viewed simply as impractical and unhelpful for the task of spending their budgets on purportedly achievable development aims. In contrast, conceptualisation of foreign aid projects in a more narrowly technical and de-politicised framework serves numerous bureaucratic functions. It builds organisational confidence (at least for public consumption) that a project's goals are achievable. This, in turn, speeds project approval, assisting the administrator to spend his budget allocation by the annual deadline, while strengthening his argument for budget increments in subsequent years. It provides a convenient framework for eventual project evaluation, based on purportedly measurable indicators – which is a bureaucratic requirement for apparent accountability and the demonstration of so-called 'value for money'. Finally (and this is particularly notable in biodiversity conservation projects, for which there is a limited constituency in countries like Cameroon), a down-playing of awkward issues relating to local political context helps to preserve the necessary organisational fiction of foreign aid programmes that donors' projects are always funded at the request of the host governments. Although this principle is embodied in the enabling legislation and charters of virtually all multinational and bilateral aid organisations (not to mention being entailed in the currently fashionable discourse of community participation), it is becoming an increasingly threadbare fiction in the case of programmes designed to achieve environmental conditionalities – which are often simply a Northern-mandated gun held to the heads of indebted Third World governments.

Current development programmes focusing on forest conservation and management, despite their participatory rhetoric, have a latent, if not manifest interest in misunderstanding the modes of resource control and appropriation of present-day forest societies. Certain key concepts, including terms such as 'community', 'indigenous peoples', 'stake-holders', 'common property', 'sustainable management', 'biodiversity conservation', play important roles, within the development and conservation policy discourses, of enabling business-as-usual by obscuring fundamental areas of contradiction. While such an analysis of the role of discursive categories in the bureaucratic functioning of Northern donor institutions and NGOs appears to be broadly applicable to most programmes of overseas development and global resource management, the theme of our present book encourages us to look beyond the immediate pragmatic level and consider more abstract issues. In the case of discourse about rainforest, which concerns us here, I have been repeatedly struck by the timeless, unhistoricised character of the images commonly employed therein[5] and, in thinking about the relation between myth and rainforest in this context, I was stimulated to pose the questions in my title – whose forest? whose myth? Although Headland's (1997) recent article on ecological revisionism makes the point that the term 'myth' is commonly used simply to denigrate opponents' positions in these debates, it seems to me that the discourse current in rainforest conservation circles shares some substantive similarities with mythic discourse in its common acceptation.

In his now-classic analysis of mythic time perspective, Lévi-Strauss (1962) made a basic distinction between 'cold', tradition-oriented, primitive societies that are said to be characterised by timeless, mythic modes of thought, versus 'hot', modern or modernising societies in which history and notions of progress predominate. However, in my view, the material we have considered in this chapter cannot be said to conform to this opposition – quite the contrary! If such a binary opposition is appropriate in analysing rainforest discourses at all (and I doubt that it is, given its evident ethnocentrism), I would be inclined to argue that it was the 'traditional', precolonial Beti whose conception of their occupation of the forest was notably historical in character, given that it focused on a process of forest penetration and conversion over time, linked with particular experiences of political group formation. In contrast, the conceptions of human–forest interactions presently used by multi-lateral institutions, NGOs and Northern donor governments in their policy formulations and fund-raising literature, often display a more timeless, idealised and mythic character. We have seen that this is the case with regard to commonly used conceptions of 'pristine' rainforest and 'indigenous' peoples, both of which suggest that there are environments and peoples who, thanks to their timeless lack of involvement with the transformative effects of societies-in-history, constitute suitable candidates for eternal preservation. From an anthropological perspective, following the work of Mary Douglas (1966, 1970) and Pierre Bourdieu (1977), the presence of such naturalising logics in current rainforest discourses can be interpreted as a clear case of culturally valued categories being sustained by appeals to extra-social processes.

To take another term which has frequently appeared in this chapter, I would argue that a word like 'community', as presently used in notions of 'traditional' or 'indigenous' communities or 'community-based conservation' or 'community forest management', serves a myth-like legitimating function in constructing idealised (and often idealistic), de-historicised social scenarios that underpin policy conceptions and discourses. Embodied in these notions of community is an image of a small-scale, culturally uniform collectivity, governed by an integrated code of customs or traditions which provides effective mechanisms of sustainable resource allocation and dispute regulation. Absent from this conceptualisation are all the elements of cultural or class difference, of legal pluralism, of articulations with the state or other aspects of the public sector or more global institutions that would call into question the putative autonomy of this idealised 'community', or render it problematic for cooption to the project of rainforest conservation and management. While such a view is very congenial as a support for neoliberal policies of decentralisation and other modes of attack on the state – an appealingly cheap and local solution – it can only be sustained by treating the 'community' as an unexamined 'black box', as has been the case thus far in Cameroon.

If myths can be understood as powerfully evocative stories which enunciate foundational cultural understandings, we have seen that mythic narratives are certainly prevalent in rainforest discourse. In the past, colonial administrators found it convenient to employ the legal fiction that large tracts of land were 'vacant and without master' and could therefore be claimed by the colonial state. Apart from the evident convenience of this view in legitimating colonial land expropriation, it conformed to European mythic perceptions of primitive societies as living through communal effort, directly from nature, without the institution of private property. Modern-day overseas aid and conservation institutions are presently active in formulating new laws and policies, which depend for their existence on other historical and social fictions perpetuated by persons who themselves do not live in these rainforest environments and who are answerable to political and donor constituencies imbued with environmentalist views of rather different origins (see, for example Guha and Martinez-Alier 1997).

To the extent that such views remain useful for global resource managers, they are likely to be perpetuated by appeals to the mythic perceptions of nature and community we have discussed above. However, we can also detect different conceptions of time operating within the environmentalist camp, which have more authoritarian, top-down implications. For example, for the radical preservationist wing of the ecology movement, indigenous

peoples cannot be trusted to look after Nature, and they are unhappy with
pragmatic attempts by certain mainstream environmentalist groups to strike
a deal with the people who inhabit these areas (cf. Guha and Martinez-Alier
1997: 93). Likewise, for an increasing number of global resource managers,
the complexity of dealing with local politics is leading to an exasperation
with community property notions (see also Gartlan or Allo above on
indigenous peoples) – and there is a temptation to strike long-term deals with
large expatriate logging companies (as in the World Bank's favoured first
draft of Cameroon's recent national forestry law), which seem easier to deal
with. In these latter cases, we tend to encounter 'hotter' conceptions of time
– a modernist, apocalyptic, neo-Malthusian rhetoric – in contrast to the
mythic timelessness of pristine nature. And we also tend to encounter more
explicitly interventionist tactics, legitimated by the perception of immediate
and dire threat to the primordial 'right' of Nature to exist. Ultimately, of
course, these two conceptions of time can be seen as a logically linked pair
of binary oppositions, which can be transformed as needed to legitimate
different forms of intervention by the global in the local – to validate policies
based on authoritarian intervention or on participatory partnership.
However, as these policies are operated at present in the Cameroon
rainforest, neither holds promise for the future – a future in which local
societies will necessarily be implicated, and much more on their own terms.

NOTES

1. Information for the present paper was collected in the course of a collective research
   project funded from 1992 to 1995 by the Economic and Social Research Council's (UK)
   Global Environmental Change Programme under the title 'The Cultural Context of
   Rainforest Conservation in West Africa'. The researchers were Paul Richards, Michael
   Rowlands, Barrie Sharpe and Philip Burnham, with Ruth Malleson as a research
   assistant. Monica Graziani also worked on a similar research theme with funding from
   an ESRC doctoral studentship and has made a substantial contribution to our joint
   work. Funding by the ESRC is gratefully acknowledged. However, the ESRC bears no
   responsibility for the arguments advanced in this paper, which are the author's own.
2. I say 'conventionally' because the figure of 20 million ha of humid forest is one that is
   recycled in many Cameroonian forestry documents, often without supporting reference.
   Another commonly-cited figure is 22 million ha. Other authors have given different
   figures. For example, Sayer (1992: 5) gives 25.6 million ha of forest, citing World Bank
   figures from 1989 (World Bank 1989). As Fairhead and Leach (1998) have recently
   pointed out, such figures are potentially subject to manipulation and need to be treated
   with caution unless carefully confirmed. Different authors and/or organisations use
   different definitions of what constitutes 'forest', with commercial logging interests often
   differing significantly from conservation organisations on this point. These differing
   definitions can then be used to support differing claims about rates of deforestation.
3. Such organisations include the World Bank, UNESCO, the ILO and the International
   Work Group for Indigenous Affairs.
4. It is interesting to note that although at the World Rainforest Movement's Annual
   Meeting in 1992, 'the International Alliance of the Indigenous Peoples of the Tropical
   Forest developed a charter that was signed and approved by 28 indigenous peoples'

organisations ... (only one of which was from Africa), and subsequently supported by
25 international NGOs' (Dyson 1992: 219), this alliance between Northern 'Green'
NGOs and the indigenous peoples movement has found little favour in Africa.
5. Even the notion of 'sustainability', although it may appear at first glance to have
everything to do with issues of duration, time and possibly history, often implies a
timeless, utopian view of a potentially steady-state world when used in much environmentalist discourse. On the other hand, more practical users of the term (such as the
World Bank or USAID) often have remarkably short time-frames in mind, which are
closely linked with the project cycles of their development projects.

REFERENCES

Allo, A. 1991. 'Linking local socio-economic development activities to park management
in the WWF-Korup project: Mundemba, Cameroon', in D. Kabala (ed.) *Symposium on
the Dja Faunal Reserve*. Paris: UNESCO.
Bourdieu, P. 1977. *Outline of a Theory of Practice*. Cambridge: Cambridge University Press.
Brown, N. 1998. 'Degeneration versus regeneration – logging in tropical rainforests', in
F.B. Goldsmith (ed.) *Tropical Rainforest: A Wider Perspective*. London: Chapman & Hall,
pp. 43–73.
Burnham, P. 1996. *The Politics of Cultural Difference in Northern Cameroon*. Edinburgh:
Edinburgh University Press.
Cleaver, K. 1992. 'Deforestation in the western and central African forest: the agricultural
and demographic causes, and some solutions', in K. Cleaver, M. Munasinghe, M. Dyson,
N. Egli, A. Peuker and F. Wencélius (eds) *Conservation of West and Central African
Rainforests*. World Bank Environment Paper No. 1. Washington, DC: The World Bank,
pp. 65–78.
Clements, F.E. 1916. *Plant Succession: An Analysis of the Development of Vegetation*.
Washington, DC: Carnegie Institution.
Copet, E. 1977. 'Nguelebok: essai d'analyse de l'organisation sociale des Mkao Mbogendi',
Doctoral thesis. Paris: Université de Paris X.
Copet-Rougier, E. 1990. 'Le clan, le lieu, l'alliance', in F. Héritier-Augé and E. Copet-
Rougier (eds) *Les Complexités de l'alliance*. Paris: Editions des Archives Contemporaines.
de Maret, P. and Trefon, T. 1998. 'Road building in Central Africa: foolproof development
or a good way to get stuck in the mud?', Avenir des Peuples des Forêts Tropicales Briefing
Note No. 16. Brussels: APFT Coordination Unit.
Denevan, W. 1992. 'The pristine myth: the landscape of the Americas in 1492', *Annals of
the Association of American Geographers* 82: 369–85.
Diaw, M. 1997. '*Si, nda bot* and *ayong*: shifting cultivation, land use and property rights in
southern Cameroon', Overseas Development Institute Rural Development Forestry
Network Paper 21e. London: Overseas Development Institute.
Douglas, M. 1966. *Purity and Danger*. London: Routledge & Kegan Paul.
—— 1970. *Natural Symbols*. London: Barrie & Rockliff.
Dounias, E. 1993. 'Dynamique et gestion différentielle du système de production à
dominante agricole des Mvae du Sud-Cameroun forestier', Doctoral thesis. Montpellier:
Université des Sciences et Techniques du Languedoc.
—— 1996. 'Recrûs forestiers post-agricoles: perceptions et usages chez les Mvae du Sud-
Cameroun', *Journal d'Agriculture Traditionelle et Botanique Appliqué* 38 (1): 153–78.
Dyson, M. 1992. 'Concern for forest peoples: a touchstone of a sustainable development
policy', in K. Cleaver, M. Munasinghe, M. Dyson, N. Egli, A. Peuker and F. Wencélius
(eds) *Conservation of West and Central African Rainforests*. World Bank Environment Paper
No. 1. Washington, DC: The World Bank, pp. 212–21.

Egbe, S. 1996. 'Forest tenure and access to forestry resources in Cameroon: an overview', paper prepared for Franco-British Conference on Land Tenure and Resource Access in West Africa in Dakar, Senegal. London: International Institute for Environment and Development.

Ekoko, F. 1997. 'The political economy of the 1994 Cameroon Forestry Law', unpublished paper presented at the African Regional Hearing of the World Commission on Forests and Sustainable Development, Yaounde.

Fairhead, J. and Leach, M. 1998. *Reframing Deforestation*. London: Routledge.

FAO. 1985. *The Tropical Forestry Action Plan*. Rome: Food and Agriculture Organisation, in association with IBRD, WRI and UNDP.

Ferguson, J. 1994. *The Anti-Politics Machine*. Minneapolis: University of Minnesota Press.

Fisiy, C. 1996. 'Techniques of land acquisition: the concept of "Crown land" in colonial and postcolonial Cameroon', in R. Debusmann and S. Arnold (eds) *Land Law and Land Ownership in Africa*. Bayreuth African Studies No. 41. Bayreuth: Eckhard Breitinger, pp. 223–54.

Fondo, S. n.d. 'The structure of the logging industry and sustainable forest management in Cameroon', unpublished report prepared for Worldwide Fund for Nature, Cameroon.

Furze, B., De Lacy, T. and Birckhead, J. 1996. *Culture, Conservation and Biodiversity*. Chichester: John Wiley & Sons.

Gartlan, S. 1989. *La Conservation des ecosystèmes forestiers du Cameroun*. Gland: International Union for the Conservation of Nature.

—— 1997. 'Every man for himself and God against all: history, social science and the conservation of nature', paper presented to the Worldwide Fund for Nature Annual Conference on People and Conservation.

Giles-Vernick, T. 1996. 'A dead people? Migrants, land and history in the rainforests of the Central African Republic', PhD dissertation, Johns Hopkins University.

Goldman, M. 1998. 'Inventing the commons: theories and practices of the commons' professional', in M. Goldman (ed.) *Privatizing Nature: Political Struggles for the Global Commons*. London: Pluto Press, pp. 20–53.

Guha, R. and Martinez-Alier, J. 1997. *Varieties of Environmentalism: Essays North and South*. London: Earthscan Publications.

Guyer, J. 1984. *Family and Farm in Southern Cameroon*. Boston: Boston University African Studies Center.

Hardin, G. 1968. 'The tragedy of the commons', *Science* 162: 1243–8.

Headland, Thomas. 1997. 'Revisionism in ecological anthropology', *Current Anthropology* 38(4): 605–30.

ITTO. 1998. *Annual Review and Assessment of World Tropical Timber Situation 1998*. (Internet www.itto.or.jp), Yokohama: International Tropical Timber Organization.

IUCN (Inter-Commission Task Force on Indigenous Peoples). 1997. *Indigenous Peoples and Sustainability: Cases and Actions*. Utrecht: International Books.

Jacobs, Marius. 1988. *The Tropical Rain Forest: A First Encounter*. Berlin: Springer Verlag.

Jua, Nantang. 1989. 'The petty bourgeoisie and the politics of social justice in Cameroon', in P. Geschiere and P. Konings (eds) *Conference on the Political Economy of Cameroon – Historical Perspectives*. Research Report No. 35. Leiden: Leiden University African Studies Centre, pp. 737–55.

Laburthe-Tolra, Philippe. 1977. 'Minlaaba', Doctoral thesis. Atelier de l'Université de Lille III.

—— 1981. *Les Seigneurs de la forêt*. Paris: Publications de la Sorbonne.

—— 1985. *Initiations et sociétés secrètes au Cameroun – essai sur la religion Beti*. Paris: Karthala.

Leplaideur, A. 1985. *Les Systèmes agricoles en Zone Forestière: les paysans du Centre et du Sud Cameroun*. Paris: CIRAD-IRAT.

Letouzey, R. 1985. 'Notice de la carte phytogéographique du Cameroun au 1/500,000°. Document TV pour légende feuille B et cartes 3, 5, et 6', Toulouse: Institut de la Carte Internationale de la Végétation.

Lévi-Strauss, Claude. 1962. *The Savage Mind.* Chicago: University of Chicago Press.

Marsden, David. 1994. 'Indigenous management and the management of indigenous knowledge', in S. Wright (ed.) *The Anthropology of Organisations.* London: Routledge, pp. 41–55.

Milol, Adonis. 1998. 'Gestion des forêts communautaires au Cameroun: vers une nouvelle hierarchisation des chefferies traditionnelles?', in *L'Homme et la Forêt Tropicale* (Xèmes Journées de la Société d'Ecologie Humaine), Marseille: Université de Provence.

MINEF (Ministry of Environment and Forestry, Cameroon). 1995. *National Forestry Action Programme of Cameroon.* Yaounde: Ministry of Environment and Forestry.

Moye, M. 1998. 'Feasibility research and consultations for the creation of a conservation trust fund in Cameroon', unpublished consultancy report prepared for Worldwide Fund for Nature, Cameroon.

Nguiffo, Samuel-Alain. 1994. *La Nouvelle Legislation forestière au Cameroun.* Yaounde: Fondation Friedrich Ebert.

—— 1998. 'In defence of the commons: forest battles in southern Cameroon', in M. Goldman (ed.) *Privatizing Nature: Political Struggles for the Global Commons.* London: Pluto Press, pp. 102–19.

Rainforest Foundation. 1998. *Out of Commission: the Environmental and Social Impacts of European Union Development Funding in Tropical Forest Areas.* London: Rainforest Foundation.

Richards, P.W. 1973. 'Africa, the "odd man out"', in B. Meggers (ed.) *Tropical Forest Ecosystems.* Washington, DC: Smithsonian Institution, pp. 21–6.

Richards, P. 1996. 'Forest indigenous peoples: concept, critique and cases', *Proceedings of the Royal Society of Edinburgh* 104B: 349–65.

Sayer, J.A. 1992. 'Development assistance strategies to conserve Africa's rainforests', in K. Cleaver, M. Munasinghe, M. Dyson, N. Egli, A. Peuker and F. Wencélius (eds) *Conservation of West and Central African Rainforests.* World Bank Environment Paper No. 1. Washington, DC: The World Bank, pp. 3–9.

Schneemann, Jochem. 1994. *Étude sur l'utilisation de l'arbre Moabi dans l'Est-Cameroun.* Yaounde: SNV.

Sharpe, Barrie. 1998a. 'Forest peoples and conservation initiatives: the cultural context of rainforest conservation in West Africa', in F.B. Goldsmith (ed.) *Tropical Rainforest: A Wider Perspective.* London: Chapman & Hall, pp. 77–97.

—— 1998b. '"First the forest ...": conservation, "community" and "participation" in south-west Cameroon', *Africa* 68(1): 25–45.

Tchomba, Gilbert. 1992. 'Echec d'une politique économique fictive', *La Nouvelle Expression* 28 April.

von Benda-Beckmann, Franz. 1993. 'Scapegoat and magic charm: law in development theory and practice', in Mark Hobart (ed.) *An Anthropological Critique of Development: The Growth of Ignorance.* London: Routledge, pp. 116–34.

Weber, Jacques. 1977. 'Structures agraires et évolution des milieux ruraux: le cas de la région cacaoyère du Centre-Sud Cameroun', Cahiers ORSTOM, Série Sciences Humaines, 16 (2).

World Bank. 1989. *Sub-Saharan Africa: From Crisis to Sustainable Growth.* Washington, DC: The World Bank.

3 THE LAND PEOPLE WORK AND THE LAND THE ECOLOGISTS WANT: INDIGENOUS LAND VALORISATION IN A GREEK ISLAND COMMUNITY THREATENED BY CONSERVATION LAW

Dimitrios Theodossopoulos

This chapter explores the interface of land and law in local action and discourse in the context of indigenous protest against environmental conservation in a Greek island community. Vassilikos, the community in question, is located on the island of Zakynthos in south-west Greece. Its inhabitants are people whose livelihoods had been until recently solely dependent on farming, although, nowadays, they try to enter the flourishing tourist economy. Their efforts to take advantage of the opportunities offered by tourism are hastened by some new prohibitions on their locally perceived 'right' (*dikaioma*) to control their land. The prohibitions are related to the establishment of a Marine National Park in the vicinity and have instigated fervent opposition, resentment and some mobilisation to confront collectively the legal status quo of the restrictions. The pathways of action followed by the local protagonists, all rooted in a culturally constituted pattern of dealing with the state and its officials, have mostly remained unsuccessful.

As recently as 30 or 40 years ago landownership in Vassilikos was restricted to a few privileged families, and access to land for peasant labourers was controlled by powerful landlords, who were the heads or heirs of those families. Acquiring land of their 'own' was a particularly difficult process for the landless labourers of Vassilikos, which is why the ownership of land is considered to be of special symbolic significance in the community. Since the 1970s most of the local people have acquired small plots of land and have effectively developed small-scale tourism enterprises without totally abandoning farming and cultivation. The establishment of the National Park, however, has threatened some of the local people with serious legal restrictions on the freedom to develop their own land.

The conservation law, as this is applied in Vassilikos, challenges the local understanding of landownership, since without completely expropriating the land from its owners, it denies them the right to control some of its productive resources. The local landowners alienated from what they perceive to be 'a proper and entirely legitimate relationship with one's land', directly confront the legal restrictions imposed. They formulate instead their own version of 'justice' and 'legitimacy', articulating unwritten and customary notions of 'ownership' with formal and juridical ones. In the context of the environmental dispute, diverging categories of meaning about land merge in a constantly transforming discourse, which reflects the unwillingness of the landed actors to become parted from their land.

My ethnographic account in this chapter focuses on the significance of land and landownership for the inhabitants of Vassilikos. It further portrays the skill and ingenuity of the local protagonists in creating new versions of 'legitimacy', according to which the symbolic valorisation of land can hardly ever be separated from the indigenous articulation of ownership and justice. My analysis also addresses the issue of indigenous confrontation with the law in Vassilikos, and reflects on the work of other ethnographers (Campbell 1964; Loizos 1975; Herzfeld 1991, 1992) who have underlined the awkward relationship between Greek actors and the agents of the state. In the sections that follow, the legal dimension of land relations is examined in the context of the post-feudal regulations on access to cultivated land that persisted in Vassilikos until the 1970s, as well as the current restrictions on tourist development due to conservation. The mythic or symbolic relationship with the land is manifested in the multitude of cultural significations of land and landownership. The purpose of the chapter is to reveal how the inhabitants of Vassilikos, the Vassilikiots, deal with legal constraints by creatively bringing together heterogeneous elements of land valorisation with notions of justice.

THE LAND OF LAW IN THE PAST

Vassilikos has been inhabited since antiquity,[1] but the memories handed down to most present-day Vassilikiots go back to 'the times of the Venetians', the period when the island was a Venetian colony (1485–1797). When the Venetians took official control of the island, they found the land in a state of complete desolation. A violent Ottoman raid (1479) had devastated the island's resources and population (Konomos 1981). Most of the land was deserted and the once-cultivated fields covered with wild vegetation due to neglect. The Venetians immediately issued proclamations to all the neighbouring Venetian provinces on mainland Greece welcoming new settlers to the island. Vassilikiots refer to those years of depopulation as the time when 'the land was deserted':

The land was deserted (*erimi*). Two families came from the Peloponnese, two families with sheep ... They came to Zakynthos to escape Turkish rule.

Then the Venetians issued an announcement (*vgalan firmani*) and noblemen (*arhontes*) came to settle on the island.

You see, at this time it was not forbidden by law to cut down trees (*longous*) and bushes (*thamnous*). If you could find deserted land you could settle on it ... and that was (considered) appropriate and legal!

During 'the times of the Venetians', the most fertile parts of the island were divided up among feudal lords, the descendants of Italian or Greek soldiers and officials, who had served the Venetian Republic. Some of those families already had noble titles; others acquired them later. The land on those feudal estates was cultivated by Greek-speaking tenant farmers (*sembroi*),[2] who were entitled only to a small percentage of the agricultural produce. The Venetian landlords effectively introduced Western European feudalism on Zakynthos along with a system of unwritten guidelines governing the economic and social relationship between the landless and the landed aristocracy. In the Venetian social context, the term *sembroi* was synonymous to the term 'serfs'; it denoted an occupational identity (the cultivators of someone else's land) and a social position (being landless, illiterate and dweller of the countryside).[3] Zakynthian *sembroi* were subject to customary expectations, unwritten rules and a landlord's personal sense of justice. It is said in Vassilikos that 'the old landlords had rights of life and death' over 'their' *sembroi*. In narratives from the distant past, the landlords (*oi afendades*) figure as the embodiment of law and authority: 'in the old days', Vassilikiots describe, 'the landlord (*o afendis*) was the law (*o nomos*) on his land'.

In the first part of the 19th century Zakynthos became a British protectorate. The British did not radically challenge the pre-existing social divisions of the local society (Konomos 1983, 1985; Hannell 1989). The wealthiest Zakynthian men sustained the older tradition of receiving their higher education – medicine and law were the favourite subjects – in northern Italy (cf. Pratt 1978: 42, 45; Hannell 1989: 111). Unsurprisingly, the most popular language among the elite was Italian, which was also the official language for practising law (Hannell 1989: 111). Legal representation of the illiterate and, primarily, Greek-speaking *sembroi* was thus seriously impaired. In court, landlords were always the winners and justice remained out of reach for the peasant labourers of the countryside (1989: 125–6).

It was only after 1864, when Zakynthos was incorporated into the young Greek state, that the power of the aristocracy was drastically limited. The integration of the island society into the national economy and administration deprived the old ruling class of several hereditary privileges. By the turn of the 20th century, the Zakynthian middle class residing in the island's capital, had gained a dominant position in local political and social life. Unlike the Zakynthian middle class, however, the peasant labourers living in the island's countryside remained dependent on the landlords until as recently as the Second World War, and in some isolated areas such as

Vassilikos, until even later. In fact, until the 1960s, most inhabitants of Vassilikos were tenant farmers (*sembroi*) working on the estates of landlords. They were entrusted by their landlords with parcels of land to cultivate, and were entitled in return to a small portion – usually approximately one fourth (*quarto*) – of the agricultural produce.

The exact percentage of the produce allocated to the tenant farmer varied according to the characteristics of the cultivation in question, its duration, the labour required, the cost of fertilisers, and the fertility or accessibility of particular plots of land. Most of those separate parameters affecting different kinds of cultivation or different types of land were regulated – in a sense they were accounted for – by several standardised types of economic arrangements which were known in Zakynthos as *sembremata*. *Sembremata* were unwritten sets of rules for managing the economic interaction between landlords (*afendes*) and labourers (*kopiastes*).[4] They provided a blueprint for negotiating the actual terms of cultivation, the expectations of the landlords and the responsibilities of the labourers.[5] Most of those standardised sets of economic arrangements were highly unfavourable to the tenant farmers and their logic was deeply embedded in the feudal tradition of the past.

In the period before and after the Second World War, two-thirds of the cultivated land in Vassilikos was part of an old, single estate. The legitimate heirs to this estate were two brothers, members of an old, noble Zakynthian family. The older brother was named and referred to by the villagers by his title, *kontes* (count). He was the master (*afentis*) of the land, and the local *sembroi* were entirely dependent upon him. In the late 1960s, his property was inherited by his nephew, an educated man who disapproved of the noticeable remnants of feudalism in the village. He sold plots of land at relatively low prices to local people, who had been working on the estate of his father and uncle for many years. Despite this disposal he still owns most of the land in the area, since, being the only heir of the estate, he inherited a huge amount of land.[6] Most of the villagers – but especially the senior ones – still treat him with the kind of respect that is highly reminiscent of the past.

The remaining third of the cultivated land in Vassilikos was owned by landlords of upper middle-class origin, wealthy people living in the capital of the island. These smaller landlords, in the past, despite their bourgeois origin, employed the pre-existing customary system of rights and regulations for the cultivation of their land (*sembremata*). Like the aristocrat landlords, this second category of landowners were approached by their tenants with a combination of respect and fear. Similarly, the term 'master' (*afentis*) was used by all *sembroi* to refer to these bourgeois landlords. Since the 1970s, some of those landlords have lost or sold their land in Vassilikos. Others divided their landed property into smaller plots inherited by numerous descendants in accordance with the widespread Greek inheritance law, which has always encouraged land fragmentation to subvert the formation and proliferation of large land estates (Herzfeld 1985b: 167–83).

The older Vassilikiots have vivid memories of the time when they were landless labourers (*sembroi*) working and living on the land of powerful landlords. This is how a 70-year-old man talks about that time:

Most of the time, the landlord used to put you on some piece of land (*htima*), according to the size of the family you had, for example, and how much land you could cultivate. Sometimes, the landlord would replace his serfs; for some reason he may not have wanted them to stay. In this case, he could give them three months' notice to find another place. Sometimes, though, one family might have stayed in the same place for many years ...

And a younger, 50-year-old Vassilikiot, adds:

The landlord was the law (*o nomos*) on his land. If he *liked* you or your *wife* that was good: you could stay. If he didn't ...

While a third, even younger Vassilikiot, further explains:

Many families used to stay on the same plot of land for years. Often, sons were cultivating the land that was previously cultivated by their fathers. But this was not *their* land. It was the landlord's land. He used to ask them to sign a contract every four years, declaring that they had just arrived on his land. In this way they couldn't claim ownership of the land.

According to state legislation if someone is 'using', that is living on or cultivating, someone else's land for a period of more than 20 years he may claim ownership of this particular piece of land (cf. Handman 1987: 51). This law is referred to in the Greek legislation as *hrisiktisia* and accounts for those cases where the landlords insisted that the *sembroi* should move to another piece of land or sign a contract stating that they were new to the land. Du Boulay (1974: 269–70), in her classic ethnography of a Greek-mountain community, refers to this law with its formal name, *Nomos Katohis* (the Law of Possession), and states that her informants, like my Vassilikiots, considered it to be the source of contention and enmity among fellow villagers.

Unlike the fertile land on the plains, mountainous areas with land less suitable for intensive cultivation never attracted the interest of landlords. In the absence of the aristocracy, land titles and other legal documents, some landless Vassilikiots managed to clear neighbouring bush and enlarge their smallholdings – a popular strategy among Greek agriculturalists (Handman 1987: 50–1; Herzfeld 1985b: 169, 181). Memories of 'clearing bush' always refer to a shadowy and unspecified era in the past, the time when state legislation had little restraining power on the everyday practices of landed or landless actors.[7] Men and women in Vassilikos are always fascinated when they talk about clearing 'deserted, uncultivated lands':

Some families on the mountainous area of Xirokastelo always (*apo anekathen*) had land of their own. Their land used to be scrub (*lagadia*) and they cleared it (*ta xehersosan*). No one knows exactly how they got this land.

Nowadays, it is forbidden to cut scrub. In the past people used to find empty stretches of scrubland and cleared them (*tis xehersosan*); as did the people of Xirokastelo, for example.

In the years following the Second World War there was increasing pressure on Zakynthian landlords with big estates to sell or distribute plots of land to landless farmers. This situation had an effect on Vassilikos, which was, due to its geographical isolation, less attuned to the social changes that had been occurring in other parts of the island from the beginning of the century. Some Vassilikiots refer to incidents in which landlords were murdered in other Zakynthian villages in the late 1940s. The civil war which took place on mainland Greece between left- and right-wing forces, contributed to the creation of an atmosphere of general confusion, where social tensions at a local level were often resolved by murder (cf. du Boulay 1974: 238–42; Handman 1987: 59–60, 62–3; Hart 1992: 78–80). Most people in Vassilikos believe that those incidents made the landlords insecure enough to start selling their land. This argument rests on the popular assumption that, the more landless people that existed in the village, the greater the likelihood for dissatisfaction culminating in social unrest. In fact, as soon as the growing demand for landownership became overwhelming, the inhabitants of Vassilikos became increasingly aware that the exploitative economic arrangements of the past could not be further tolerated in the mid-20th century. They started criticising some of their fellow landless villagers for being 'faithful-to-the-master' (*afentopistoi*), and tried harder to enlarge their smallholdings.

For the people of Vassilikos acquiring 'land of their own' was the realisation of a lifelong goal and the result of persistent effort. Within a period of 40 years, they escaped from a situation of complete landlessness, to a comparatively comfortable economic position. Nowadays, almost every Vassilikiot possesses some land suitable to be used either for cultivation and animal husbandry or as the basis for small-scale tourist enterprise. Several local farmers still cultivate land owned by landlords or the landlords' descendants, according to economic arrangements which have been modified so as to allow a greater profit for the peasant labourer (*kopiastis*). Most of the local people wish to expand their land holdings so as to allow for more productive economic activities, related either to animal husbandry or tourism. For them the struggle to acquire land is a process which is not yet fully complete.

'PROGRESS' AND LEGAL IMPEDIMENTS IN THE PRESENT

During the last two decades the living standard of the people of Vassilikos has been increasingly improving. The gradual introduction of tourism to the community, provided Vassilikiots with new economic alternatives. Small-scale economic enterprises like 'rooms for rent', mini-markets, *tavernas*, car and motorbike rentals gradually appeared everywhere in Vassilikos. The new entrepreneurs had the opportunity to give their households a transfusion of cash, while at the same time, their periodic engagement with tourism did not necessitate a complete abandonment of their farming activities. As I have argued elsewhere (Theodossopoulos 1997a, 1997b: 253–4, 1999: 3), tourism and agriculture are not necessarily antagonistic. In Vassilikos, the traditional farming products are readily absorbed by the growing tourist market[8], while tourist enterprises benefit from the aura of tradition associated with the consumption or display of 'original', local produce or handicrafts. 'Tourism keeps (*krata*) our children in Vassilikos', the older people explain, 'the young men don't have to look for jobs elsewhere, as we did in the 1960s and 1970s'.

In Vassilikos tourism is not developed on a grand scale, but is a small-scale, household-based enterprise (cf. Galani-Moutafi 1993: 250) closely associated with the land. Most households have 'rooms for rent' built on or adjacent to their farmland. Most families run a *taverna* or a restaurant, which is built under their living quarters or on some other part of the household's cultivated land. The members of the Vassilikiot households participate in these enterprises collectively – that is, each member does what s/he can – devoting the same kind of effort and commitment to it that they do to joint economic activities related to agriculture: 'tourist jobs and farming both demand a struggle (*agona*)' the local people maintain.[9]

Tourism in Vassilikos is understood as a benevolent economic force that makes life in the village viable. It does not merely ensure the continuation and reproduction of the local community in anthropological terms. 'It makes life in the village comfortable and worth living', as the local women and men put it.[10] It is like an entrance ticket to prosperity, a 'fair' reward for the difficulties Vassilikiots have endured in the past. Provided that most Vassilikiots 'own some land of their own' on which they can develop tourism, and are, in general, released from the exploitative conditions of their feudal past, the 'progress or prosperity' (*prokopi*) they have awaited for so long is within the reach of the average household.

An unexpected impediment, however, threatens to hinder the steady pace of this 'process'. Some of the beaches of Vassilikos are important breeding sites for the Mediterranean Loggerhead turtle,[11] a species threatened with extinction. Since the mid-1980s, Greek and international groups of environmentalists have been persistently lobbying in favour of the establishment of a National Park, which will include the relevant beaches and prohibit development on the adjoining land. The environmentalists maintain that for the turtles' egg-laying to take place, the basic requirements are a minimum of noise and light pollution on the land surrounding the 'egg-laying beaches', and an almost total absence of people on the beaches themselves. In other words, the prerequisites for turtle breeding and the development of tourism appear to be mutually exclusive, or this is what the conservationists seem to demonstrate with 'hard' scientific data.

The Greek government, on the other hand, maintains an encouraging policy towards the development of tourism. Yet on the issue of the turtle conservation programme in Vassilikos, the continuous pressure of the environmentalists in Athens was effective enough to secure legislative approval for the creation of a National Park. The state had no alternative but to promote conservation by law, in a reluctant effort to get 'in line' with the pro-environment regulations of the European Union. In 1983, for example, a Presidential decree prohibited any construction on the land adjacent to the turtle breeding sites and, three years later, a new law formally approved the creation of a Marine Conservation Park. Since then, state legislation has inhibited tourism development in the area without providing any compensation to the affected landowners.

The affected landowners were informed that they did not lose the legal possession of their property. They were, in fact, allowed to exercise all forms of traditional farming economic activity on their 'conserved' land. They were also told that the current conservation measures were temporary and that a more drastic solution to their problem will be offered in the near future. The reluctance of the state bureaucracy to pay the cost of conservation was thus officially rationalised by a rhetoric of incompleteness and temporality. Under the pretext that more environmental planning should be completed and critically examined, delay and postponement in finalising the conservation measures was instituted as the official policy of the state. As Herzfeld has noted in a conservation dispute in Crete, when bureaucracy and the need of precise documentation is involved 'nothing is more permanent ... than the temporary' (1991: 251).

In due time, the long bureaucratic delays frustrated both the environmentalists, who sought to guarantee the survival of the turtles, and the local landowners, who could not afford 'to fall behind' (*na minoun piso*) in the pursuit of tourism development and, thus, deprive their families of 'progress or prosperity' (*prokopi*). It is not surprising, then, if, during the last 15 years, relations between the defenders of conservation and the inhabitants of Vassilikos have become seriously strained. Vassilikiots consider the 'ecologists' – a term they use to refer to the environmentalists – responsible for the conservation prohibitions, and realised that their presence on the island would only be a source of trouble for them. After waiting in vain to be compensated for their expropriated property, they collectively declared their opposition to the National Park and harassed – by constant threats and, in some cases, physical violence – the various groups of conservationists attempting to gain a foothold on their land.

In addition to those measures, the affected landowners consistently and demonstrably ignored the conservation laws. They kept on building illegal constructions next to one beach or renting sun-umbrellas on the other. On several occasions the police and various civil officials attempted to stop the erection of illegal buildings constructed on the conservation area. They always returned to their headquarters spectacularly unsuccessful. As I will describe in detail in the following sections, law enforcement of the restrictions related to the conservation legislation (cf. Herzfeld 1991), or even hunting regulations (cf. Theodossopoulos 1997a), is very ineffective in Vassilikos. The local spirit of resistance dramatically displayed in stances of 'performative excellence' – to quote Herzfeld (1985a: 16) – successfully undermines the reluctant efforts of the local authorities to impose the legal conventions. Narratives such as the following were often heard in the village, during the time I was conducting my fieldwork:

They tried to pull down the new illegal constructions (*aphthereta*) today. But *one of the owners* (:his name is explicitly stated) was waiting for them. He went down the road with a gun and he stood in front of the bulldozer and the Public Prosecutor. He said: 'Get down, if anyone dares (*opoios einai antras as katevei kato*). You will not pull down my house on my land, which I own with legal papers. Come on, give me back the taxes for the purchase. Why didn't you stop me, when I was paying the taxes?

The affected landowners found themselves owning land over which they had no control, while other Zakynthians in neighbouring areas were developing tourism on their own land and making a great deal of profit. This situation was locally interpreted as a 'great injustice', a violation of people's 'basic right' (*vasiko dikaioma*) to 'do whatever they want with their own land'. I will end this section with an extract from a report written by a group of Vassilikiot landowners affected by the conservation legislation. The report is addressed to the Prefect of Zakynthos and neatly portrays what the Vassilikiots understand as legitimate landownership:

This land which we possess today belongs to us. It was bought by our grandfathers and our parents in 1955. They didn't usurp this land from anybody else. Nobody gave this land to us for free. This land is the outcome of the labour and sweat of three generations, who lived and toiled all their lives, having as their only dream to possess this land, their land ...

We believe that the land owned by any villager, who is a Greek [citizen], belongs to him ... Or do you think that his land belongs to the state, so as to be under the state's control and under anybody chosen by any government in power?[12]

LOCAL ACTORS IN CONFRONTATION WITH THE LAW

In local narratives about the recent past, Vassilikiots locate the agents of state law in the island's capital (*sti Hora*), a place once visited only by men, and in fact by those men who had the 'know how' of public affairs. Three hours journey by cart on the main earth road was the spatio-temporal distance separating the self from civil servants and most representatives of the law. With the notable exception of the school teacher, the priest and the president of the local council – the last two positions being held by permanent

inhabitants of the community – Vassilikiots had few opportunities to engage
in a direct interaction with the representatives of the state. In the context of
this relative isolation, the landlords, individuals well-connected with the
outside world,[13] could exercise real authority on the common villagers. 'The
landlord' *(o afentis)*, as the native commentary already presented demonstrates, personified the local version of the law. 'He' *(sic)*, also, embodied – as
a patron – the only reliable (or less reliable) source of representation in
dealing with the state.

In contexts other than the immediate locality of the village, Vassilikiots
have always found themselves in a disadvantaged position. 'What could the
unpolished and illiterate villager *(o axestos kai agramatos horiatis)* do in front
of the people of the law? *(brosta stous anthropous tou nomou?)*', is the rhetorical
question phrased repeatedly by the older Vassilikiots. Their accounts of
examples of bureaucratic mistreatment and state injustice are numerous
and colourfully depicted. The indigenous self in these accounts is always
portrayed as the innocent victim of unscrupulous state officials, who enact
a prescribed form of 'indifference' by actively defying any attempt by the local
protagonists to personalise the legal transaction (Herzfeld 1992).

The painful Vassilikiot confrontations with bureaucrats and state officials
resonate with a broader, recurrent theme in the anthropological literature
that focuses on Greek-speaking communities: the indigenous insecurity,
inadequacy, mistrust and frustration in formal and informal dealings with
the law (Campbell 1964; Loizos 1975; Slaughter and Kasimis 1986: 118;
Herzfeld 1991, 1992). In a well-known analysis of the politics of patronage
among the Sarakatsani pastoralists of northern Greece, Campbell vividly
sketches the hesitation and awkwardness of the shepherds in formal
encounters with civil servants and other administrators (1964: 241–3). The
shepherds, who were usually not favoured by legislation (1964: 239),
developed a generalised disbelief in the power of justice to deliver (1964:
257). The indigenous distrust of the law, according to Campbell, is only part
of the broader structural contradictions arising out of the uncomfortable –
but often mutually profitable – coexistence of a hierarchically, top-down-
instituted system of state administration (1964: 258) with an equally
hierarchical, but emerging from below, system of patronage (1964: 260–1).

Another central theme emanating from Campbell's study of the relationship between Greek indigenous actors and the representatives of state is the
family-oriented logic of the former (1964: 215, 235, 238, 246). The
Sarakatsani do not expect government officials – 'people who share with
[them] no bond of kinship or community' (1964: 246) – to safeguard their
civil rights or pay impartial attention to their legal claims. The same theme
is further explored by Loizos (1975) in his ethnography on politics in a
wealthy farming community in Cyprus. The Cypriot villagers studied by
Loizos, although wealthier and more cooperative with non-kin than the
Sarakatsani, appeared similarly hesitant and anxious in their dealings with
the law and state officials (1975: 121, 202). The older among them would

approach with suspicion the representatives of the state, since they consider it highly improbable – almost unreasonable – to expect favours or benefits from unrelated people (1975: 121, 200). From their point of view, state benefits and legal rights are issues 'out' of control for the local self (1975: 4, 121). When it comes to political representation, a firm belief in the effectiveness of personalised relationships impels the same people to rely on the elite leadership of educated relatives (1975: 203, 228). Several ethnographic examples offered by Loizos (1975) show that when farmers pursue their rights against the state, relationships defined by kinship often provide a model for relating to bureaucracy and the law.

In Vassilikos, local actors pursuing their cause against bureaucracy often adopt kinship metaphors. Those Vassilikiots who are more directly affected by the constraining measures of ecological conservation have succeeded in uniting the majority of their fellow villagers in support of their cause. Webs of kinship, which in Vassilikos are bilaterally traced, facilitate the tuning of the local protest in a unified direction. The mobilisation of relatives offers additional connections to the wider society. As a young Vassilikiot man once explained to me, 'having the support of your relative is one thing, but having the support of your relative's patron is even better'. Like the shepherds studied by Campbell (1964) or the farmers studied by Loizos (1975), Vassilikiots heavily depend on relatives, patrons and educated local elites in claiming their civil rights. Those 'parallel' strategies – to evoke Campbell's (1964: 260) 'parallel hierarchies' – are usually effective, but in the case of environmental legislation are proven feeble. From the point of view of the Vassilikiots, bureaucratic exclusion is instituted in the name of endangered species with which the human protagonists share no 'common substance' (Herzfeld 1992: 177).

Herzfeld (1991) has examined an ethnographic case that has many similarities with my data in Vassilikos. In the Cretan town of Rethemnos, the owners of old 'Renaissance and Turkish' houses are effectively stopped from renovating or rebuilding their property (Herzfeld 1991, 1992: 160). Those affected by the restrictions of archaeological conservation have developed hostile attitudes towards bureaucracy and the agents of the state. Their predicament is rationalised by a stereotypical blame of the agents of the state. Herzfeld treats this generalised blame as a social strategy; 'stereotypical expectations about bureaucratic unfairness offsets [people's] sense of personal failure' he explains (1992: 4, 165). But when local actors are deprived of any available option of tracking 'justice' in the world of bureaucracy they might resort to illegal measures. Some Rethemniots defy the state law by illegally demolishing and/or reconstructing their properties overnight (Herzfeld 1991: 5, 229). Building before the arrival of authorities is a successful strategy in Greece. Local actors very well know that the police will be hesitant to take further action when faced with a *fait accompli* (1991: 229).

Identical strategies are also practised in Vassilikos. Frustrated local people, after waiting for years for some compensation or other solution, reluctantly make the decision to build 'overnight' in the restricted area. At the subsequent arrival of the police they forcefully protest by shouting, waving guns or openly contesting the law. Here is a typical example of resistance narrated by a 55-year-old man in Vassilikos:

> Listen what happened today in Dafni [one of the turtle-beaches under conservationist protection]:
>
> The police and a bulldozer from the town attempted to demolish the newly constructed houses and the little tavern ... But then, one of the landowners approached the bulldozer with his hunting rifle. 'This is my land', he said to the driver and the civil servants from the town. 'This is my land, and you'd better go away ...' He was so angry that he could even have murdered someone. The people from the town saw that he was 'determined' (*apophasismenos*) and left.

Vassilikiots very well know that the state authorities will almost certainly back off when confronted with a determined crowd of local people. When women and old men are part of an agitated crowd, the protest obtains an air of legitimacy, one the surprised police officers cannot ignore. The safest thing for them to do is leave, since, as Herzfeld puts it, 'what is built cannot be unbuilt' (1991: 248).

For several years since the establishment of the Marine National Park, small groups of Vassilikiot men, with no access to legal avenues for developing tourism, have defended their sun-umbrella and canoe-hiring enterprises at places where tourist activity is strictly prohibited by the conservation legislation. The conservationists – horrified at the sight of sun-umbrellas perched on the sandy beaches where turtles usually lay their eggs – persistently called for the support of various law enforcement officers. But the local protagonists, through protest enhanced by daring instances of challenging the law, carried on with their illegal enterprises. They have been, however, obviously agitated by the continuous obstruction of the police. 'This is not a decent life', one of the Vassilikiot sun-umbrella entrepreneurs explained to me, 'every couple of weeks or so, I have to struggle with the police to keep this business running ... those people do not understand that we have families and children to feed ...'

Similar performances of resistance to the law are enacted in Vassilikos almost every year during the prohibited spring turtle-dove hunt. Vassilikiot hunters theatrically display their disregard for the hunting regulations, claiming that the authorities 'cannot stop them from hunting on their land'. Although the number of turtle-doves is drastically diminishing – a serious predicament according to the hunters themselves – the local hunters argue that their 'passion' for hunting is uncontrollable and beyond any rational calculation. Like some Kalymnian men, studied by Sutton (1998: 57–76), who persistently throw dynamite during the Easter celebration despite fatal accidents and some considerable public dissatisfaction, Vassilikiot hunters are content to recite versions of their own idiosyncratic process of legitimisation. 'We will go on hunting and nobody will dare to stop us ... ' they openly declare, 'this is our land and this is *our* way ... we will be hunting on our land for ever, like we always did ...'.

On those rare occasions when the patrol car of the Forestry Department or the police approaches the village, the hunters, whose presence was previously conspicuously manifested, predictably disappear. Every car that heads towards Vassilikos on the single village road can be viewed from the neighbouring houses and the message is easily spread by telephone or other means. Some of the hunters claim that they have connections in the Forestry Department or in the police headquarters and are, therefore, in a position to know well in advance an imminent inspection patrol. Obviously indirect connections of this sort – despite the failure to safeguard the interests of Vassilikiots against the conservation legislation – are particularly effective in the case of illegal hunting. It must be noted, however, that the local hunters' noisy performances of illegality hardly compare with the frustration and anguish experienced by some of them when resisting restrictions relating to land access. As I will describe in the following section, the indigenous relationship with the land is too intimate and too complex to be easily compromised.

THE SIGNIFICATION OF LAND IN THE INDIGENOUS DISCOURSE

When God expelled Adam and Eve from Paradise, God gave them this land and said: 'This land is for you, to work it hard and earn your bread (*to psomi sas*) from it.' This is what we do all the time. We work the land. We care for the animals and everything living on it.

This is how Vassilikiots relate to their relationship with their land; a relationship loaded with meaning and signification. The same land Vassilikiots work and pragmatically utilise, is portrayed in narrative in the most affective, idealistic terms. Vassilikiots talk a lot about their land; they talk about it poetically, metaphorically, emphatically. They refer to landownership as their achievement. Their 'own land' is what they acquired after years of hard effort, their reward for being patient and diligent during the times of landlessness and poverty. Landownership is the tangible evidence that all the sweat and toil (*mohthos*) they have spent, has not been wasted or 'lost' (*den hathike*). Their land is proof that they have escaped the fate of the landless tenant (*tin moira tou ftohou sembrou*) and have a place, their place in the sun (*ston ilio moira*).

More importantly, Vassilikiots' landownership is a sign of self-determination, the solid foundation of Vassilikiots' current efforts for 'a better life'. Nowadays, landownership is a sound claim, a guarantee, for a legitimate entrance to the economy of tourism. It is locally articulated that all people, who share a bond with the land of Vassilikos, deserve (*axizoun*) to benefit from it. Landownership, coupled with descent from people who have lived or worked on the land of Vassilikos, gives access to a locally perceived moral right to seek employment in local tourist enterprises. The mere idea of non-local or non-Zakynthian people making a profit out of tourism on the land of Vassilikos, makes the indigenous inhabitants furious. Most of them consider tourism – or one's right to profit from it – as the best locally available alternative to poverty. Non-Vassilikiots seeking employment in tourism, despite recurrent exceptions (cf. Galani-Moutafi 1993: 250–1; Kenna 1993: 87–8), are usually not welcomed.[14]

Apart from being a prerequisite for entering tourism, land is conceived by Vassilikiots as the safe foundation from which one can embark on insecure ventures like tourism. 'Tourism doesn't always do well' (*den vgainei*), the local protagonists maintain. This is why one's own land is locally described as one's bedrock for dealing with unpredictable loss or lack of success. Alternative sources of income based on land, like cultivation and animal husbandry, are the safety valve for fluctuations in the tourism economy. Most Vassilikiots still practise traditional farming activities. Some 'keep' animals and make considerable profit out of cheese-making, others retain large olive groves, construct greenhouses for vegetables or cultivate vegetables and fruit (especially tomatoes and melons) on summer gardens in the open. The large majority of Vassilikiots maintain the identity of the farmer (*agrotis*) and like all farmers proudly depend on their land. As they put it, 'if tourism doesn't do well, the land will be here for us'.

The relationship of Mediterranean agriculturalists with their land and its multiple, 'thick' signification is well attested in the regional literature. Several classic anthropological monographs have emphasised the varying sets of value land has for farming people in the Mediterranean. As Davis (1973: 73) argues, 'land has more than purely economic uses', and these are, in fact, numerous. It influences marriage strategies, strengthens ties of unity among households, and constitutes an imperishable part of a households' history and a households' collective identity (Lison-Tolosana 1966; du Boulay 1974; Pina-Cabral 1986). It signifies self-sufficiency, security, status, political influence and the independence of household members – especially female ones – from disreputable paid labour (Davis 1973; Loizos 1975). A working relationship with the land is synonymous with responsibility, power, vitality and good health (Pina-Cabral 1986: 25, 152–3, 208).

In the Vassilikiot discourse, all the above-mentioned sets of value assigned to landownership are presented as self-evident facts. The landed actors of Vassilikos explicitly point out that their relationship with the land – 'their land' – is a very serious one. The non-local participant in a relevant conversation is not even allowed to question this point.

But this is my land, the land my father secured with sweat and effort. What do you expect me to do? Offer it as present to the ecologists? (*Na tin hariso stous ecologous?*)

These are serious matters (*sovara pragmata*), my dear (*matia mou*). We are talking about people's land (*ti gi ton anthropon*) ... the land of our fathers, the land we work, the land we sweat over ... people's legal land ...

Here, the multiplicity of meanings attached to the land adds to the weight of the land–actor relationship. The polysemic signification of the land is readily translated into evidence with argumentative power. In conversations about conservation, meanings drawn from land symbolism merge with practical considerations and aspirations for material and social progress (*prokopi*). As such, the ancestors' sweat and suffering embodies all current dreams for economic growth. Metaphors about the land marry tradition with development, while divergent sets of meanings, that sharply clash with each other in the context of other conversations,[15] regroup and unite to challenge the validity of conservation law.

I can't sell my land. I can't see the land of my father being sold to foreigners and especially to the 'ecologists' ... I want to keep my land and make something nice on it.

This is the land I worked. This is the land I ploughed with a wooden plough. [It is] here that I struggled (*edo palepsa*), [it is] here that I'll grow into an old man (*edo tha geraso*).

CONCLUSION

The examples presented in the previous sections demonstrate that, in the context of the environmental dispute in Vassilikos, the indigenous confrontation with the law is more successful when it takes place within the physical space of the community. Far away from home the local actors tend to appear intimidated by the formality and impersonality of the bureaucracy (cf. Campbell 1964; Loizos 1975; Herzfeld 1992). Alienated by officialdom they usually prefer compromise (*symvivasmos*) to direct confrontation in court (cf. Papataxiarchis 1990: 366–8). More importantly, their resistance to the law is not aimed at the abolition or modification of the law itself, but rather towards blocking its application at the local level. Thus the scope of the Vassilikiot opposition to conservation is limited to opposing or defying the application of the conservation restrictions on their land. This can be achieved by collective protest that involves the mobilisation of an extensive kinship network and frequent dramatic instances of their determination. Reliance on one's kin, one's patrons or one's kin's patrons could extend support to various levels of official administration (cf. Loizos 1975). But when it comes to direct representation in the process of making laws, local actors remain – to use Ardener's (1975: 21–2) term – 'muted'. Despite their articulacy in local conversation, Vassilikiot men and women simply do not speak the language understood by the agents of the law. In their struggle against environmental conservation they could only resort to strategic, but ephemeral resistance to the laws made by 'others' for them.

In the cultural context of modern Greece, the indigenous rationality in dealing with the law and the state radically diverges from official thinking (Herzfeld 1991: 159). This explains the frustration of the indigenous actors in the official settings where the law is represented and enacted. The local notions of justice and fairness, however, are not completely divorced from legal terminology. In fact, the local rhetoric often contains elements of the official one (1991: 257); they are just only too well incorporated within a rich body of less official – but laden with symbolic potential – cultural signi-fications. As I have described in the previous section, the local protagonists frequently refer to the land titles they hold or the land taxes they have paid. But the potential weight of these more formal, or more 'eligible', assertions is frequently overshadowed by the influx of several other sets of value attributed to landownership.

Land valorisation in Vassilikos addresses an impressive array of meaningful associations. Like elsewhere in the Mediterranean, landowner-ship plays a crucial role in shaping household identity, material self-sufficiency, moral independence, marriage strategies, prestige and political influence (cf. Lison-Tolosona 1966; Davis 1973; du Boulay 1973; Loizos 1975; Pina-Cabral 1986). In a cultural context where self-interest and well-being are understood in terms of household-oriented priorities (cf. du Boulay 1974: 169–70; Loizos 1975: 66, 291, Hirschon 1989: 104, 141, 260), the constant evocation of diverse forms of land valorisation indirectly legitimises the relationship between landed actors and their land. A moral connection is drawn between the benefit from land's productive resources and the right of accessing or controlling the land. The moral and the legal sig-nificance of the land are thus combined in a unique rhetorical form that constantly reflects on what constitutes justice at the local level. As Campbell puts it, 'if the law does not allow a man to protect the interests and dignity of his family, then it does not represent justice' (Campbell 1964: 215).

In local conversation about the land, polysemy brings about certainty rather than confusion. Different sets of values point in the same direction, and Vassilikiots are, indeed, certain. Their claim of control over their property is not perceived as merely valid; it is understood as rightful and just (*dikio*). Repetition empowers local argument, while the richness of cultural justifi-cation allows no space for doubt. God's trust in the farmer's guardianship of the land, the sweat of Adam or of the grandfathers, and the right to develop one's own land, become part of the same powerful rhetoric. Defying conser-vation law engenders a moral quality legitimised – in fact, naturalised – by the discursive unravelling of layers of cultural justification. In the context of Vassilikiot resistance to conservation legislation, 'the land of myth' – that is the multiply-signified, traditional or less traditional relationship with the land – is inseparable from moral law. As Vassilikiots themselves put it:

This is our land here. This is our property. We've paid taxes for it. We've worked hard on it for generations. Like our fathers did, as we do now ... Our job is to care for the land ... This is why God gave Adam the land ... because the land needs care ...

NOTES

I would like thank Elisabeth Kirtsoglou, Shanell Vaughn, Roger Smedley and Allen Abramson for their comments and suggestions during the preparation of this chapter.

1. See, Sordinas (1993), Kourtesi-Philipaki (1993), Kalligas (1993); also Thucydides (I, 47; II, 66).
2. Most of the people who later composed the peasant population of Zakynthos arrived on the island at the beginning of the 16th century from Venetian provinces on mainland Greece which were threatened by Ottoman expansion.
3. Unlike Zakynthos, in rural areas of the south-western Peloponnese, that part of mainland Greece that lies opposite Zakynthos, the term *sembroi* refers to people who participate in a more egalitarian relationship. *Sembroi* could be two individual farmers cooperating in the cultivation of their respective plots of land for their mutual benefit.
4. Different kinds of *sembremata* arrangements regulated different kinds of cultivation and animal husbandry. For more information on particular, standardised *sembremata* arrangements and the actual negotiation between labourers and landlords, see Theo-dossopoulos (1997a: 33–8, 72–8, 108–9). For an examination of similar arrangements on Corfu, see Couroucli (1985: 87–94).
5. The landlords, who were usually absent during the course of the negotiations, were represented by their overseers.
6. Some Vassilikiots argue that his father and uncle deliberately planned their parenthood so as to avoid the fragmentation of their property, a practice customary in Zakynthos' feudal past.
7. Handman (1987) states that the villagers of Pournari (Pouri) on Mount Pillion spent a great deal of effort clearing neighbouring bush, taking advantage of the leniency of the state legislation before the Second World War. After cultivating the cleared land for a period of 20 years, they had the opportunity to legally claim ownership of it (Handman 1987: 50–1).
8. This positive relationship of tourism and agriculture is not representative of a widespread phenomenon in island Greece. Kenna (1993: 86), for example, reports that in Anafi agriculture is not rejuvenated by the introduction of tourism.
9. In Vassilikos, like many other parts of rural Greece (Friedl 1962: 75; du Boulay 1974: 56; Kenna 1990: 149–50; Hart 1992: 65; Dubisch 1995: 215), the term 'struggle' (*agonas*) is widely used by both men and women to denote manual labour invested in farming and household-related responsibilities. The same term, when applied to labour invested in tourism, indicates the integration of small-scale tourism enterprises into the local, household-oriented economic logic.
10. Both women and men in Vassilikos are involved in the emerging economy of tourism. As Galani-Moutafi (1993, 1994) demonstrates, after the introduction of tourism into previously predominantly rural communities women were provided with new oppor-tunities to further strengthen their economic role in their respective households. For women's new employment opportunities in tourism, also see Kenna (1993: 85–6).
11. Loggerhead Sea Turtle, *Caretta caretta*.
12. This report is entitled '*Memorandum from the owners of landed property at Gerakas, Dafni and Sekania in Vassilikos Community*'. Gerakas, Dafni and Sekania are the disputed turtle-beaches in Vassilikos.
13. Most landlords of either aristocratic or bourgeois origin were residents of the island's capital (Zakynthos or Hora). Some were even residing in Athens. All were perceived

by the landless labourers of Vassilikos as 'town dwellers', 'proper people (*anthropoi*) with manners and knowledge of the world (*kosmos*)'.

14. In practice, there are notable exceptions of non-local Greek workers or even Albanian wage labourers being hired by Vassilikiot tourist entrepreneurs. As the local people get better acquainted with the newcomers the more likely it is that they become treated as an exception that proves the rule. 'Albanians are thieves', most Vassilikiots will claim, 'but my Albanian [the one working on ego's land] is a good man.' Similar expressions are applied to non-local Greek workers.

15. Two separate conflicting discourses about tourism and agriculture exist in Vassilikos. The first epitomises the advantages of traditional peasant economic activities and underscores the disadvantages of tourism. The second argues for the reverse: the discomforts of the peasant lifestyle are emphasised, while the benefits of tourism are highlighted. Between those two ideological poles, represented by some older people who consistently express their nostalgia for the vanishing farming lifestyle and some young men who persistently criticise the lifestyle of the old-fashioned agriculturalists, exist the great majority of Vassilikiot men and women, who are perfectly capable of contributing to both discourses, at different instances, provoked by different economic or social dynamics. For example, a tourist season which is not particularly profitable, or various incidents of tourists behaving 'improperly', could instigate a discussion in which the negative aspects of tourism are vividly elaborated and the old peasant ideals revered. The same rhetorical fervour is often expressed at the disappointment of a poor olive harvest or a prolonged drought; but this time it is the 'misery' of peasant life which is portrayed, and unrewarded agricultural labour that is overstated.

REFERENCES

Ardener, E. 1975. 'The problem revisited', in S. Ardener (ed.) *Perceiving Women*. London: Malaby Press.

Campbell, J.K. 1964. *Honour, Family and Patronage: A Study of the Institutions and Moral Values in a Greek Mountain Community*. Oxford: Oxford University Press.

Couroucli, M. 1985. *Les Oliviers du lignage: une Grèce de tradition Venitienne*. Paris: Maisonneuve et Larose.

Davis, J. 1973. *Land and Family in Pisticci*. London: Athlone Press.

Dubisch, J. 1995. *In a Different Place: Pilgrimage, Gender, and Politics of a Greek Island Shrine*. Princeton, NJ: Princeton University Press.

du Boulay, J. 1974. *Portrait of a Greek Mountain Village*. Oxford: Clarendon Press.

Friedl, E. 1962. *Vassilika: A Village in Modern Greece*. New York: Holt Rinehart & Winston.

Galani-Moutafi, V. 1993. 'From agriculture to tourism: property, labour, gender and kinship in a Greek island village (part one)', *Journal of Modern Greek Studies* 11: 241–70.

—— 1994. 'From agriculture to tourism: property, labour, gender and kinship in a Greek island village (part two)', *Journal of Modern Greek Studies* 12: 113–31.

Hart, L.K. 1992. *Time, Religion, and Social Experience in Rural Greece*. Lanham: Rowman & Littlefield Publishers.

Handman, M.E. 1987. *Via kai poniria: antres kai gynaikes s' ena elliniko horio*. Athens: Ekdoseis Kastanioti.

Hannell, D. 1989. 'The Ionian islands under the British protectorate: social and economic problems', *Journal of Modern Greek Studies* 7: 105–32.

Herzfeld, M. 1985a. *The Poetics of Manhood: Contest and Identity in a Cretan Mountain Village*. Princeton, NJ: Princeton University Press.

—— 1985b. '"Law" and "custom": ethnography of and in Greek national identity', *Journal of Modern Greek Studies* 3: 167–85.

—— 1991. *A Place in History: Social and Monumental Time in a Cretan Town*. Princeton, NJ: Princeton University Press.

—— 1992. *The Social Production of Indifference: Exploring the Symbolic Roots of Western Bureaucracy*. Chicago: University of Chicago Press.

Hirschon, R. 1989. *Heirs of the Greek Catastrophe: The Social Life of Asia Minor Refugees in Piraeus*. Oxford: Clarendon Press.

Kalligas, P.G. 1993. 'Oikisi stin arhaia Zakyntho', in *Oi oikismoi tis Zakynthou apo tin arhaeotita mehri to 1953*. Athens: Etaeria Zakynthiakon Spoudon.

Kenna, M.E. 1990. 'Family, economy and community on a Greek island', in *Family, Economy and Community*. Cardiff: University of Wales Press.

—— 1993. 'Return migrants and tourism development: an example from the Cyclades', *Journal of Modern Greek Studies* 11:60–74.

Konomos, K. 1981. *Zakynthos, pentakosia hronia: politiki istoria (teyhos A)*. Athens: K. Michalas.

—— 1983. *Zakynthos, pentakosia hronia: politiki istoria (teyhos B)*. Athens: K. Michalas.

—— 1985. *Zakynthos, pentakosia hronia: politiki istoria (teyhos Γ)*. Athens: K. Michalas.

Kourtesi-Philipaki, G. 1993. 'I proistoriki katikisi tis Zakynthou', in *Oi oikismoi tis Zakynthou apo tin arhaeotita mehri to 1953*. Athens: Etaeria Zakynthiakon Spoudon.

Lison-Tolosana, C. 1966. *Belmonte de los Caballeros: A Sociological Study of a Spanish Town*. Oxford: Clarendon Press.

Loizos, P. 1975. *The Greek Gift: Politics in a Greek Cypriot Village*. Oxford: Basil Blackwell.

Papataxiarchis, E. 1990. 'Dia tin systasin kai ofelian tis koinotitos tou horiou: sheseis kai symvola tis entopiotitas se mia Aegiki koinonia', in M. Kouminon and E. Papataxiarchis (eds) *Koinotita, Koinonia kai ideologia: Kostandinos Karavidas kai i provlimatilci ton koinonikon epistimon*. Athens; Ekdoseis Papazisi.

Pina-Cabral, J. 1986. *Sons of Adam, Daughters of Eve: The Peasant Worldview of the Alto Minho*. Oxford: Clarendon Press.

Pratt, M. 1978. *Britain's Greek Empire*. London: Rex Collings.

Slaughter, C. and Kasimis, C. 1986. 'Some social-anthropological aspects of Boeotian rural society: a field report', *Byzantine and Modern Greek Studies* 10: 103–60.

Sordinas, A. 1993. 'Lithina ergaleia proimotatis typologias sti Zakyntho', in *Oi oikismoi tis Zakynthou apo tin arhaeotita mehri to 1953*. Athens: Etaeria Zakynthiakon Spoudon.

Sutton, D.E. 1998. *Memories Cast in Stone: The Relevance of the Past in Everyday Life*. Oxford: Berg.

Theodossopoulos, D. 1997a. '"What use is the turtle?": cultural perceptions of land, work, animals and "ecologists" in a Greek farming community', unpublished PhD thesis, University of London.

—— 1997b. 'Turtles, farmers and "ecologists": the cultural reason behind a community's resistance to environmental conservation', *Journal of Mediterranean Studies* 7(2): 250–67.

—— 1999. 'The pace of the work and the logic of the harvest: women, labour and the olive harvest in a Greek island community', *Journal of the Royal Anthropological Institute* (NS) 5: 611–26.

Thucydides. *History of the Peloponnesian War: Books I and II*. With an English translation by C. Forster Smith. London: William Heinemann Ltd, 1919.

4 TRACT: LOCKE, HEIDEGGER AND SCRUFFY HIPPIES IN TREES

Paul Durman

This chapter, taking a philosophical approach, reflects on the protest in 1997 against the expansion of Manchester's Ringway airport, 'The Campaign Against Runway Two' (CAR2). It confronts the thorny problem of reconciling understandings of land as a resource and as an 'object' of our subjective responses. The land dispute under examination it is not merely a conflict over land usage. In fact, there is much more to the usage of land than its practical or technical dimensions. To facilitate this view, I call on Locke's theoretical reflections as a paradigm for understanding liberal property values. His arguments have played a well-documented role in dispossessing cultures – and indigenous people – of their lands. Heidegger's 'The Question Concerning Technology' (1977) is also discussed in the latter stages of the chapter. It adds a further dimension to this dispute and sheds light on the character of the protesters' actions.

I argue that the protest under examination is a creative act of political significance in response to the development of the Bollin Valley area. Starting with a description of the protest site and the social groups to be found there, I proceed to an investigation of John Locke's philosophy as a means of understanding the logic of claim rights to property. In a subsequent section, this discussion is complemented by an application of Martin Heidegger's work, which theoretically unlocks and reveals the structure of the relationship between people and the land. In the conclusion I draw all these philosophical threads together by examining the limits of a Lockean approach and the relevance of Heidegger's hermeneutic analysis in the context of the events that took place during the protest over Runway Two.

MEETING THE LAND

Driving past Manchester Airport on the A 538 in April of 1997 you would have found it difficult to see the tree protesters of the 'Coalition Against Runway Two'. The first signs of the protest's physical presence are the ribbons, tin foil and bells tied to the gap in the hedge where the public footpath leads on to the site. This is the only entrance into the valley now that the right to evict has been won in the courts. Behind the hedge earthworks rise up. These were built to deflect noise from the road and they obscure any view of what lies beyond. Rounding the crest only vague hints of blue and white tarpaulins can be seen in the trees. Between us and the wood there is a field criss-crossed with JCB tracks, cut up by small earthworks and separated from where we stand by a steel mesh fence patrolled by police and security guards. The policeman who opens the gate for us is friendly and informative.

Once the wood is entered the scene changes; Cliff Richard camp, no longer accessible at ground level, is enclosed against the threat of eviction by earthworks, branches and fencing appropriated from the security cordon. Overhead, rope walkways thread their way between the trees; some of these walkways are as high as 80 feet above the ground. Making our way through the waterlogged valley we pass a sign informing us to keep to the path so as not to disturb the foxes and come out into the river valley itself: a flat meadow, the meandering line of the river marked by poplar trees. We meet a couple of protesters who rechristen us Poochie and Green and we are taken to Wild Garlic camp.

The atmosphere is easy going but there is an undercurrent of anxiety as the eviction is expected any day. There is no overt organisation and tasks are accomplished on a voluntary basis underwritten by peer pressure. Food is obtained through donations from shoppers and from food discarded by the supermarkets because it has reached its sell-by date. Wood is scavenged from the ground, but fetching water is the hardest task, involving long walks to friendly farmers some distance from the camps. This involves walking through the fences and the possibility that security will refuse entry back onto site. Meals are communal and usually involve jokes, stories and possibly even songs.

There are in total six camps; Cliff Richard, River Rats, Flywood, Jimi Hendrix, Wild Garlic and Zion Tree spread out around the Bollin Valley. At night there is occasional activity by the police – the protesters call it 'harassment'. Dark vans might pull up on the perimeter road, indistinct figures might move by the fences and start rumours that they were preparing for a dawn eviction. Halogen spotlights would shine into the trees, illuminating and blinding their occupants. Music, chicken noises and excerpts from *Bugs Bunny* might be even heard: 'We're gonna get the wabbit, we're gonna get the wabbit.'

By night powerful lights on 30 pylons shine into the camps, powered by generators that constantly rumble in the background. By every generator is a portakabin staffed by security. The security are paid £3.50 per hour and are drawn from the dole offices of Manchester, some on pain of losing their benefit, they allege. Talking to the security gives you the impression that they are not particularly committed to their employers, and there is some tacit support for the protest. There is a hierarchy amongst the security, designated by the colour of their hats; white hats are the lowest tier, then yellow, with at least one to every portakabin. Red hats are supervisors who come around to give the orders, frequently accompanied by the police. And very rarely seen but always commented on, blue-hatted officials of Manchester Airport. They are commented on because, of course, their presence suggests decisions are being made.

In defending the Bollin Valley from development the protesters use a variety of tactics. Most obviously, their physical presence is an obstacle to the machinery necessary to modify the land. This strategy is strengthened by using methods which make the protesters' removal very difficult for bailiffs during the eviction. Locking-on is the most successful and popular tactic. A lock-on is created by setting an iron ring into concrete. A tube is then placed around it and further concrete is poured around until it sets. The protesters wear padlocks or wire bracelets constantly so they can lock-on at a moment's notice to the nearest point. It is impossible to remove a protester with bolt croppers because his or her arm is now buried inside a concrete tube. The concrete must first be broken before the lock-on can be removed with bolt croppers. When lock-ons are placed in tunnels or in trees they are particularly successful as it is difficult to get the machinery necessary into place. Sometimes a lock-on is placed around the neck which makes the operation to remove it very delicate, possibly threatening the protester's life. Protesters may also suspend themselves on platforms which are strung between the trees. The ropes cannot be cut without threatening injury because the platform's stability relies on the tension of the ropes between the trees. It is difficult to pluck the protester off the platform because of obstruction by overhead branches.

Tunnels not only make extraction of protesters difficult but help the occupation of the trees by making it difficult to bring in the 'cherry-picker' platforms which take the bailiffs up into the trees to cut protesters free. Heavy machinery would collapse the tunnels killing the occupants. This was a real fear for the authorities during the eviction; there were several press releases expressing concern about the welfare of protesters by representatives of Manchester Airport Authority, and re-couching the eviction in terms of a rescue project. The death of a protester would be a PR disaster for them. When heavy plant moves onto site protesters also form a human barrier above the tunnels linking arms or locking-on to each other to make removal by security more difficult. Other protesters dance around the machinery which is protected by a cordon of security guards to prevent sabotage. Machinery is sabotaged when there is the opportunity, although some protesters feel damage to property goes beyond the remit of the protest.

TAKING THE LAND: JOHN LOCKE'S ARGUMENTS FOR ENCLOSURE AND PRIVATE PROPERTY

John Locke's celebrated argument for the moral grounding of property rights sits within the context of the political debates raging in England following the English Civil War. Specifically the argument was constructed to refute Robert Filmer's argument for unlimited private property. Filmer's argument is essentially libertarian, granting unlimited control of that which is owned (Tully 1993). Locke wishes to show that property is grounded in a moral framework: that far from it being a liberty, it is based on a claim for sustenance which demands duties as well as granting rights. Both Filmer and Locke take as their starting points the passage in scripture, Genesis 1.28. However, where Filmer argues that this passage confers private and exclusive property to Adam and his heirs (an argument for divinely granted kingship), Locke claims it to be conferring common property to all of humanity.

Locke employs this passage in his argument, but significantly he does not argue *from* scripture per se, but rather from the standpoint of natural law. In a state of nature, he assumes, the earth and all upon it is owned in common by all mankind. This premise is based upon the claim that we all have a right to preservation. The Earth is a gift *given* to us for this sake: for our survival and enjoyment. The other strand of his argument is the inalienable right to one's own person, and to the labour of one's own person. From these premises spring the right to private ownership and the moral provisos which bind it, and are intended to avoid a despotic dominion which would exclude a part of humanity from the means to sustenance. I summarise the structure of his argument below:

1. God has given to Humanity the earth and the reason to make use of it to its best advantage.
2. A man (sic) owns his own body and its labour.

It follows that property is acquired:

3. By mixing his labour with something the man comes to own it. Thereby taking it out of a state of nature and annexing it from the common.

Property is limited as follows:

4. A man may have property only in so much as 'enough and good' (Locke 1993: Ch. 5, § 27) is left for others.
5. A man may benefit from his property in so much as what is produced does not spoil or go to waste.

The provisos as stated by Locke are: a man may have property only in so much as 'enough and as good is left for others' (Locke 1993: Ch. 5, § 27); a man may benefit from his property in so much as what is produced 'does not spoil or go to waste' (Locke 1993: Ch. 5, § 31). Locke's approach certainly diverges greatly from Filmer's libertarian view of property, but some clarification is needed as to how Locke moves from common ownership to private property. The mechanism that Locke uses is labour and his task is to show that this annexes from what is held in common in a morally coherent fashion. It is in this ingenious move that Locke also leaves the land vulnerable to the type of exploitation that the protests at CAR2 object to. He argues that because the land is given for mankind's sustenance, and because this is its purpose, private property is a more efficient means of sustenance. The latter assumption leads us to an additional proposition: since property is the most effective means to use the land for human sustenance, it is a positive moral duty to enclose it and remove it from the common. Locke also holds that private property in land improves the land by making it more productive. The improvement wrought by the application of labour grounds private property in the moral force of the Divine Grant of the land. It is this that both justifies and limits private property.

This rather elegant argument, from its basic premises, unfolds a moral framework that justifies, indeed demands private property, while at the same time, it provides a moral limit to acquisition. There are some further assumptions within this argument which arbitrarily attribute a certain character to the land and pre-judge the relationship(s) that humanity has with it. As I have already stated, Locke's argument binds property into the necessity of a moral framework: property does not stand alone as a liberty. Rather it is based on the claim to sustenance and is bounded by the rights of others. The same right to preservation. In this structure of property rights, Locke defends the land in as much as 'sufficient and good' must be left for others, the land's productivity should not be damaged. This point seems to provide some hope of a Green ethic impinging on property rights. However, there are, I believe, three moves in Locke's theory of property which mitigate against him addressing the concerns of protests such as CAR2.

Locke's moral framework, while binding the use of property and its distribution, also leaves the land vulnerable. His framework concerns itself with human preservation. This priority given to human preservation, when it is conjoined with the labour theory of value embedded in Locke's work, reveals a particular relationship with the land. His original premise taken from scripture – the proposition that the earth is granted to humanity for its sustenance and enjoyment – leaves the land open to exploitative practices. The proviso of leaving 'sufficient and good' becomes ineffective when what is settled, within our practices, of what 'sufficient and good' amounts to changes when those very practices change. In a technological society 'sufficient and good' could be a functioning car park, a motorway interchange or an airport runway. Likewise and conversely, 'sufficient and good' could be the enjoyment of natural fecundity or the absence of air pollution. The land for Locke is represented as a means to an end, the end of human preservation.

By presenting the land as *given*, Locke has not considered the manner in which it is given. When he then goes on to ground private property in the moral right to preservation, by arguing that private property is the most efficient means of achieving this preservation, he identifies human labour as the power that provides for our preservation. [enclosing the commons for]

For it is labour indeed that puts the difference of value on everything... I think it will [preser] be but a very modest computation to say, that of the products of the earth useful to the [vation] life of man nine tenths are the effects of labour: nay, if we will rightly estimate things as they come to our use... we shall find, that in most of them ninety-nine hundredths are wholly to be put on the account of labour. (Locke 1993: Ch. 5, § 40)

With these arguments Locke gives the land a certain description, a purely instrumental one. To this end the fecundity of the earth and the agency of nature are reduced to inert properties, manipulable by human agency. Here, it becomes possible to see how Locke has been misunderstood as arguing for property as dominion – what he is, in fact, arguing against in his confrontation with Filmer's work. This approach is necessary, however, to validate his justification of private property:

And therefore he that encloses land and has a greater plenty of the conveniences of life from ten acres, than he could have from a hundred left to nature, may truly be said, to give ninety acres to mankind. (Locke 1993: Ch. 5, § 37)

Locke gives the moral force to the proprietor of the land and the onus of proof that land is spoiled or wasted to the other claimants. To judge what is good and what would constitute improvement depends on the description under which the land is encountered. Such issues are settleable within a community of valuers that share a common form of life, a common way-of-being-with-the-land. A farmer can judge another farmer's treatment of his land because they share a similar set of judgements and values regarding the treatment of the land and what counts as 'sufficient and good', or 'improvement'. What the protest against Runway Two is challenging relates to the bases of the interpretation of such value judgements. Locke grounds the interpretation of these judgements in the application of labour, within a framework that lends itself to the instrumentalising character of such development projects. In fact Locke's terms mitigate against the kind of reading of our relationship with the land that the protesters might like to give.

The earth presents itself to Locke as a means, as an instrument. For the protesters of Runway Two the earth is understood in broader terms. While certainly it remains an instrument within their practices it is also considered as fecund and full of life. To many of the protesters land or 'nature' is considered as life-giving. In contrast to the purely instrumental portrait of the land provided by Locke, the protesters approach the land as a source of life. The relationship between people and the land is treated as wider than that of the relationship between a user and a resource and a sense of engagement with the land is identified. This sheds some light on the dissatisfaction the groups involved felt with the proposal to move flora and fauna to another site, a move that appears to treat the threat to the wildlife as merely another mechanical problem capable of a practical solution. For the protesters the wider issue of *how* the land is grasped is of greater importance. It is this issue that I shall explore with some considerable help from Martin Heidegger.

GRASPING THE LAND: HEIDEGGER AND THE INSTRUMENTALISATION OF THE LAND

Heidegger presents the world as revealed to us within our practices. 'The Question Concerning Technology' (1977), in particular, deals with the issue of technological practices: the tension arising out of the instrumental apprehension of nature explicit in technological relations and the rendering of nature as a phenomenon implicit in the technological way-of-Being. His work is employed here to examine critically the Lockean view of the land, which makes the land amenable to technological appropriation, and to show that a purely Lockean approach does not allow us to 'read' the protest at Runway Two in a meaningful way.

Heidegger in *Being and Time* (1962) introduces a descriptive theory of Being. Human beings are presented as fundamentally engaged, embodied agents. This is a radical refutation of a strong rationalist and empiricist position that holds true knowledge of the world to be the outcome of disengaged inspection of the world. Heidegger places the engaged view prior to the disengaged. The engaged agent experiences the world as ready-to-hand, that is as apprehended through the practices, projects and passions of the agent. Thus, the meaning the world has for us, our understandings of it, is bound up in the way we deal with it practically. These practices are held within the cultural context of the agent.

Heidegger's example is of a hammer, understood primarily in terms of its use, in terms of hammering. It is located within a workshop of tools, a physicality understood as a set of practices, of enframement of the world, revealed through the application of the tools. The workshop provides the hammer with context. This is how it is *primally* experienced, it is only through a conscious disengagement with it, that we get to see the hammer as an object separate from its use. Further it is this *primal* engaged experience of the hammer that reveals its true character, its essence. A hammer *is* for hammering, it exists to bang nails into wood, build tables, build houses and so on. Heidegger, then, is seeking the essence of things in the way they are concretely revealed in our practices, rather than in the Platonic fashion as some *idea* removed from the actual and present object. As a result of this approach, what grows into an ontological theory of engaged *Being* reveals the structure of the world as being dependent on the enframement of the way-of-Being implicate with that world. The objects within that world are apprehended (physically and mentally) in terms of the projects, practices and passions of the particular way-of-being.

Following Heidegger's emphasis on the physical engagement with the world, I will do some small violence to his language and call this apprehension in the ready-to-hand the 'grasping of the world' to facilitate my discussion of the Runway Two protest. For the protesters land presents itself in a ready-to-hand fashion: they grasp it through their projects and practices, it enters their lives and culture in terms of tangible experiences. The Bollin Valley is perceived by them as ready-to-hand, it is grasped, as a natural sanctuary to be defended against the grasp of the economic project. It is to be defended against the expansion of Manchester Ringway, in the same manner that Twyford Down, Fairmile and Newbury were defended by similar protests. All these protests manifest a clash between the ways in which the land is grasped by protesters and developers, between the way the land reveals itself essentially to each party.

According to Heidegger, all ways-of-being, existential choices about what we should be and how we should live, entail finding the world in a certain ready-to-hand fashion. All passions and practices apprehend the world according to their own instrumentalising needs. In 'The Question Concerning Technology', Heidegger discusses the particular way-of-being that he calls technological. He discusses the common conceptions of technology which he differentiates into two basic descriptions: first, technology as a means to an end (the instrumental description), and second, technology as a human activity (the anthropological description). Heidegger takes issue with these definitions, not on the grounds that they are not correct, but rather on the grounds that they are inadequate to reveal some important truth about the 'essence' of technology. While accepting the instrumentality of technology he maintains that causality is not purely instrumental. He traces these concepts back to Ancient Greek philosophy and concludes that the original meaning of technology has been degraded through the ages. Heidegger attempts to recover it.

Along his hermeneutic journey Heidegger identifies the crucial point of falling into an instrumental understanding of causality as the translation of the Greek *aletheia* to the Roman *veritas*. The former means 'revealing' while the later is normally taken to be correct or accurate representation. The importance of understanding this apprehension of causality is that technology does more than bring about effects instrumentally. Although its Greek root *techne*, which means 'use', is instrumental in meaning, it also applies to handicraft and creative pursuits. It was considered in Ancient Greece that *techne* had the character of *poiesis*, which means the 'bringing-forth' of something. This latter concept is also connected with *physis*, the power of nature, the bringing-forth of something within itself. Heidegger's example is of a blossom blooming. For *poiesis*, however, it is the bringing-forth of something in something else, for instance, poetry or creativity in the artist.

There is a strong purpose to this journey into the linguistic and conceptual framework of the Ancient Greeks. Heidegger attempts to show us that the way we think about technology blinds us to something startling about it. From the original definitions of technology, he maintains, we can see that the notion of causality, the idea of 'bringing-forth' a new outcome, is not present. Either technology is seen as the instrument in our hands or as a cultural activity. If we bring together Heidegger's points about the grasping of the world in terms of our practices and the nature of technology we can begin to conceptualise the thread of his reasoning. It is not just that technology is a means to an end, but rather that technology enframes the whole of our world in the character of its demands.

Modern technology is not only different in degree, but also different in kind to the technology of the ancients. It surrounds us and orders the world. It takes the world as raw material and shapes it, treating all materials as instrumentally available to be shaped and changed. The phrase Heidegger uses is 'ordering'; the character which the objects of the world take on is that of 'standing reserve', waiting as resources to be ordered by the dictates of technology. Heidegger is talking about the 'essence' of technology, about technology as a way-of-Being. The real danger he sees here is that the instrumentalising picture of the world blinds us to the fact that there is more to causality than instrument and that there is more to technology than instrumentality. Technology 'enframes' the world in this way. The land, the goods of nature, even human beings get drawn in as 'standing reserve'. In this process we are pulled towards an understanding of the world that is merely mechanical, one that presumes that more precise use of technology will save us from the dangers that technology generates.

We come back again to Heidegger's distinction between *aletheia* (bringing-forth) and *veritas* (accurate representation). Technology, working in the manner of exact science, plots and scales the world accurately to manipulate it towards projected ends. In the process, it loses the faculty of perceiving its own unique way of changing the world. Of course, it must be acknowledged that the way the world is revealed by technology is not necessarily untrue. If the world was not amenable to a technological interpretation then technological way-of-being would not hold coherently together. Rather than technology itself being a lie, its danger lies, according to Heidegger, in the totalising effect that excludes and downgrades other sensibilities, even those of which it partakes itself.

This is perhaps the most difficult part of Heidegger's hermeneutic analysis of technology. It may be clear that technology becomes a way-of-being, one with a totalising effect on the world we live in. This effect implies that only certain kinds of truths and perceptions of the world count as truth (that is: physical facts). Heidegger's even more challenging proposition addresses the possibility that there is more to technology than its portrayal of the world as instrumental. To help us understand this, we have to familiarise ourselves with Heidegger's conception of what it is to be. The German word for Being that he uses is *Dasein*, literally: 'Being-there'. To be is to be situated and to have a way-of-being. What distinguishes the being of *Dasein* from the being of the things we find in the world, whose existence is as occurrentness (that is as objects), is that for *Dasein* its existence is an issue for itself.

Our own being is an important issue for us, and this is why we reflect on our way-of-being. By questioning our own way-of-being we can make choices that alter that way of being. It is not, for Heidegger, that we can escape to some objective standpoint from which to review our existence, but rather we can clear a space within our being that allows the revealing of truths about our way-of-being. There is the ability in any extant *Dasein* (which, for us, is human being) to comprehend in more than a purely instrumental fashion our existential choices, from within those choices. So we can alter our practices if we find them wanting or we can find ourselves living under different passions, if life reveals the existent passions to be hollow and devoid of meaning. It is this ability that enables us to escape from falling completely into the totalising effect of technology. Human beings have the power of choice, albeit a conditioned choice. This ability exists even within the totalising technological way-of-being where instrumentality is dominant.

At the end of 'The Question Concerning Technology' Heidegger returns to the notion of causality that is *poiesis* (bringing-forth). He quotes Holderlin (somewhat cryptically):

> But where the danger is, grows
> the saving power also. (Heidegger 1977: 34)

Then he attempts to draw our attention to the fact that despite technology's totalising and instrumental portrayal of the world, technology also partakes in additional descriptions under which causality can be understood. In other words, technology too has *poiesis* and this is what Heidegger equates with 'the saving power' in the lines of Holderlin. *Poiesis*, or bringing-forth differs from the instrumental conception of causality. *Poiesis*, as an essentially creative notion of causality, points towards a poetic saving power (hence his quotation of Holderlin's poetry).

In the following section I will attempt to show how *poiesis* is expressed in direct action protests in the technological society. The rhetoric of empowerment and the lack of hierarchical structure of the protest camps at Runway Two concords very well with the notion of *poiesis*, while direct action partakes of and expresses the notion of causality expressed by *poiesis*.

BACK TO THE PROTEST SITE

To the airport the land stands as an economic resource, as a potential for profit. It is a resource to be used in the expansion of the airport's business, a defined tract of land abstractly represented by a project, as well as existing physically. It is signified as an economic entity that both facilitates development and resists it. Through the application of the airport's project the land is transformed into the required physical base for the airport's operation. Such a land, defined in those narrow, instrumental terms, resists human action upon it in as much as effort is required to 'develop' it. It must be transformed from its current state to the state required for its effective use. Physically this requires the filling of the Bollin Valley with several thousand tons of rubble and the levelling of a number of farmhouses. The airport will then be able to run two runways, one for inward and another for outward bound flights. In terms of economic strategy it also puts Ringway in a stronger position against any proposals for competing airports in the north-west, such as Liverpool for instance, thereby protecting its market and the profitability of its operation.

The land then is conceived of as a means to economic production and dominance. The revenue gained by its use is the motivator for this particular use of the land and the means of enframing the land in question. It not only drives the project, but it also determines the way in which the land is apprehended. The land is to be utilised in the achievement of this project, which is presented to the local population as a desirable one in terms of jobs and the economic wealth it will provide. The goods gained by building the airport more than offset the goods lost in its construction. The goods lost, in this case, are the ability to enjoy the valley, the loss of farm land, some destruction of the local flora and fauna, the peace and quiet of the residents of the area, and the decreased air quality and so forth. This is the basis on which the Manchester Airport Authority enframes the issue of development as well as the land utilised. In the context of a strict cost-benefit analysis, this latter category of goods lost should also have a price attached to them. It is here that the enframement of development reaches the limits of legal experience. In other words, the law has never been challenged to provide a mechanism by which the worth of such 'goods' is valued.

When the planning proposal for the second runway was challenged at the public enquiry the Manchester Airport Authority offered to relocate flora and fauna from the Bollin Valley to another location. This was unacceptable to the direct action networks. Politically this addresses only one of a cluster of issues that surround the building of the runway. The protest, while focused at Runway Two, draws on misgivings about transport expansion in general. It rests on a set of fundamentally different significations of the land. It is evoked in and given life through the method of physically defending land from development. The protesters perceive the land through an intense and emotional relationship with it, springing from a signification of the land as threatened by the expansion of Manchester Airport. The Bollin Valley signifies for them a place of cultural involvement (through their own experiences of protest) and a place where a 'natural' environment has been allowed to flourish. Because the protesters are physically and practically involved with the land on a daily basis the land is woven into their lives.

For the protesters, the defence of the land was not merely a legal or intellectual issue. An intense emotional engagement was consequent on the commitment of many of the protesters to defend the land. Their engagement led to polar opposition: their proposed scheme of protest was not merely reforming – it did not seek to negotiate an accommodation with the Runway Two project – it directly challenged the Runway Two project. This does not mean that the other protagonists in this conflict did not themselves develop intense relationships as a result of it. What characterises the difference between the protesters and the developers is the direction of their concerns. The form of engagement that the agents of development had with the land was concerned primarily with the land as it was coopted, and represented within an economic and technological enterprise. The very land that held these divergent meanings is now transformed into a different place from which passenger jets will shuttle people to and from Manchester.

Heidegger in 'The Question Concerning Technology' presents an open discourse which does not look for a settled rendering of the issues, but opens up a response to technology which he believes frees us from the dangers inherent in it. I see the protest at Runway Two as displaying the feature of *poiesis*. Despite the political character of the issues involved *poiesis* is a significant feature which reveals the deep-seated differences between the ways the land is signified for the two parties. My purpose here is not to conclude with a normative solution to such conflicts, but rather to open up the discourse on land by showing its essentially shifting significance and hence the ambiguity inherent in any attempt to essentialise it.

It could be that the poetic tendency of human beings is merely an epiphenomenon which subsists upon ways-of-being conditioned by the practical demands of the economic and technological character of our society. It could be that, although we may feel the passion and admire it, such protest has no real efficacy in the world. This is, for Heidegger the danger of technology – namely, that it limits our vision of what constitutes an effective causal relation. There is, I would claim, efficacy in the protesters' vision and in their actions because they open up and reveal a different character of the land. They perceive the land as more than just resources and reveal it as threatened but defensible. Beyond a purely instrumental approach, the protesters treat the land as a defined piece of landscape but also as 'Land' or 'Nature', as full of significance and meaning beyond the facts of its physical constitution and the legal binds that situate this resource within our community. Thus by revealing a 'different land', the protesters actively engage in the act of *poesis*.

The protesters, in physically defending the land, whether that be by locking themselves to trees, blockading themselves in tunnels in the earth or hanging on suspended platforms between trees, demonstrate the truth of their apprehension of the land. The vitality of their actions reveals the land differently from the ordering of the land as standing reserve by the technological. Instrumentality is eschewed. The person is not attempting to be master of the process, because the process (the technological) is perceived as unmasterable. Rather the protesters give themselves over to their passion for the land (signified as endangered, and as a treasure) and in so doing they evoke a powerful response in those who witness it. The protesters, removed by crane and bolt croppers, arrested, processed, charged, abandon themselves to the instrumentality of technology. At the same time the meaning and intent of their actions remain free of instrumentality because the causal power that these actions have is that of *aletheia* (bringing-forth) rather than that of calculating the correct actions *(veritas)* to bring about the required change: be that conceived as lobbying or negotiating with the project.

TOWARDS A CONCLUSION

A Lockean approach to the dispute over Runway Two requires a consideration of the land in terms of its functional value. As such, this approach fails to acknowledge the point and character of the protest. On the other hand, it would be rather simplistic to consider the developers of the protest site as having a unitary position in relation to land in general or to Bollin Valley in particular. It is also the case, however, that the grounds for development rest *per definitionem* on certain purely instrumental assumptions about the land. Furthermore, the manner in which this instrumentality is apprehended and applied to the land is within the framework of a totalising technology. This is why I maintain that a natural law approach (*à la* Locke) is inadequate – despite the fact that it rests on moral guidelines that provide grounds for protest over land use. Most importantly, though, it should be noted that without the introduction of Heideggerian sensibility the dispute becomes trivialised as one over land use.

Heidegger's assertion that *poesis* is 'the saving power' finds some reflection in the events at the Bollin Valley. The crucial fact in the interaction between the conflicting visions of the land held by developers and protesters respectively, is the refusal of the latter to accept the relocation of flora and fauna as a suitable response to their objection to the airport expansion. This is an essentially instrumental gesture, which, in the same manner as the other facets of the Runway project, treats the land as material to be modified for the desired end. While political and environmental concerns are involved in the protest, the character of the protesters' actions (locking-on, suspending themselves on platforms between trees or concealing themselves in tunnels to make the movement of machinery impossible) signify the land as a different entity. Whereas the developers approach the land as an instrument and resource for the realisation of a technological project, the protesters apprehend the land through their passionate relationship with it and as a result they reveal it as a distinct actuality. The engagement with the Bollin Valley that the protesters enacted revealed the land as a place of diverse possibilities while the passions of the protest revealed it as beautiful and worthy of preserving. The character of the protest, however it may appeal to romantic pastoral visions of land and environment, was also, I would claim, reflecting the technological. It responds to many of the characteristics that Heidegger identifies as technological. What distinguishes modern technology from the ancient Greek notion of *techne* is the challenging of nature by the demands of a particular way-of-being that orders the world.

The protest at the Bollin Valley stood as a direct challenge to the runway development. It was uncompromising in its stance; it ordered the cessation of the project. Yet at the same time, for many, this very land was held as sacred. During the occupation of the site by the protesters a Native American Chief visited the land and blessed the trees. Conversely, the technological approach challenges any sense of sacredness of the land. It merely sees it as material; dissectible, rearrangeable, manipulable. The challenge thrown back at the technological project is to see the land as more than this, to recognise it as a place full of possibilities, a place vitalising to the beings who live there. In the protesters' view, land is life giving in a more rounded manner than the provision of resources for our practices. It is a place that affirms life. Nevertheless, one cannot argue that the protesters care about the land and the developers do not. Rather, it is the case that the care each party has in the land reveals their respective passions and projects. The care they exhibit reveals the manner in which they apprehend the land and at the same time the land itself is revealed differently through distinct notions of care.

It is the originality of the protest that generates such a resonance with the *poiesis* of Heidegger. The protest is essentially a creative act which stands against the appropriation of the land within the totalising instrumentality of the technological way-of-being. It is a response, a bringing-forth of truths which are otherwise hidden by the technological, truths which become commodified in the economic instrument and language of such projects as Runway Two. It is here that we find Locke both necessary and wanting. He is wanting in as much as his analysis of property rights cannot grasp the essentially creative tenor of relationships with the land. The dispute over CAR2 is an example of this. At the same time, Locke's approach is also necessary in the sense that eventually the renegotiation of ways-of-being must take place. The mundanity of pragmatic political solutions is inescapable, but a closed, Lockean discourse on the land degrades sensibilities and responses vital to a lived relationship with it. It is true that, in the political and legal sphere, settlements that allow for the practical business of living on and from the land are necessary. However, when operating within the Lockean framework one must remain cautious that this perspective is mostly instrumental, as well as dismissive of other sensibilities.

The tensions in these two philosophical approaches are mirrored in the tensions inherent in Western European apprehension of the land. An analysis of the dispute at Manchester Airport reveals the ambivalence in our relationship with the land. At one and the same time we depend on land as a resource, a facility for our practices and we experience it as an actual entity in its own right. As an entity, subjectively experienced as 'Land', it is the environment we live in and to which we respond. What appears to be a value-neutral analysis (in the manner of Locke), may in fact, within the totalised world of the technological, already be carrying a heavy burden of judgements about the land. It may at the same time exclude sensibilities that do not rest upon functional apprehensions of the land. Ultimately offering only a closed discourse that pre-judges the land as instrument and degrades our other sensibilities towards land as 'Land' or 'Nature', which form the basis of our pre-considered experience of it.

REFERENCES

Heidegger, M. 1962. *Being and Time*, trans. from the 7th German edn by J. Macquarrie and E. Robinson. Oxford: Blackwell Publishers.
—— 1977. 'The Question Concerning Technology', in *Basic Writings*. London: Routledge & Kegan Paul.
Locke, J. 1993. *Two Treatises of Government*, ed. Mark Goldie. London: Everyman.
Tully, J. 1993. *Locke in Contexts*. Cambridge: Cambridge University Press.

5 NOT SO BLACK AND WHITE: THE EFFECTS OF ABORIGINAL LAW ON AUSTRALIAN LEGISLATION

Veronica Strang

In conflicts over land rights, it is popularly assumed that indigenous relations with land will invariably be 'corrupted' or forcibly overwhelmed by the supposedly simpler and more material values of European concepts of land ownership and use. Many indigenous groups and their supporters see the foregrounding of material values in capitalist economies as a hegemonic threat. However, although Western relations with land may be overtly dominated by such values, they are far from simple, and the appropriation and consumption of other physical and cultural landscapes is not without its effects. Battles over land, though invariably contentious and unequal, involve the explication and exchange of values, providing all parties with exposure to alternative conceptual frames and qualitatively different environmental relations. Even where groups remain locked in conflicts over land, the mere fact that they are forced to represent their values to each other opens the door to the influence of 'other' ideologies.

This chapter considers how Aboriginal cultural landscapes have permeated and influenced the ways in which European Australians now relate to the land, encouraging them to explore and thus to give a greater emphasis to the ways in which history, spiritual being, aesthetic meaning, social relations and concepts of nature are located in their own mythic landscapes. This subtle but persistent influence is discernible in an increasingly sophisticated discourse concerned with European Australians' affective attachment to land (see Read 1996) which underpins debates on 'cultural heritage', and it can also be charted in the rapid growth of the environmental movement, in art and literature, and other media. Most tangibly, it is demonstrated by a consistent pattern of changes in legislation over time, not only in laws concerned with land rights and ownership, but also in the recent proliferation of legislation dealing with environmental protection and heritage issues.

In principle, legislation in Australia can be described as a recursive expression of a consensus on values or, perhaps more realistically, as a reflection of the aspirations and negotiations of powerful groups and alliances. The mythic and legal boundaries which laws attempt to delineate are, simultaneously, broad statements of the dominant cultural values, and metaphors of the intellectual, spatial and economic boundaries which define social identities. The creation of legislation illustrates the dynamics – and the tensions – between the Aboriginal population and the other landowners and users in Australia: the pastoralists and farmers, the environmentalists, and the mining, fishing and tourist industries. The ways in which legislation is developed over time provide a graph of changes in cultural beliefs and values.

This chapter is based on ethnographic research in Far North Queensland which focused on the environmental relationships of most of these groups, including the Aboriginal community of Kowanyama on the western coast of the Cape York Peninsula. Their long-term conflicts over land and resources have forced all of the participants to make their values explicit in a dialogue which is made manifest through changes in State and Federal legislation. As Ritchie (1996) points out (citing Stewart 1991), the process itself – the creation of legislative definitions of beliefs and values – has been a catalyst for change in Aboriginal communities. It would be ethnocentric to assume that European Australians are immune to concomitant influences through their involvement in the dialogue. This chapter argues that the shifts in European Australian legislation provide evidence that they are not.

In recent decades, as in other parts of the country, there has been a re-intensification of the conflicts over land. Aboriginal communities have gained much self-determination, political involvement and greater equity with the rest of the population, and they have learned to present their claims to the land in a way that other Australians can understand. One outcome of this, after 200 years of denial, was the government's admission that the Aboriginal people of Australia did indeed own the land prior to colonial settlement. The resulting Native Title Act (1992) placed land rights centre stage in the political theatre and caused bitter acrimony, culminating in a change of government and massive efforts to override the Native Title Act with new legislation.

The land rights issue continues to polarise communities within Australia, but this chapter argues that, subsumed by the raised voices, there is an underlying convergence of Aboriginal and European values relating to land. The Native Title Act not only emerged from a greater understanding of Aboriginal Law, but is also an indication of how much it has influenced European Australian discourses about land. Within the last century, despite political suppression, Aboriginal visions of the landscape and ways of evaluating land have seeped quietly into the wider Australian imagination, creating new ways of thinking about and interacting with the environment, and encouraging the formulation and expression of affective values in relation to place. This is increasingly reflected in the legislation which attempts to define people's rights and responsibilities in land. To consider this convergence it is necessary to step back a little, to the early days of settlement, and examine two very different relationships with the same environment, and the legislation which upheld the appropriation of Aboriginal land.

A BLACK AND WHITE HISTORY OF LAW AND LAND

In the 1700s and 1800s, European settlers left their homelands, their familiar social landscapes, their sentimental attachments and all of the things which to them denoted 'civilisation'. They came to Australia in search of economic opportunities, and found their new environment frighteningly harsh, with its unfamiliar climatic extremes, vast, 'empty' spaces, poisonous creatures and hostile 'savages'. Their diaries of settlement depict a mythic landscape in which the foreground is dominated by a heroic endeavour to subdue 'Nature' and make it productive in accordance with their aims. In the loneliness of the outback they battled against the elements to carve a life, enduring hardship and deprivation in order to achieve economic stability.

In contrast, the Aboriginal people of Australia had been there, in the archaeological record, for at least 40,000 years, and in their own words 'since the beginning to us' (Alma Wason in Strang 1997). As hunter-gatherers, their lives were wholly bound up with the land: their economic sustainability was reliant upon intimate knowledge of the landscape, and their entire social and spiritual existence was mediated by the land and the ancestral beings embedded in it, whose lives they were spiritually directed to emulate (cf. Altman 1984; Williams and Hunn 1986; Morphy 1988; Ingold et al. 1988; Jones 1990).

The two systems of law relating to land reflected these wholly different environmental relationships. Though, in practice, they had many more complex ways of interacting with the land, the settlers brought with them an individuated concept of property in which land was presented predominantly as a material object, entirely alienable and secular.[1] Legal ownership was based wholly on economic principles, and the investment of labour in the land, made evident through production. The newly measured boundaries 'staking out' the land delineated the ownership of a commercial resource. The land was thus commoditised, and any legal responsibility to care for it, if acknowledged at all, fell awkwardly between the temporary control of individuals and the distant sovereignty of the state. In this early struggle, the social and spiritual dimensions of the landscape were largely obscured by an intense focus on everyday economic activities. People remained linked to social networks in distant homelands, and conformed to spiritual beliefs with little or no location in their immediate environs.

Aboriginal land ownership, on the other hand, was (and remains) inalienable, communal and based entirely on spiritual and social identity. In Queensland, as in the rest of Australia, local descent groups are organised according to Ancestral Law in which ancestral beings, having re-entered the land after the creative era of the Dreamtime, remained there as totemic foci for their clans of human descendants. These ancestral ties bind people to their 'country' as part of a structural whole, giving title to the land and explicit responsibility to each totemic clan to care for it 'for all time'. Articulating with the ideologically 'fixed' charter of Ancestral Law, complex systems of marriage law and exchange ensure a sufficiently flexible balance between people and resources (cf. Morphy 1988). Clan country is defined by its totemic beings: their tracks, their creation of features of the landscape and, most particularly, the places where their ancestral power is most intensely concentrated. Ancestral Law is therefore centred on such sacred sites rather than peripheral boundaries, and through these it meshes the mythic, legal, social and economic landscapes of Aboriginal people into a tightly holistic body of knowledge.

The colonising Europeans, unwilling or unable to discern the collective property rights inherent in a socially and spiritually based system of land tenure, at first declared Australia to be *terra nullius* – empty land. By the 1800s, however, it was obvious that this was a fallacy and that Australia contained many Aboriginal people who both used and managed the land, living in readily definable 'territories' they considered their own. But, as Reynolds points out, it was easier to turn a blind eye to this. 'The theory of an uninhabited continent was just too convenient to surrender lightly' (Reynolds 1987: 32).

Various justifications were made: the settlers had arrived with evolutionary ideas that saw human development as proceeding through various stages, from hunting and gathering, through pastoralism, to agriculture and 'civilised' living. Seeing the simple technology, the lack of physical boundaries around land and the apparently nomadic lifestyle of the Aboriginal people, they concluded that they were 'less advanced' and had no notion of land as property:

In the first two stages of social life, while men were hunters and shepherds, there scarce could be any notion of landed property ... In this vagrant life men have scarce any connection with land more than with air or water. A field of grass might be considered to belong to a horde or class, while they were in possession; and so might the air they breathed and the water which they drank: but the moment they removed to another quarter, there no longer subsisted a connection between them and the field that was deserted. It lay open to newcomers who had the same right as if it had not been formerly occupied. (Home 1761: 94–95)

Arguments, that the Aboriginal people were 'heathens' or had been 'conquered' were also made, although these were equally insupportable in either moral or legal terms. As Reynolds comments, this denied that Aboriginal people had ever owned the land, and deprived them of a defensible legal position. 'The intellectual and moral gymnastics required to sustain that position have been quite extraordinary' (Reynolds 1987: 2). In 1847 a legal wrangle over land resulted in the following ruling:

We are of the opinion, then, that the waste lands of this colony are, and ever have been, from the time of its first settlement in 1788, in the Crown. (*Attorney General* v. *Brown* in McCorquodale 1987: 243)

Thus, by imposing a legal model based on Cartesian principles, and dividing land into material areas of economic utility leased or owned by individuals, the settlers effectively overrode all Aboriginal claims to the land. Fence-lines chopped the land into various forms of tenure: freehold, leasehold and multiple variations on these themes. Only the 'leftover' land remained directly under the aegis of the Crown.

In the early days of contact, the open warfare over land and the subsequent disparity in power relations between Aboriginal and European Australians were such that a dialogue about land rights was not feasible.[2] Far North Queensland, being a remote area, was settled much later than much of the eastern seaboard, remaining relatively undisturbed, except for a few sea and overland explorations, until the late 1800s, when a gold rush brought mining camps and thus the establishment of cattle stations to feed them. The widespread genocide of the Aboriginal inhabitants of the peninsula led to the setting up of a number of Christian missions to provide a measure of protection for some Aboriginal groups. Grudgingly, and despite vociferous protests from neighbouring cattle properties, some land was handed over to the missions to provide Aboriginal Reserve areas. Other Aboriginal groups managed to remain on their own country by accepting the settlers' use of the land and – with Hobson's choice – providing labour for them in exchange for flour, sugar and tobacco, and general domestic support for their families.

By the 1940s–50s, a more amicable *modus vivendi* had developed and there was a brief 'Golden Age' of relative harmony and stability in which the land was used jointly. Aboriginal people found cattle work relatively easy to encompass, as it drew on their knowledge about the environment and permitted regular interaction with their own 'country'. Their traditional uses of the land were sufficiently different from those of the settlers that they could often, without inviting conflict, continue to exploit the natural resources of the area and maintain spiritual and social connections with their clan country.

During this period, both Aboriginal and European Australians alike maintained belief in their ownership of the land. Though involved in the economic structures of the settlers, Aboriginal people continued to 'hold' their own law, which in their terms gave them inalienable land ownership: 'Aboriginal people on pastoral leases have never ceased seeing the land as their own' (Rowse 1988). This was relatively uncontroversial at the time, and it is worth bearing in mind that, as Tehan points out: 'the notion of native title co-existing with both public and private interests is not new. Nor is the notion of co-existence of rights and interests in land in the Australian property law system' (1997: 3).

Australia therefore encompassed two systems of land tenure, and two economic systems driven by completely different cultural values and visions of landscape. This was quite manageable because the two populations continued to live very separate lives. Aboriginal people had been largely pushed off their own country, but they often retained access to it. Though the colonial government gave them no legal rights to own land under European law, there were various legislative efforts to give them special rights of usufruct, mainly in order that they might continue to feed themselves. For example, in 1928 a Bird's Protection Ordinance (Northern Territories) allowed an exemption for Aborigines to kill protected species for food, and, similarly, the Fisheries and Oyster Farms (Amendment) Act of 1957 allowed them to fish the inland waterways without a licence. Some provision was made to set aside some Crown land for their 'use and benefit' – provided that it was not subject to contract or purchase – for example in the Crown Lands Ordinance of 1923 (NT). Over time, as some understanding grew of their very different relationship with land, efforts were made to prevent the destruction of Aboriginal relics or sacred sites. Thus the Police and Police Offences Ordinance of 1954 (NT) made it an offence to 'wilfully or negligently deface, damage, uncover, expose, excavate or otherwise interfere with Aboriginal ceremonial, burial or initiation grounds or to remove native relics or curios'.

These small accommodations permitted some decades of stability, but the 'false harmony' could not continue indefinitely. The 1960s brought the introduction of legislation for Award Wages, which required pastoralists to pay wages to all stock workers where they had previously been able to get Aboriginal labour in exchange for a few supplies. This resulted in the expulsion of whole Aboriginal communities from many cattle stations. This commercialisation of relations coincided with considerable economic growth in Australia, and increasing use of the land – and pressure upon it – by other interest groups such as miners, tourists and fishermen. In the outback there was an influx of technology and better communication with urban centres, and the mining industry burgeoned, threatening Aboriginal ties with land in a new way: 'mining was alarmingly insensitive either deliberately or not to Aboriginal religious sentiments' (Kolig 1987: 110).

As Aboriginal people became more threatened by the changes and more familiar with the *realpolitik* of European land use, the two value systems clashed and the need for re-negotiation became inescapable. Previously, believing that they could not truly be alienated from their land, Aboriginal groups had not attempted to challenge the legality of the 'white feller' type of ownership. However, they now had to face up to the fact that European Australians did not consider Aboriginal ownership to be valid. Although they might be allowed to use Crown land while no one else wanted it, they were not given title to it, and increasingly often, as soon as any valuable resources were discovered on the land, their rights were ignored. Vastly outnumbered – representing only a few per cent of the rapidly growing

Australian population – and still held firmly under the paternal thumb of Church and state, Aboriginal people were poorly placed to assert their rights to land, but they began, nonetheless, to campaign for their rights, enlisting the help of anthropologists in their efforts to communicate with Australian jurisprudence. As Ritchie says: 'Anthropology provided the conceptual framework enabling legislators to contrive a patch to cover the moral and political lacunae resulting from the failure to recognise Aboriginal rights in common law' (1996: 276).

TURNING THE TIDE

In the legal battles that resulted from the land rights campaign of the 1960s and 1970s, the Australian courts experienced considerable difficulty in understanding Aboriginal proprietary concepts in which economic and religious ties to land were coterminous. In the Gove hearings of 1968–70, the Yolngu people in north-east Arnhem Land sought recognition of their prior title to the land, in opposition to the Nabalco aluminium company.

His Honour Justice Blackburn in his decision found the system underlying the Aboriginal claim to be a system of law, but he did not accept that the Aboriginal claimants held proprietary interests in the land under Australian law. (Merlan and Rumsey 1982: Appendix 5)

The court upheld the view that the Yolngu system lacked concepts of property that exist in other legal systems, preferring to see land as 'attributed' to people rather than being owned by them. However, Aboriginal people refused to give up, and more liberal European Australian voices began to speak up alongside them. In 1973 the Woodward Commission was established 'to investigate how Aboriginal rights to land might best be recognised'.

During the 1970s Aboriginal mission communities such as Kowanyama became much more autonomous, and urban Aboriginal groups began to move away from the towns and cities, creating outstations in order to re-establish a more 'traditional' social and cultural life. In 1978, in a major step away from the historic paternalism of the State Government, the Aboriginal and Torres Strait Islanders (Queensland Reserves and Communities Self-Management) Act empowered the people living on reserves to control and manage their own affairs. The Woodward Commission began to formalise a translation of Aboriginal Law into European terms, and the Northern Territories, with its large and less scattered Aboriginal population, led the way towards re-instituting Aboriginal landownership with the Aboriginal Land Rights (NT) Act of 1976. This was 'one of the most far-reaching advances in vesting title to land in corporate bodies representing Aborigines' (McCorquodale 1987: 13).

The Aboriginal Land Rights Act established Aboriginal Land Trusts and enabled Land Councils to protect and secure Aboriginal land on behalf of the traditional owners, assert Land Claims and reconcile disputes and conflicts. It made a workable definition of 'traditional ownership'. Though it applied largely European ideas about genealogical descent as the criteria for group membership, the new law allowed for collective ownership by a group defined by social[3] and spiritual ties as well as traditional economic rights to the land. It acknowledged the landownership of a local descent group of Aborigines who had:

Common spiritual affiliations to a site on the land, and primary spiritual responsibility for that site and for the land, and who were entitled by Aboriginal tradition to forage as of right over that land. (Government of the Northern Territories, 1976. Aboriginal Land Rights Act (NT), 1976)

Thus the Land Rights Act introduced for the first time into the European legislative process an alternative model of relations to land in which ownership was not only collective but – crucially – based on spiritual and social connection with place. This model presented a clear challenge to the dominant European legal model in which land was neatly compartmentalised as a material resource and social and spiritual issues relating to land were generally situated outside legal boundaries. A string of land claims followed the new legislation, beginning in 1979 with Borroloola. Of particular importance was the controversial reclaiming of Uluru (Ayers Rock), which brought the tenets of this alternative model squarely into mainstream discourses about land. The ongoing legislative debate continued to provide a focal point for dialogues between Aboriginal people and the wider population, and anthropologists played a valuable role as 'translators' of Aboriginal cosmological concepts, beliefs, laws and values.[4]

At first, fitting the highly complex and tightly holistic form of Aboriginal Law into the explicit and narrowly specialised European Australian legal framework proved immensely difficult. There was much polarisation between Aboriginal and non-Aboriginal representations of landownership and Australian courts, largely unfamiliar with Aboriginal culture, found its complexities baffling. Evidence from Aboriginal witnesses invariably stressed the affective aspects of their relationship with the land. For example, in the claim by the Walpiri and Kartangarurru-Kurintji people, Galarrwuy Yunipingu said:

The land is my backbone. I only stand straight, happy and proud and not ashamed about my colour because I still have land. The land is the art. I can paint, dance, create and sing as my ancestors did before me. My people recorded these things about our land this way, so that I and all others like me can do the same. (Peterson et al. 1978: 98)

Initially, in the land claim hearings, European Australians generally conducted a much more pragmatic defence, largely preoccupied with juridical issues such as whether land had already been alienated from the Crown and who, if anyone, would be economically disadvantaged by the granting of the land to Aboriginal people. However, in the arena of the hearings, Aboriginal Law was steadily demytisfied and its values made explicit: what had been closed and seemingly impenetrable became open and gradually comprehensible as the depth and meaning underlying Aboriginal attachments to land were elucidated. European Australians began to understand a different way of interacting with the land, and to see more clearly the complexities of their own mythic landscapes. Thus the conflicts enabled an intensive educative process to take place in which, through familiarisation with Aboriginal beliefs and values, European Australians were encouraged to re-evaluate their own relations with land. Over time, even within the constraints of the legal proceedings, they began to formulate a discourse encompassing more affective issues.

The shifting dynamics of the land claim debate echoed important demographic and cultural changes in Australia. By the second half of the century, many pioneering communities had put down roots and built attachments to place, abandoning their mythic 'homelands' and encoding deeper social and spiritual meanings in the landscape they had previously perceived as hostile. There are some peculiar ironies here. The pastoralists have had, on the one hand, more exposure than anyone to Aboriginal ways of interacting with the land. They worked alongside Aboriginal stock workers for many decades, and were for much of this time almost wholly dependent, not just on their labour, but on their intimate knowledge about the environment. It could be argued that it is this that has encouraged them to develop their own local knowledges and their affective connections with place. It is therefore deeply ironic that this common ground, this very attachment to place, means that they are the group most virulently opposed to Aboriginal efforts to reclaim their land. There is also a social pressure here. Being educationally and economically low in social status, and fervently conservative, many pastoralists are particularly anxious to differentiate themselves from Aboriginal people. However, their discourses about the land and their 'heritage' suggest that even in this most bitter of conflicts, their exposure to Aboriginal values has been more influential than they would probably care to admit.

In the post-war period there was also increasing divergence between the resource-based land users – pastoralists, farmers and miners – and the other, more urbanised, 'white-collar' sectors of the population. The rapid growth of the urban population and a diversification of educational and economic opportunities resulted in a wider diversity of views and a more liberal political arena. For urban Australians, life became less marginal economically, and more technology and infrastructure permitted greater recreational use of the land. Tourism – bird watching, fishing, exploring, camping out – provided people with a different, purely sensual and creative kind of environmental interaction which encouraged aesthetic and subjective responses to the landscape which resonated more readily with Aboriginal values (see Strang 1996).

By the late 1970s, the land rights discourse was achieving wide coverage in mainstream media, educating the general population about an indigenous environmental relationship. At the same time, some groups within the urban population, in particular those inclined to use the land mainly for aesthetic and recreational purposes, were developing environmental concerns and New Age spiritual beliefs more located in 'Nature' than in an abstract Christian heaven. As in other parts of the world (for example, North America), these issues were increasingly conflated, and many people began to see indigenous groups as having wiser, more sustainable ecological relationships and more desirable environmental values. A burgeoning 'Green' movement became vociferous about issues such as the land degradation caused by the pastoral and mining industries, the need to maintain biodiversity, and a host of other concerns about the lack of sustainability and environmental responsibility in modern Australian economic activities. There was considerable overlap between this sector of the population and the increasingly liberal groups who were supportive of Aboriginal land rights and open to Aboriginal ideas.

These changes in values were expressed in the late 1970s and 1980s in a plethora of new legislation designed to give greater protection to the environment. At a Federal level there were acts such as the National Parks and Wildlife Conservation Act (1975), the Endangered Species Protection Act (1992) and the National Environmental Protection Council Act (1994). In Queensland, there was the Fauna Conservation Act (1974–89); the Rural Land Protection Acts (1985, 1988, 1989); the Soil Conservation Act (1986); the State Environment Act (1988); the Nature Conservation Act (1992); and, during the same period, a host of Clean Air Acts, Clean Water Acts, Forestry Acts and Mineral Resources Acts.

With some – albeit partial – understanding of Aboriginal attachment to the land and a growing appreciation of the vast depth of knowledge contained in their traditional bush lore, many Australians saw Aboriginal interests as being naturally aligned to those of the growing environmental movement. A convenient tie was made between attempts to protect large areas of land for conservation purposes and Aboriginal use of such land. In 1975 the National Parks and Wildlife Conservation Act acknowledged Aboriginal 'traditional rights in relation to the land' and mandated the National Parks Director to 'assist and cooperate with Aborigines in managing land for the protection and conservation of wildlife in the land and the protection of natural features of that land'. For the first time, therefore, Aboriginal people were cast as 'the experts' – guardians of a particular kind of knowledge, and a particular way of interacting with the land. It is no coincidence that the first Aborginal Land Rights Act (NT) followed shortly thereafter (in 1976).

THE MYTH OF HERITAGE

You might think cultural heritage is only about the grand old house on the hill. But it's much more than that. It's the rough and ready cottage, the bent and broken bridge, a landscape of spiritual importance, or even a modern building ... Our cultural heritage creates special meaning for us as individuals and members of a community. But we need to protect these icons of our past and present for the future. (Queensland State Government, 1998: 2–4 web site)

In recent years, there have been some critical changes in the European Australian cultural landscape. One such change, which is highly suggestive of Aboriginal influence, is the way in which non-Aboriginal Australians have begun to articulate ideas about their own attachment to place in a discourse about 'cultural heritage' which focuses specifically on the location of social being in the land. With most of the population now living in urban centres, 'frontier' life in the outback has become a romanticised centre-piece of Australian identity, a source of imaginative imagery celebrated, in part, because of its perceived interaction with the land.[5]

The heritage movement in Australia, more than any other, expresses real changes in the relationship between people and land. In essence, it sets aside material economic values and reifies and makes explicit the mythic dimensions of landscape: the historic connections, the social, spiritual and aesthetic meanings, and the affective attachments to places that are held in the landscape of the imagination. It is also inextricably linked to national constructions of identity and its perceived boundaries. This shift in values and explication of the mythic qualities of landscape has been reflected in new organisations and legislation. In 1975 the Australian Heritage Commission was established to administer a national register of 'natural and cultural' sites.[6] In Queensland there was, significantly, a blending of environmental and heritage issues with the amalgamation of various State Government departments into a new Department of Environment and Heritage. Authority for its activities was provided by a revamped National Trust of Queensland Act (1963–81, 1989), the Heritage Building Protection Act (1990, 1992), the Cultural Record Act (1987) and the Queensland Heritage Act (1992). The latter is notably focused on sites of European heritage, suggesting an underlying political agenda to stress the importance of European Australian history and attachment to place:

Queenslanders are fortunate because our state has a wide range of items and places relating to settlement since 1823 ... They may have played an important part in our history, or have architectural, archaeological or scientific values ... The Act refers to the conservation of 'places' of aesthetic, historic, scientific or social significance or other special value to our community and to future generations. These values are referred to as the 'cultural heritage significance' of a place. (Queensland State Government, 1992: 2)

These more complex values have now entered the everyday language of modern Australian society, posing a challenge to reductive notions of land as a mere economic resource. They have come in part from the pressure of international debates about environmental issues; from economic changes shifting people away from resource to service industries; and from the simple passage of time and the cumulative effects of interaction with place. However, the extraordinary burgeoning of the environmental and heritage movements in Australia, hard on the heels of the raging debates about land rights, suggests that there is a further influence – that the values promulgated by Aboriginal groups have served to educate the European Australian population about the mythic elements of their own relations to land. The new environmental and heritage legislation is highly redolent of the kinds of attachments to land so clearly expressed by Aboriginal groups in their struggles for land rights in the 1970s. It focuses on long-term relations with land, and on the embedding of personal and communal narrative, social and spiritual meaning in the landscape.

The new legislation therefore seems to reflect some genuine changes in the environmental values of European Australians, though it is also necessary to ask whether the heritage movement is, in part, a cynical appropriation of Aboriginal discourses in an attempt to defend the land against being reclaimed ('we white Australians have deep attachments to place too'). There are some obviously appropriative moves by politicians such as Pauline Hanson, of the 'One Nation' Party, who in her maiden speech (10 September 1996) attempted to whip up a constituency of what she calls the 'forgotten people' the 'homely working-class battlers' and 'vernacular Australians' by suggesting they are victims of inequalities which favour Aboriginal people, giving them more access to land and money, while failing to acknowledge the settlers' investment of labour in the land.

Clearly there is much variation in the motives of the many different groups involved: the pastoralists, for example, have been largely concerned to assert their own claims to the land and deny those of the Aboriginal population, but most of the other groups in the debate have become noticeably more sympathetic to Aboriginal land claims. It is also difficult to disentangle cause and effect: whatever the original motivations for encouraging a dialogue about social and spiritual attachment to place, this foregrounding serves to strengthen these kinds of values and, indirectly, to enable greater understanding of Aboriginal relations with land.

Making an investment in the education of the various protagonists in the land rights battles has paid off for Aboriginal people. Now, instead of being merely marginalised as 'the Aboriginal Problem', they have been recast as an exotic and positive part of the 'National Heritage'. This represents, to some degree, yet another conflation of Aboriginality and Nature, as happens so frequently with indigenous groups whose way of life is perceived as intrinsically more 'natural'. However, it has brought Aboriginal concerns right into the centre of Australian society, and greatly increased appreciation and respect for Aboriginal culture. The first sites nominated for World Heritage Listing in Australia were places such as Kakadu or Uluru, which were considered to have outstanding natural features as well as importance in terms of 'preserving Aboriginal heritage'. The Aboriginal communities in some of the listed places made astute use of the process to strengthen their claims to the land: 'the people at Uluru were instrumental and supportive in getting Uluru on the World Heritage List ... They saw it as related to land tenure, a way of becoming more secure' (Sullivan in Australian Heritage Commission 1990: 49).

The discursive common ground between Western concepts of 'heritage' and the holistic nature of indigenous relations with land has been a powerful impetus for the land rights movement. Once the media, the intelligentsia and large sections of the Australian population began to get some insight into the complexities of Aboriginal culture and its concepts of landownership, land rights could no longer be suppressed. Even in the more conservative parts of Australia, legislation began to open up land to be reclaimed.

In Queensland, the late 1980s brought some transferral of reserve land to Aboriginal groups as Deed of Grant in Trust (DOGIT). For example, in 1987, Kowanyama was 'handed over' to the Aboriginal Council, although the new law provided little control over exploration and mining on the reserve. In 1991 the Queensland Aboriginal Land Act made it possible for traditional Aboriginal owners to claim gazetted National Parks and vacant Crown land, and to gain legal title to their DOGIT land. It followed previous acts in requiring 'traditional affiliation': common spiritual and other associations with the land, rights in relation to the land, and responsibilities for it under Aboriginal tradition. It also added a new criterion: 'historical association', which meant that the claimants had to satisfy the Tribunal that their ancestors had lived on or used the land for a substantial period of time. In addition, in an attempt to respond to some of the growing demands to improve the social and economic opportunities for Aboriginal groups, the legislation permitted the Tribunal to grant temporary leases if it judged that the granting of the claim would 'help Aboriginal and Torres Strait Islander people help themselves to regain or improve or maintain their economic independence and cultural integrity' (Queensland State Government 1992: 7).[7]

Although the Land Act in Queensland theoretically gave Aboriginal Trustees the right to hold title to the land, it was not particularly radical, fairly effectively preserving the status quo. It only applied to vacant Crown land (of which there is little), to DOGIT land that had been effectively Aboriginal land for some time, or to National Parks. In the latter case it offered largely nominal title, since Aboriginal 'owners' then had to lease the land straight back to the State Government to be run as a National Park. The 'joint management' basis of claims in National Parks perpetuates earlier efforts to encourage a convenient alliance between Aboriginal people and conservationists. Despite the good intentions of some environmentalists to acknowledge 'indigenous interests', Aboriginal influence on this eager and liberal group has only been partial. Though keen to embrace 'indigenous values' at an abstract level, in practice many environmentalists remain focused on their own aims and wedded to more familiar land management principles, which means that there are still some real incompatibilities in this arranged marriage. In some instances, conservation groups have expressed antipathy to hunting and gathering activities in national parks, and this has encouraged Aboriginal groups to see them as just another set of invaders seeking to impose their wishes. As Hill says: 'Indigenous people do not share the explicit interest in the goals of nature conservation of the Government agencies. Rather they wish to become involved primarily because the land is theirs' (Hill 1992: 19).[8]

There are other ramifications for Aboriginal communities in terms of their freedom to change and adapt as they please. Ranger comments that alliance with environmentalists represents a 'double trap' because it 'glorifies a static, essentialist definition of Aboriginal identity ... On the other hand, if Aboriginal communities come to terms with mining concerns in return for royalties they can be savagely denounced for betraying "Aboriginality"' (Ranger 1993: 15–16).

The legislation permitting the claiming of National Parks was greeted with dismay by some conservation groups, and their concerns were widely sensationalised in the media: 'Environmentalists fear the new Nature Conservation Act will allow Aborigines to exclude whites from some areas in national parks ... the legislation would result in national parks becoming Aboriginal enclaves' (*Gold Coast Bulletin* 4 April 1992).

So the combination of Aboriginal and conservation interests was (and remains) rather difficult. Some environmentalists are concerned about land rights leading to untrammelled hunting and fishing in the National Parks; the State and Federal Governments are anxious for expedient solutions to land rights issues; and Aboriginal communities remain dubious about becoming 'co-managers' alongside powerful groups whose underlying message is that they must adopt Western values in order to regain their land. In any case, they have found the adoption of other methods and discourses somewhat unavoidable, responding to the threat of dominance by conservationist groups by, as Hill says, attempting 'to establish their own credibility as land and natural resource managers in the western scientific sense' (Hill 1992: 19).

In attempting to participate in the decision-making, Aboriginal communities have begun to adopt the language of 'biodiversity' and express concerns about 'pollution' and 'land degradation'. In this sense, their own relationship with the land has shifted slightly to encompass concepts of land management which frame the environment in more material or 'scientific' terms. This suggests some convergence with European visions of the land, but it is fairly superficial: Aboriginal discourses about land, and their priorities and values, have remained immensely consistent throughout the land claim process.

The 1991 Land Act presented Aboriginal people with a difficult choice: whether to continue along the road of becoming 'Western-style' land managers, accepting somewhat nominal title, leasing their land back to the State Government and sharing control of it, or whether to wait and hope for a way to regain their land on their own terms. However, it was at about this time that all the persistent efforts to educate the majority population about Aboriginal Law paid off. In 1992, the High Court of Australia reached the historic Mabo decision, and ruled that an Aboriginal form of property in land had existed before the colonial invasion. This finding established the reality of native title, reversing the fallacy of *terra nullius* that had permitted the Crown to assume title to the land. It acknowledged that:

Aboriginal and Torres Strait Islander rights of ownership existed before non-Aboriginal settlement, and may still exist where the connection with the land has been maintained and title has not been extinguished. (Council for Aboriginal Reconciliation 1993: 5)

By doing away with the bizarre conceit that this continent had no owners prior to the settlement of Europeans, Mabo establishes a fundamental truth and lays the basis for justice. (Paul Keating, speech at Redfern Park, 10 December 1992)

Although the decision recognised native title, it also judged it to have been extinguished by the actions of the Crown in granting freehold title, long-term leasehold or by using the land in a way that prevented traditional use. It left questions about certain types of leasehold unanswered, and, despite Government reassurances, many parts of European Australian society – in particular the mining and pastoral industries – reacted with anger and deep concern about the security of their own tenure.

OUTBACK BACKLASH

The Mabo decision exposed some major divides in Australian society. While a large part of the urban population had been embracing changes in their cultural landscapes and exploring the social, spiritual and affective issues in their relations to land, other highly conservative groups – particularly those most involved with the land in economic terms – had retained visions of the landscape and their place in it which had changed very little since the early days of settlement. The liberal Government's leadership in encouraging progress in Aboriginal land rights posed a serious threat to the economic security of these groups and to their sense of identity. In Queensland, where some people were already incensed by the new Land Act and by Aboriginal people purchasing failed cattle stations and becoming politically active, tensions reached a new height. Throughout Australia, the media had a field day with headlines like 'Native title a terrifying concept' (*Sunday Telegraph*, 6 June 1993) and 'Mabo: the fallout' (*Sydney Morning Herald*, 9 June 1993). As the hysteria grew, writers warned of the dangers of 'pandering to the rednecks ... The danger of a white backlash against Mabo can be seen on every hand. The old racist dog is off the chain again' (*Sydney Morning Herald*, 12 June 1993).

A fierce battle ensued between the more conservative States and the liberal Federal Government: 'PM, States deadlocked over Mabo' (*The Australian*, 9

June 1993); 'Hall of shame for anti-Mabo premiers' (*The Australian*, 31 August 1993). Wild interpretations of the meaning of the Mabo decision were made by various industries, the media, politicians and Aboriginal groups. Hundreds of land claims were submitted, considerable 'grandstanding' took place, and there was a deafening call for new legislation to validate all existing leases and provide solid reassurance for farmers, pastoralists and miners that the world was not about to end.

With some urgency, the Federal Government produced the Commonwealth's Native Title Bill 1993. This was heralded by some as the first steps towards genuine reconciliation between Aboriginal people and the rest of the Australian population. But in other areas, bitter conflicts surfaced, particularly where mining interests were concerned, or where areas are seen as desirable tourist destinations. Mining and pastoral interests loudly denied the validity of Aboriginal Law and were openly cynical about Aboriginal land care. The tone of the following extracts illustrates the diversity of the positions taken:

Opposition spokesman on Aboriginal affairs, Mr. Keith Hamilton, said Mabo was the greatest step in race relations since the 1967 referendum and the Racial Discrimination Act of 1975. 'Mr Keating has successfully achieved a milestone in Australia's history. His determination to pass the Mabo legislation is evidence of a new era.' (*News-Mail*, 23 December 1993)

Native title bill sets scene for race war. (*News-Mail*, 3 December 1993)

The best description of the relationship between traditional Aboriginals and land seems to be that of custodianship ... The bleeding heart nonsense about the traditional Aboriginal care of the land is just that ... In fact the traditional Aboriginal routinely ritually sacked and burned that land to the limit of nature to regenerate, by burning and hunting. (Andrew White, a former exploration manager for COMALCO, in *The Cairns Post*, 9 May 1990)

The Chief Executive Officers of the major companies affiliated with the Australian Mining Industry Council believe the Commonwealth's Native Title Bill 1993 is unworkable ... it is imperative that existing titles are properly validated ... The continuing uncertainty will jeopardise development, diminish and delay investment, and reduce economic growth and employment opportunities. It will cause investment to be diverted away from Australia. All Australians, including Aboriginal Australians, will bear the ultimate cost. (Mining Industry Council statement in *The Courier-Mail*, 11 December 1993)

States such as Western Australia and Queensland, being heavily dominated by resource-based industries, rushed to create legislation which attempted to extinguish Native Title at a State level. In Western Australia a new Land Administration Bill was created to enable pastoralists to conduct tourism, horticultural and agricultural ventures, and in Queensland the State Government tabled legislation and offered 30-year interest-free loans to make it possible for pastoral leases to be upgraded to freehold, thus achieving *de facto* extinguishment of Aboriginal rights. There were considerable environmental as well as political costs in this move: 'The amendments are irresponsible and will inevitably result in massive damage and loss if upgrades are permitted on fragile pastoral lands ... Currently, lease conditions enable governments to ensure that pastoral land is looked after. Upgrades will reduce this ability or remove it entirely, ensuring further degradation and loss (ANTAR web site 1998: 2).

Despite these die-hard efforts, the pastoralists' anxieties were further exacerbated in December 1996 by the High Court's decision on the land claim submitted by the Wik and Thayorre Aboriginal communities just north of Kowanyama.[9] In *Wik Peoples* v. *the Federal Government*, the court ruled that pastoral leases did not confer rights of exclusive possession on the lessees, and that they did not necessarily extinguish Native Title. This was greeted with a roar of protest, with Don McDonald, president of Queensland's National Party (largely composed of pastoralists) calling for the extinguishment of Native Title: 'For farmers to continue to invest in [land] and operate successfully they must know they have security of tenure and sole occupancy' (National Party Press Release, 16 April 1997).

The backlash from these immensely powerful lobby groups contributed in 1996 to a change in Federal Government, bringing in conservatives determined to 'amend' the Native Title legislation. This, they maintained, was to provide certainty and thus stability for the primary industries, and to secure the way forward for development of the land. Opposition to Aboriginal Land Rights was further demonstrated in 1998 by a sudden upsurge in support for the 'One Nation' Party in Queensland's State elections. 'One Nation' is a radical far-right group committed to re-establishing a 'white Australia' immigration policy and undoing any legislation advantaging Aboriginal people or enabling them to reclaim their land. Though the support for this extreme (and some would say intensely racist) party was a considerable embarrassment to many people in Australia, the constituency for the 'One Nation' party and its spokeswoman Pauline Hanson lay in the outback rural areas, with the pastoral and farming industries. It reflected the economic pressures which forced many pastoralists to sell their properties (while observing some Aboriginal groups regaining rights to land) and it also tapped a deep vein of hostility towards Aboriginal people, left over from colonial conflicts. Perhaps most importantly, this political extremism emerged partly from the passionate desire of rural Australians to hold on to what they saw as their land, thus suggesting that, while it may be 'anti-Aboriginal' in its political stance, it may – ironically – reflect some degree of absorption of Aboriginal ideas and values about attachment to land.

The conservative Federal Government, while being careful not to support 'One Nation' openly, was also listening to the concerns of Australia's primary industries. It responded to the High Court's Wik decision with a ten-point amendment plan which proposed massive curtailments of the hard-won land rights, including the validation of the unlawful mining and pastoral leases given by State Governments in an attempt to deny Native Title. This was criticised by the Australian Law Reform Commission as being 'very likely' to breach Australia's obligations under international law (*Native Title Research Unit Newsletter*, September 1997: 12), and in August 1997, a UN report criticised the Federal Government's approach to land rights as 'wrought with discriminatory and colonial biases' (*The Australian*, 1 August 1997). In the same year, the Northern Land Council leader Galarrwuy Yunupingu refused to attend meetings about native title in Canberra until the Federal Government demonstrated 'respect for, and a willingness to come to grips with, what native title means for Aboriginal people ... [it] is not just about pieces of whitefella paper, it is the customary law and customary system which still governs us' (*Native Title Newsletter*, 21 October 1997: 14).

CONCLUSION

The dialogue about land and law therefore remains immensely contentious, but the battle lines and boundaries have shifted and blurred. Some things have remained constant: the Aboriginal community, throughout the maelstrom of change in the 20th century, has firmly maintained its own sense of identity and a clear vision of its particular relationship with land. Another stubborn rock is provided by the more conservative pastoralists and miners, whose desire to hold the land and whose antipathy to Aboriginal claims is thoroughly entrenched. Their self-identity is bound up in the mythic frontier imagery, with the 'lone heroes', the pioneers of colonial settlement and an adversarial interaction with the land.

However, these groups represent a very small proportion of the Australian population, and the mainstream has changed course considerably: it has absorbed the discourses of the land claim process; it has embraced the new environmental movement and – to some degree – its location of spiritual and moral meaning in the landscape (often through the borrowed imagery of indigenous groups); it has introduced deeply affective concepts of 'heritage' into its visions of the land. In the process the landscape has been re-evaluated, bringing to the foreground more complex values and beliefs which resonate with many Australians' unmet yearnings to reach beyond a heavily economic and technological interaction with nature and find a sense of place. Though most Australians' readings of the land remain embedded in very different practices and founded on a much more material cosmology, this suggests some convergence with Aboriginal values. Such convergence is demonstrated by the way in which Aboriginal concepts are regularly echoed in efforts to articulate this new environmental relationship. This can be seen as a positive outcome of long and determined efforts to educate European Australians about a different cultural landscape, or – less positively – as a mere appropriation of Aboriginal ideas which may be used to counter their claims to the land.

Wherever groups sit within this spectrum though, this new discourse has transformed Australian views on land rights, challenging many of the important precepts of European Australian identity and opening deep rifts between different sectors of Australian society. Like the early divisions between missionaries and settlers, it exposes the tensions between educational and economic classes, between rural and urban populations, between different parts of the country and between some of the States and the Federal Government. At times the vitriol of the debate seems even to threaten the nation's economic and social stability.

Nevertheless, progress towards reconciliation is being made. Although some of the opponents of Native Title are powerful and highly vocal, the majority of Australians are now clearly inclined to move towards compromise and reconciliation. Many people have no problem with the concept of sharing the land: by September 1997, Australians for Native Title and reconciliation (ANTAR) had received over 40,000 signatures in support of its citizen's petition against the dismantling of the Native Title legislation.[10] Another on-line piece of activism is represented by 'The Sorry Book': 'By signing my name in this book, I record my deep regret for the injustices suffered by indigenous Australians as a result of European settlement' (ANTAR 1998: 2). Many social scientists and legal experts are now closely involved in the process of reconciliation: 'The prerequisite for all this is for industry and government to accept that indigenous peoples now are an integral part of Australia's political framework ... They must be an equal partner in negotiations' (Farley 1997: 4).

So although extremely conservative groups have been able to push politicians to temper the effects of the new Native Title legislation, they have been unable to resist a groundswell of popular opinion in favour of reconciliation and negotiation rather than litigation. This is demonstrated by many new attempts to create regional agreements over land use and access (see Edmunds 1998, 1999). These offer to all parties in the conflict the possibility of avoiding lengthy and expensive legal battles and tailoring the agreement to suit the particular case. Some, such as Uluru, seem to have been more or less successful, and some hope was offered by the *Cape York Regional Agreement* (Cape York Land Council 1996)[11] which was initiated in response to the Wik claim. The Wik participants agreed that:

pastoral leaseholders are entitled to enjoy their rights, industry and lifestyle; that Aboriginal people are entitled to enjoy their rights, industry and culture; that all pastoral leases should be secure against native title claim, provided that traditional Aboriginal people be entitled to access to their traditional lands for traditional purposes. (Cape York Regional Agreement, CYRA web site)

Joint management agreements have also continued on a smaller scale in the National Parks, for example in the Capital Territory the Ngunnawal people have negotiated a management agreement in the Namadgi National Park, and in Kowanyama itself the Aboriginal community is a leading participant in the Mitchell River Watershed Catchment Management Group (MRWCMG) which it initiated in order to open up a discourse with other land users on a range of resource management issues within the watershed.

Kowanyama has responded to the legislative tug of war in a number of ways: the Community Council, elected when Kowanyama was given the Deed of Grant in Trust Land in 1987, provides avenues of communication with the State and Federal Governments. In the late 1980s, the Council set up an Aboriginal Land and Natural Resources Management Office, which as well as employing Rangers to manage the land, has developed a wide network of contacts with different industries and professional experts from Australia and overseas. This has helped to give the community more of a 'voice' in political negotiations. Similarly, the MRWCMG, though initiated ostensibly to provide a forum for the discussion of common environmental problems in the watershed, is a nexus of local relationships for the Aboriginal community. This has enabled it to establish itself firmly as a 'player' in nego-tiations about land on Cape York. The MRWCMG meets regularly, providing opportunities for Aboriginal representatives to maintain a dialogue with all the different groups within the catchment, including those – such as the miners and pastoralists – with whom it has the widest political divisions.

The European-style Community Council in Kowanyama has recently been supplemented by a gerontocratic *Counsel* [sic] of Elders, which provides 'traditional' leadership and advice for the community. The elders make con-siderable efforts to provide education about Aboriginal culture and relations with land, both in Kowanyama (to the children at school) and externally, to visitors and groups outside the community. Many different members of the community are thus involved in a subtle but highly political process of educating the Australian population about Aboriginal landownership and the case for land rights. In this way the community ensures that the values which underpin Aboriginal culture are communicated effectively in every possible arena, in every negotiation and in every representation of the community to the wider population.

This process of negotiation and education is being duplicated in many Aboriginal communities, maintaining a steady pressure on the legislative process. In the course of such negotiations, and in the more formal legislative arena, the boundaries between groups and on the land itself are explored and tested, and often renegotiated. Values and visions are exchanged and different kinds of attachment to land are communicated. In this sense, knowledge is power, because once shared, this knowledge cannot be readily erased, even by the most conservative groups who are most unwilling to admit Aboriginal influence. In the last century, Aboriginal groups have incorporated the parts of European law and land management which they find useful or expedient. At the same time, the clarity and intensity of Aboriginal relations to land have provided an irresistible mirage for the more mobile, homeless European Australians, offering a vision of wholeness, of connection with nature, which they find deeply seductive. Even in the crisp dry language of European law this subtle but powerful influence is evident in the patterns of legislative change which can be charted over time. Laws have expanded beyond the limitations of delineating property boundaries to encompass caring for the land, developing long-term sustainability, and, in the concept of heritage, expressing the breadth and depth of social and spiritual meaning embedded in the land. So in the new millennium the picture is not so black and white: Australian law has, in fact, taken on many of the values integral to Aboriginal Law, integrating mythic and legal lands into a more holistic landscape.

NOTES

1. The 1722 Privy Council had determined that 'if there be a new and uninhabited country found by English subjects, as the law is the birthright of every subject, so wherever they go they carry their law with them'.
2. A detailed history of the settlement of the Cape York Peninsula is provided in Strang (1997).
3. The Land Act has been criticised as a model because it catered mainly for the kinds of social organisation found specifically in northern Australia.
4. In 1983 the Queensland Association of Professional Anthropologists and Archaeologists (QAPAA) recommended to the Aboriginal Land Enquiry that the most appropriate form of land title which could be awarded to Aborginal groups would be inalienable freehold title - 'an estate in fee simple' with the explicit provision that the interest in the land may not be sold or disposed of. This is in keeping with the NT Land Rights Act of 1976 and the Pitjantjatjara Land Rights Act of 1981:

    Q.A.P.A.A. believes (a) that the only acceptable form of title to be granted over Aboriginal lands in both Western Australia and Queensland is inalienable freehold title; and (b) that such granting of land should be by an Act of Parliament and variable only by another Act of Parliament. (Henderson, 1983:4)

5. Ironically, the heritage movement has been generated by a greater distance between people and the land, and greater fluidity and uncertainty in social relations. The removal of the steadier boundaries of rural life seemed, in a way, to make identity more uncertain and contested. As Tonkin points out (1992:130), majority identities, if unchallenged, 'can become naturalised as reality', but if that solid ground is removed, they become, like minority identities, more self-conscious. It is reasonable to assume, therefore, that they are more in need of the explicitly foundational imageries of 'heritage'.
6. Heritage Management was further empowered by the Natural Heritage Trust of Australia Act in 1997.
7. This last criterion can only produce a lease for a set period of time, not title, and does not apply to National Parks or transferred land.
8. In 1996 an Aboriginal man, Murrandoo Yanner, was charged under the Nature Conservation Act for spearing crocodiles, and, although he was acquitted by the courts, the State Government in Queensland appealed the decision.
9. The Wik groups made a land claim in 1993, arguing that native title coexisted with pastoral leases. When their federal case was unsuccessful, their High Court appeal produced a ruling that native title could only be extinguished by a written law or act of government in which this was shown as a 'clear and plain' intention, and that the statute creating pastoral leases showed no such intention.

10. The ANTAR petition states that:

> The Government's draft legislation is mean-spirited and racially contemptuous. It involves a distinction that is based on race - in that it seeks to extinguish only those property rights held by Indigenous people. There is no need to extinguish anyone's rights. Under an alternative based on co-existence, local Aboriginal people, farmers, miners and other stakeholders can negotiate their own agreements about land use. The Government should acknowledge that its proposals are unworkable, divisive and a threat to reconciliation. (ANTAR web site 1998: 6)
>
> Extinguishment is completely unnecessary, irrational and will not deliver the certainty which everyone understandably wants. Aboriginal people themselves have consistently argued that existing pastoralists' rights should be guaranteed and are calling for coexistence as the way forward ... Retrospective validation of the unlawful State government grants is a shameful act.
>
> States like Queensland, eager to flout the Native Title Act, will now be rewarded for their unlawful and racially contemptuous behaviour ... The amendments are unlawful in that they extinguish the property rights of one race only ... the amendments are environmentally irresponsible and will inevitably result in massive damage and loss if upgrades are permitted on fragile pastoral lands. (ANTAR, web site, 1998:2)

11. The *Cape York Regional Agreement* was signed in 1996 by the Cape York Land Council, the Peninsula Regional Council of the Aboriginal and Torres Strait Islander Commission, the Australian Conservation Foundation, the Wilderness Society and the Cattlemen's Union of Australia. Though it has by no means been unproblematic, many people still regard such regional agreements as a useful potential avenue for resolving the conflicts over land.

REFERENCES

Altman, J.C. 1984. 'Hunter-gatherer subsistence production in Arnhem Land: the original affluent society hypothesis reexamined', *Mankind* 14(3): 179–90.

ANTAR (Australians for Native Title and Reconciliation). 1998. *The Native Title Bill and What You Can Do about It.* ANTAR web site, http://www.antar.org.au/

Attwood, B. 1996. *In the Age of Mabo: History, Aborigines and Australia.* Sydney: Allen and Unwin.

Australian Heritage Commission. 1990. *A Sense of Place? A Conversation in Three Cultures,* Technical Publications Series No. 1. Canberra: Australian Government Publishing Service.

Cape York Land Council. 1996. *Heads of Agreement of the Cape York Regional Agreement.* Cairns: CYRA.

Cape York Regional Agreement, CYRA web site. <http: //nccnsw.org.au/member/ tws/projects/Cape_York/agreement.html>

Council for Aboriginal Reconciliation. 1993. *Making Things Right: Reconciliation After the High Court's Decision on Native Title.* Canberra: Government Publishing Service.

Edmunds, M. (ed.) 1998. *Regional Agreements: Key Issues in Australia – Volume 1, Summaries.* Canberra: Australian Institute of Aboriginal and Torres Strait Islander Studies (AITSIS).

—— 1999. *Regional Agreements: Key Issues in Australia – Volume 2, Case Studies.* Canberra: AITSIS.

Farley, R. 1997. 'Wik – The Way Forward', in *Land, Rights Laws: Issues of Native Title, Native Title Research Unit Newsletter,* Issue Paper No. 13. Canberra: Australian Institute of Aboriginal and Torres Strait Islanders Studies.

Henderson, A. 1983. 'Submission of the Queensland Association of Professional Anthropologists to the Aboriginal Land Enquiry', unpublished m.s., University of Queensland.

Hill, R. 1992. 'Models for Aboriginal involvement in natural resource management on Cape York', in *National Park Conservation*. Queensland AIR 008: 19–24.

Home, H. 1761. *Historical Law Tracts*. Edinburgh.

Horstmann, M. 1996. 'Black shadows, white shadows, grey shadows: does the Cape York Regional Agreement provide a model for the reconciliation process?', *Arena Magazine*, 22: 26–31.

Ingold, T., Riches, D. and Woodburn, J. (eds) 1988. *Hunters and Gatherers, vol. 1: History, Evolution and Social Change*. Oxford, New York, Hamburg: Berg.

Jones, R. 1990. 'Hunters of the Dreaming: some ideational, economic and ecological parameters of the Australian Aboriginal productive system', in D. Yen and J. Mummery (eds) *Pacific Production Systems: Approaches to Economic Prehistory*. New Zealand: Symposium at the XV Pacific Science Congress, Dunedin, 1983, pp. 25–53.

Kolig, E. 1987. *The Noonkanbah Story*. Dunedin, NZ: University of Otago Press.

McCorquodale, J. 1987. *Aborigines and the Law: A Digest*. Canberra: Aboriginal Studies Press.

Merlan, F. and Rumsey, A. 1982. *The Jawoyn (Katherine Area) Land Claim*. Darwin: Northern Land Council.

Morphy, H. 1988. 'Maintaining cosmic unity: ideology and the reproduction of Yolngu clans', in T. Ingold, J. Riches and J. Woodburn (eds) *Hunters and Gatherers, vol. 2: Property, Power and Ideology*. Oxford: Berg.

Peterson, N., McConvell, P., Wild, S. and Hagen R. 1978. *A Claim to Areas of Traditional Land by the Warlpiri and Kartangarurru-Kurintji*. Austalia: Central Land Council.

Queensland State Government. 1992. *Queensland Heritage Act 1992: A Guide for Heritage Property Owners*, Information leaflet, BP651, July 1992.

Queensland State Government. 1998. Department of the Environment, *Cultural Heritage* web site: http://www.env.qld.gov.au

Ranger, T. 1993. 'Aboriginal and Khoisan Studies Compared', unpublished m.s., University of Western Australia.

Read, P. 1996. *Returning to Nothing: The Meaning of Lost Places*. Cambridge, New York, Melbourne: Cambridge University Press.

Reynolds, H. 1987. *The Law of the Land*. London, Victoria, New York: Penguin.

—— 1996. 'Pastoral leases in their historical context', *Aboriginal Law Bulletin* 3(81): 9–11.

Ritchie, D. 1996. 'Constructions of Aboriginal tradition for public purpose', in S. Toussaint and J. Taylor (eds) *Applied Anthropology in Australasia*. Perth: University of Western Australia Press.

Rowse, T. 1988. 'Paternalism's changing reputation', *Mankind* 18(2): 57–73.

Stewart, J. 1991. *Report to the Minister for Aboriginal Affairs under Section 10(4) of the Aboriginal and Torres Strait Islander Heritage Protection Act 1984 on the Kakadu Conservation Zone*. Canberra: Australian Government Publishing Service.

Strang, V. 1996. 'Sustaining tourism in Far North Queensland', in M. Price (ed.) *People and Tourism in Fragile Environments*. London: John Wiley.

—— 1997. *Uncommon Ground: Cultural Landscapes and Environmental Values*. Oxford, New York: Berg.

—— 1998. 'Competing perceptions of landscape in Kowanyama, North Queensland', in P. Ucko and R. Layton (eds) *Shaping the Landscape*. London: Routledge.

—— in press. 'Aboriginal women and sacred landscapes in northern Australia', in E. Low and S. Tremayne (eds) *Women as 'Sacred Custodians' of the Earth*. Oxford: Oneworld Publishers.

Tehan, M. 1997. 'Co-existence of Interests in Land: a dominant feature of the Common Law', in *Native Title Research Unit Newsletter* 7 February 1997: 2–9. URL: http://www.aiatsis.gov.au/ntpapers/ntip12.htm

Tonkin, E. 1992. *Narrating Our Pasts: The Social Construction of Oral History*. Cambridge: Cambridge University Press.

Williams, N. and Hunn, E. (eds) 1986. *Resource Managers: North American and Australian Hunter-Gatherers*. Canberra: Australian Institute of Aboriginal Studies.

6 THE APPROPRIATION OF LANDS OF LAW BY LANDS OF MYTH IN THE CARIBBEAN REGION

Jean Besson

This chapter examines the articulation of mythical lands and legal boundaries through the case of the Caribbean region, Europe's oldest colonial sphere and the core area of African-America (Mintz 1989, 1996; Mintz and Price 1992). Lands of Law[1] have been the main basis of hegemony in the Antilles and coastal lowlands of the Americas surrounding the Caribbean Sea for over 500 years of post-conquest history, since Columbus's landfall on Guanahani in the Bahamas chain in 1492. Such land rights are reflected in persisting plantation systems and new forms of land monopoly in the bauxite mining and tourist industries. Lands of Myth[2] have been a central mode of resistant response to such constraints by Caribbean 'reconstituted peasantries' (Mintz 1989: 132)[3] from slavery to the diaspora: among slave 'proto-peasants',[4] squatters, free villagers, Rastafarians, migrant peasants and maroons. Their landholdings have been embedded in sacred rites and ancestral oral traditions reaching back to emancipation, enslavement, and the African past.

I explore these perspectives, in the main body of the chapter, in relation to eight Jamaican peasant communities constrained by land monopoly at the heart of the Caribbean region. I first outline the background theme of land monopoly and peasants in Jamaica. I then focus on the Accompong Town community, in the parish of St Elizabeth, which is the oldest corporate maroon society in the Americas (Besson 1995c; Price 1996). There rebel slaves appropriated land in the wilderness from the plantation-military regime through squatting, warfare and treaty. Modern maroons have transformed this marginal reservation into a sacred landscape, in the context of continuing attempts by external governments to undermine both the treaty and the bauxite-rich commons that remain surrounded by plantations.

I next consider Accompong's neighbouring Aberdeen community, at the junction of the maroon and non-maroon peasantries. Here Lands of Law have likewise been transformed into Lands of Myth. The Afro-Aberdonians are descended from proto-peasant slaves who appropriated plantation backlands, adjoining the maroon commons, through customary cognatic land transmission. After emancipation the freed slaves, augmented by some maroons, squatted on Crown land and plantation-mountains nearer to the plains. These lands, which were retrieved by planters and the state and sold to the ex-slaves, have been transformed into 'family lands' through customary transmission to all descendants of the original landholders. Such family land serves both as a symbol of identity for the family line and as its economic foothold, in the context of corporate plantations and the bauxite industry.

I then examine five 'free villages' and a related squatter settlement in the parish of Trelawny. The Trelawny villages were established in the vanguard of the Caribbean post-slavery flight from the estates. Here ex-slaves appropriated land from the plantations through squatting and by purchase, especially in alliance with the Baptist Church, which created freehold land settlements as captive congregations. These legal freeholds have been transformed into customary family lands in contexts of persisting plantations, escalating tourism and transnational circulatory migration. The intense land scarcity has also generated a Revival-Rastafarian[5] squatter settlement, which is currently appropriating government plantation land.

In the final section of the chapter, I show that similar appropriations of Lands of Law by Lands of Myth can be identified in peasant communities throughout the Caribbean region, where common lands and family lands articulate with unrestricted cognatic descent systems. As I discuss there, this conclusion both modifies and develops the African-American creolisation thesis advanced by Mintz and Price (1992). I also argue that the case of the Caribbean region suggests wider cross-cultural perspectives in relation to a two-dimensional view of land as both economic and symbolic, scarce and unlimited.

LAND MONOPOLY AND THE JAMAICAN PEASANTRY

The former British West Indian colony of Jamaica, with its pronounced plantation system and peasantry formations, reflects in microcosm the Caribbean dialectic between Lands of Law and Lands of Myth. The island was encountered by Columbus in 1494, two years after his Caribbean landfall; colonised by the Spanish in 1509, during the early stages of European expansion; and conquered by the British in 1655. By 1700 Jamaica was the world's leading sugar producer (Walvin 1983: 35). In the 18th century the island became 'the very centre of Negro slavery', 'the most important colony in the British Empire' and, with neighbouring French Saint-Domingue, one of the two most profitable dependencies the world has ever known based on the colonial slave–plantation system (Williams 1970: 152, 154). Plantations persisted after the abolition of slavery (1834–8) and remain entrenched in several areas of the island today, despite political independence in 1962. Jamaica has therefore been described, rightly, as the New World society in which 'the plantation system was developed to the most extreme degree and over the longest continuous period of time' (Robotham 1977: 46). Complementing this long history of plantation hegemony, which is now reinforced by land monopoly in the bauxite mining and tourist industries, has been a pronounced process of slave resistance and peasantisation.

Within these contexts the parishes of Trelawny and St Elizabeth, in west-central Jamaica, became the heart of the island's plantation system: Trelawny had more plantations and slaves than any other parish and St Elizabeth was an area of intense colonial exploitation. In 1999, the lowlands and intermontane valleys of both parishes remain dominated by sugar-cane estates producing rum and sugar for the world-economy. Such land monopoly is reinforced by bauxite mining in St Elizabeth and by tourism in Trelawny, where there are now also several papaya plantations. These large-scale landholdings are based on clear-cut rights and boundaries, originating in the island's colonially derived agrarian legal code.

Paralleling this extreme manifestation of the plantation system and other forms of land monopoly in the west-central area of Jamaica, have been pronounced examples of slave resistance and peasant adaptation. Runaway slaves found early refuge by squatting in the precipitous Cockpit Country Mountains of the interior, where the Leeward Maroon polity became established through the treaty of March 1739. In addition, a proto-peasant economy evolved among plantation slaves who cultivated food for sale and subsistence on estate backlands and mountains; a development, based on both adaptation and cultural resistance, that was particularly well-established in Trelawny. Slave revolts likewise characterised this part of the island, including the 1831 rebellion that led to the abolition of slavery throughout the British Empire.

After slavery, the Leeward Maroon polity persisted in the face of recurrent attempts by colonial and postcolonial governments to undermine their treaty and common land. Meanwhile, free villages were being established by emancipated slaves in the face of draconian planter policies and legislation designed to keep the ex-slaves as a cheap labour supply on the plantations; developments that were especially marked in Trelawny, which was typified by the bitterest plantation–peasant conflicts in the island. An overseas migration tradition likewise consolidated, including a process of circulatory migration which articulates with the diaspora in Europe and North America today. A symbolic migration to Africa also developed through the Rastafarian movement, simultaneous with the rooting of Rastafari in Caribbean land, as in the peasant communities of the west-central area of Jamaica (Besson 1995a, 1995b). These peasant formations persist today surrounded by plantations, bauxite mines, and luxury hotels. The wresting of small-holdings from the Lands of Law has been central to the peasantisation process, and these small-scale landholdings have been reinforced through sacred cosmologies and rituals; a process of appropriation that is still evolving. It was in these contexts that I undertook fieldwork during the period 1968–99 in eight peasant communities in Trelawny and St Elizabeth, where land rites are most elaborate in the isolated Accompong maroon society.

THE ACCOMPONG MAROON SOCIETY

Accompong Town is situated in northern St Elizabeth, in the deep-forested southern area of the precipitous *karst* Cockpit Country Mountains that straddle the adjoining parishes of St Elizabeth, Trelawny and St James. The village, which has a voting population of around 3,000 persons (many of whom are dispersed in Bradford and London, England), is the only surviving community of the Jamaican Leeward Maroon polity. The Leeward polity was consolidated over 250 years ago, after Jamaica's First Maroon War (1725–39), by the treaty in 1739 between the maroon leader Colonel Cudjoe and the British colonial government which was forced to sue for peace. From the early post-conquest period runaway slaves from the plantation lowlands squatted on Crown land in the interior mountain wilderness, which not only provided a refuge from European exploitation but also (as in neighbouring Cuba) had a 'symbolic and religious meaning' derived from Africa 'that gave marronage a dimension beyond mere escape' (Hennessy 1993: 4). A 'belief in the spirituality of the woods' persisted among slaves in the New World and life in the forest enabled 'a communing with Nature', with 'ancestral divinities' and with 'the Universal Mother, source of life' (ibid.: 4, quoting from Echevarría 1980: 13, 3).

The Leeward Treaty granted the maroons their freedom and 1,500 acres of common land,[6] which they had already appropriated through squatting and guerrilla warfare. By the time of the treaty, two maroon villages had been established in the Cockpits: Cudjoe's Town in St James and Accompong Town in St Elizabeth. The maroons of Cudjoe's Town were subsequently betrayed, disbanded and deported to Nova Scotia by the colonial regime after Jamaica's Second Maroon War (1795–6). Thereafter, external attempts to nullify the treaty and subdivide the Leeward Maroon commons have persisted to the present time. The Accompong maroons have firmly resisted these attempts to undermine their maroon society and common land. This resistance has been reflected in the land disputes with the colonial and post-colonial state documented by Kopytoff (1979) up to the 1970s; and in the contentions over legal boundaries and taxation throughout the period of my fieldwork in Accompong, from 1979 to 1999. In the 1990s there have also been attempts, by the Jamaica state, to impose individual alienable titles on Accompong Town's bauxite-rich inalienable common land.

From the colonial viewpoint, the treaty ceded land rights to a marginal wilderness reservation designed to confine the rebel slaves. However, from the maroon perspective this legal document became a sacred charter of corporate identity reflected in the commons (Kopytoff 1979). My fieldwork has uncovered a still-evolving symbolic landscape transforming this Land of Law into a Land of Myth, which continues to preserve the maroon polity in the face of threat and change (see also Besson 1997).

Modern maroons classify the commons into three concentric zones, deriving from their ethnohistory. The deep forest was traditionally the scene of warfare with the colonial plantation-military regime. There too the warrior-maroons hunted wild boar and gathered cocoon-beans. The forest now forms an outer boundary zone segregating maroon society from the surrounding plantations and bauxite mines, and from the Jamaican state. Contemporary maroons collect sacred medicines and fell timber here. The cultivation of provision-grounds, carved out of the forest, was combined with hunting and gathering in the rebel-slave economy and was a focus of destruction by the colonial regime. The warrior maroons also raised livestock, raided from plantations. Today provision-grounds, land cash-cropped in bananas, and pasture form an intermediate zone. At the heart of the commons is the inner residential area, with its village yards and cross-roads. House-yards are not only residential sites, but also the nuclei of the maroon economy. Here food-forests are cultivated, small livestock raised and fruit trees grown. This inner residential zone most fully incorporates the Leeward Maroon polity, which has an elected Colonel, a Maroon Council, an Abeng-Blower (who blows the sacred cow-horn that was used to communicate in guerrilla warfare) and a Secretary-of-State.

All Leeward maroons have the inalienable right to use the commons and these usufructuary rights are allocated by the Colonel and his Council, who also address internal disputes. However, within this wider context of common land, unrestricted cognatic descent groups are consolidating in relation to the customary transmission of house-yards and provision-grounds.[7] These overlapping landholding kin groups claim descent from the 'First-Time' maroon heroes and heroines, especially Colonel Cudjoe and his reputed sister Nanny, who fought the war and won the peace.

Maroon land rites reflect these themes and focus on interment in the commons. Six burial patterns can be identified, charting the landscape as sacred space. The first pattern typifies the Kindah Grove at the edge of the residential zone. Oral history states that ancestral Congo and Coromantee burial grounds are situated here. This oral tradition is reinforced by a written history of African ethnicities among the early rebel slaves (Kopytoff 1976), and by the ancient cairns and boulders overgrown with bush and encompassing the grove. Within the Kindah Grove itself is a small area of grassland and jutting limestone rocks surrounding the sacred 'Kindah Tree', representing in microcosm the *karst* topography of the Cockpit Country. The Kindah Tree, a fruitful mango tree, is rooted in myth and ethnohistory. It is said to be the place where the two rebel 'tribes' of Congos and Coromantees met to forge an alliance, through inter-marriage, in opposition to the plantation-military regime. Here, each year on or around 6 January, the 'Myal Dance' and feast is held; a ritual reaching back to Africa, slavery and marronage. Myalism was the first creole spirit-possession cult forged by the Jamaican slaves from African cosmologies; and the Myal Dance, with its death and resurrection theme, was initially performed to protect the plantation-slave communities (Patterson 1973: 185–95; Schuler 1980; Besson 1995c).

In Accompong Town today, the Myal Dance is said to commemorate both Cudjoe's birthday and the ending of the war. It is also believed to protect and re-create the contemporary community, through the possession of living females by the spirits of the male warrior-maroons. This spirit possession is enacted by maroon women directly beneath the Kindah Tree, accompanied by drummers and by the Abeng-Blower, who are male. This ritual symbolises the central role of scarce, but precious, women in reproducing the historic maroon polity. The fruitful Kindah Tree itself, with its sign proclaiming 'We are Family', symbolises the common kinship of the corporate creole community on its common land. This shared kinship is based on overlapping cognatic descent groups, interlocking bilateral kinship networks, and tendencies towards endogamy and cousin-conjugality.[8] In the 1990s, the Myal Dance has become a tourist attraction and a symbol of Jamaican nationhood, forged through a history of conflict and alliance. This, too, is now ritually enacted at the Kindah Grove, which is visited by tourists and by invited ministers of the Jamaican state with their armed bodyguards.

Beyond the Kindah Grove is the reputed resting place of Colonel Cudjoe's 'brothers' and lieutenants: Quaco, Cuffee, Johnny and Accompong; the latter being the founder of the Accompong Town community. This second burial ground, like the graves at Kindah, is marked by cairns and boulders. However, unlike the Kindah graves, which are overgrown by bush and absorbed into the wilderness, the lieutenants' graves (which are surrounded by provision-grounds and pasture) are weeded for the Myal Dance. At this time the maroons make a ritual journey from Kindah through this second grove. Non-maroons are not allowed to make this pilgrimage.

Some distance on, in the intermediate zone, is 'Old Town': the third and most sacred burial place. Old Town is located where a Cockpit valley adjoins a jutting Cockpit mountain covered profusely with cocoon-vines, which oral history states provided both camouflage and food during the First Maroon War. Modern maroons say that Old Town was Colonel Cudjoe's military camp, the mountain being his look-out to miles around, and that Cudjoe himself is buried in the valley here in a stone-marked grave. Nanny, the ritual heroine of the Windward Maroon polity in the eastern mountains of Jamaica,[9] who is claimed by Leeward maroons to have been Cudjoe's sister, is likewise said to be buried here. These reputed graves are weeded for the pilgrimage and an altar is erected for a sacrificial meal.

Even further on, into the forest, is the Peace Cave, which is said to be the scene of the successful maroon ambush of British soldiers that won the war, and the site of the signing of the treaty between Colonel Cudjoe and the colonial regime. The ritual transit from Kindah to the Peace Cave is marked by intercessions and libations to the warrior-heroes; and a rum-bottle, annually replenished, is placed for Cudjoe's spirit inside the Cave. The graves of defeated British soldiers, and maroons who fell in war, are said to be scattered all around at this fourth sacred burial ground. On their return from the Peace Cave, through Old Town and the lieutenants' graves, the maroons reconvene at Kindah to greet their non-maroon guests armed with sticks and battle-camouflaged in cocoon-vines.

This symbolic journey through sacred space and back in time is continued through a fifth burial ground within Accompong Town itself. This is the cemetery of the Presbyterian (now United) Church, which was established in the maroon society in the late 19th century (Kopytoff 1987: 473; Besson 1997). More recent ancestresses and ancestors are interred in this burial place, which symbolises the transformation from marronage and African ethnic groups to a creole maroon community. The village cemetery is a symbol of this corporate community and its common land. This mode of burial is still ongoing, reinforced by both Christian and Myal mortuary ritual.

However, during the period of my fieldwork, a sixth interment pattern has been emerging. This is burial in house-yards in modern concrete tombs.[10] This represents the nascent concretisation of the evolving cognatic descent groups, and is reinforced by Afro-Christian mortuary ritual and migrant remittances. This emerging yard-burial pattern is long-established in the Jamaican non-maroon communities that originated in the proto-peasant adaptation and the post-emancipation flight from the estates, such as Trelawny's free villages. Yard burial also typifies Accompong's neighbouring Aberdeen community, which is rooted in both the maroon and proto-peasant pasts.

THE AFRO-ABERDEEN COMMUNITY

Adjoining the Accompong Town maroon commons, in the parish of St Elizabeth, is the Aberdeen community with a population of some 16,000 adults on about 1,200 acres of mainly mountain land. Aberdeen has a more dispersed settlement pattern, on parcelled lands, than the corporate maroon village. However, as in the maroon society, Lands of Law have here also been transformed into Lands of Myth.

The Afro-Aberdonians are descended from proto-peasant slaves, who appropriated the mountain backlands of Aberdeen plantation (bordering the maroon commons) established by Alexander Forbes of Scotland's Aberdeen; in addition to cultivating the house-yards of the Aberdeen slave village. Oral traditions in both Accompong and Aberdeen recount military and conjugal alliances between the First-Time maroons and the slaves on Aberdeen estate, established by communicating through the plantation-backlands bordering the commons. This theme is underwritten by historical accounts of such alliance forged by rebel slaves. Today, many Afro-

Aberdonians have ties of kinship, marriage and descent with maroons in Accompong. In addition, Aberdonians of maroon descent retain usufructuary rights and voting status in the Leeward polity. However, the Accompong maroons contrast their tax-free common land, deriving from the treaty, with Aberdeen's taxed and parcelled lands. These comprise a core of 'family lands' co-existing with other small-scale tenures, such as purchased and rented land. On these lands Aberdonians practice mixed cultivation for subsistence and sale in public market-places, and cash-crop bananas and sugar-cane for the world-economy.

The core of family lands in Aberdeen are rooted in the customary land-transmission system of Jamaican proto-peasant slaves, who appropriated and transformed the house-yards of plantation-slave communities and the backlands and mountains of estates. In order to avoid the high cost of imported food, plantation owners allocated mountainous and hilly land (unsuited to sugar-cane production) to their slaves for provision-cultivation, in addition to the house-yards that were kept as kitchen gardens. The slaves developed their domestic economy well beyond the planter rationale, producing surpluses for sale in public market-places. By 1774, at the zenith of plantation slavery in Jamaica, slaves controlled one-fifth of the island's currency through such marketing activities (Mintz 1989: 180–213).

In addition, by the late 18th century the planter-historian Bryan Edwards noted a system of customary transmission in relation to these house-yards and provision-grounds, and in the early 19th century John Stewart observed that each slave had such rights to land (Edwards 1793, 2: 133, and Stewart 1823: 267, quoted in Mintz 1989: 187, 207). This gender equality among male and female slaves provided the foundation for their customary system of unrestricted cognatic descent and land transmission, especially given the significance of women as field slaves and the matrilateral emphasis in slave yards and communities. This cognatic system, which reversed the colonial primogeniture on which the plantation system was based[11] (as well as transforming the restricted unilineal kin groups of West and Central Africa), not only generated ever-increasing descent lines but also maximised scarce land rights as bases of identity among the chattel slaves – who were legally landless and kinless, and were property themselves. The Jamaican slave religion, Myalism, with its elaborate mortuary ritual reflecting a belief in an active spirit world including ancestral kin, reinforced this land-transmission system with its descent-based burial grounds in the house-yards of slave villages (Besson and Chevannes 1996). In the later slavery period, Myal would control Nonconformist mission Christianity: such as the Moravian Church, which missionised the Aberdonian slaves and consolidated the Aberdeen community in the late 19th century – though many Aberdonians are Pentecostalists today (cf. Austin-Broos 1997).

Oral tradition combined with written history indicates that, in the case of Aberdeen, the former proto-peasants extended the appropriation of plantation lands some years after emancipation by squatting on Crown land

and on plantation backlands south of Aberdeen estate. After legal land
retrieval, registration, land sales and taxation, the Aberdonian ex-slaves
purchased parcelled lands. These emancipated slaves formed the core of the
Aberdeen post-slavery peasant community, which was augmented by some
maroons who migrated from Accompong to live nearer to the plains. Such
'bought lands' have been transformed to 'family lands' by their descendants,
with landholdings validated by oral tradition rather than by legal
documents. These ancestral lands, which are transmitted through unrestricted cognatic descent and are characterised by burial grounds as in the
proto-peasant past, provide a foothold in the face of the surrounding bauxite
mines and corporate plantations. The process of creating family land from
purchased land continues, reinforced by burial rooted in Afro-Christian
mortuary ritual.

This appropriation of Lands of Law by Lands of Myth is exemplified by the
Aberdonian ancestor-hero, the African-Prince Maroon. Aberdeen's central
'Old Family' or unrestricted cognatic descent group (which overlaps with
an Afro-Scots non-maroon family line) traces its ancestry and family land
eight generations, through males and females, to an ancestor who is said to
have been an African Prince brought on a slave ship to Jamaica and who
escaped to Accompong Town from a plantation on the plains. One of his
descendants is said to have 'come out' from Accompong and to have
acquired, through squatting and purchase, some 16 acres of mountain land
in Aberdeen around 1845, seven years after emancipation. This land has
been orally transmitted to all of his descendants. Some members of this unrestricted landholding corporation have migrated to New York and to
Bradford, England; while others remain on the family land. Any absent
member of this dispersed kin group may return to live there or be buried on
the land, which in 1999 has at least 23 old tombs and cairns in its descent-
based burial ground.

THE FREE VILLAGES OF TRELAWNY AND THE SQUATTER SETTLEMENT
OF ZION

Ancestral family lands or Lands of Myth are also at the core of the post-emancipation villages in the neighbouring parish of Trelawny, which was the
heart of the slave-plantation economy and the vanguard of the post-slavery
flight from the estates. In the first few years after emancipation, at least 23
post-slavery villages were established in Trelawny through an alliance
between the freed slaves and the Baptist Church – which was prominent in
the anti-slavery struggle and had been the most successful Nonconformist
sect to missionise the slaves. This 'free village' movement, which was
widespread throughout the island, drew on traditions of slave resistance
including the proto-peasant adaptation (which was pronounced in
Trelawny) with its customary cognatic land-transmission system. In the five

free villages studied, oral traditions elaborate the theme of emancipated slaves appropriating small-holdings from the Lands of Law in the context of acute planter opposition to peasantisation.

In four of the villages (New Birmingham, Wilberforce, Kettering and Granville) the Baptist Church mediated between ex-slaves and planters, creating legal-freehold land settlements with colonial Christian nuclear families through the subdivision and sale of land from purchased plantations. In the fifth free village, Martha Brae, freed Baptist slaves from the surrounding estates of Holland and Irving Tower squatted on the site of a declining planter town that had been the colonial capital of Trelawny in the late 18th century. As in St Elizabeth's Aberdeen, the colonial state retrieved this 'captured land' for sale, registration and taxation; and, as in Aberdeen, the ex-slaves and their descendants created family lands from purchased lands in the process of transforming the planter town into a peasant village. A similar transformation from legal to customary freeholds has occurred in the context of imposed land settlements in the other Trelawny villages; and in all five free villages unrestricted cognatic descent lines, which transformed the European nuclear family, are anchored in these family lands (Besson 1984). As in Aberdeen, these Lands of Myth (which co-exist with other small-scale tenures) are transmitted through oral history from ancestresses and ancestors; and are typified, in varying degrees, by ancestral burial grounds. Interment in all five villages is characterised by a combination of Baptist and Revival-Zion mortuary ritual (forged through the appropriation of Baptist Christianity by Myalism), Trelawny having been at the centre of both Baptist missionising and the Myal movement in Jamaica.

These Lands of Myth perpetuate the peasant communities, which are today surrounded by vast corporate plantations and by the escalating tourist industry. New Birmingham, which was Trelawny's first free village founded in 1838 on a former coffee estate at The Alps in the northern foothills of the Cockpit country, resembles St Elizabeth's Aberdeen in its dispersed mountainous land base. Its family burial grounds are likewise very pronounced, one such family cemetery containing 34 identifiable cairns and tombs of the descendants of the ancestor-hero Archie Campbell, an emancipated slave.

The other four free villages are more nucleated on marginal land bordering plantations on the coastal plains, in an area directly inland from Jamaica's world-famous tourist coast. These villages are typified by intense land scarcity, and landholdings are measured in square feet or chains.[12] Today Wilberforce (now called Refuge), which was founded in 1838 on approximately 90 acres of hilly land now embroidered with ancestral cairns and tombs, has a population of about 400 persons in 80 households hemmed in by the 20,000 acres of the National Sugar (Long Pond) corporate sugar-estate. Granville, which was established in 1845 also on some 90 acres, now has a population of around 600 persons in 120 households on a landscape covered in ancestral graves of varying style and age surrounded by estates.

Here too ex-slaves – such as 'Hard Time', 'Mother Lawrence' and 'Queenie' (whose genealogy is traced to one of three sisters brought from Africa into slavery) – feature in relation to these Lands of Myth.

Kettering was founded in 1841 on rocky land (a former pimento estate subdivided into 400 'lots' measured in square feet) adjoining the town of Duncans. Contemporary Kettering has about 800 persons in 160 households, and parts of the free village now have to bury in the Duncans cemetery, though yard interment continues undisturbed in the more remote areas of the village. In Martha Brae, which was appropriated by ex-slaves in the 1840s, around 800 persons in 170 households are now enclosed 'like pigs in a kraal' on a ridge of approximately 30 acres by sugar and papaya estates. There, yard-burial was discontinued in the early 20th century, due to acute land scarcity, and has been replaced by interment in the free-village cemetery. However, family lands persist at the heart of the community and are still created wherever possible from minuscule plots of purchased land. Family lands in Kettering and Martha Brae are likewise imbued with ethno-history, focusing on ancestor-heroes and ancestress-heroines such as the freed slave Emanuel Scott, the slave-girl Sarah Wilson and the ex-slave 'Nana Green' (Besson, in preparation).

In all of these free villages today, the unrestricted cognatic descent system at the heart of family land maximises scarce land rights and kinship lines as bases of identity and security among descendants of chattel slaves. This non-exclusive land-transmission system also enables return and circulatory migration; and in the diaspora (for example, in London, England) small sacks of soil from family lands symbolise rights to such Lands of Myth, which are regarded as inalienable.

The unrestricted cognatic descent system also links these free villages to Zion, a squatter settlement established during the period of my long-term recurrent fieldwork in Trelawny by landless tenants from Martha Brae who 'captured' land on a part of Holland plantation owned by the Trelawny Parish Council. This satellite squatter-peasantry, some of whom migrated to Martha Brae from other Trelawny villages where they are members of Old Families experiencing land scarcity, has a history of land dispute and negotiation with the state. When I began my fieldwork in 1968 there were no houses on Holland estate. By the end of 1968 one chattel cottage had been moved there, from Martha Brae, to the Parish Council land and the household was threatened with eviction. After a court case and a compromise relocation, two more households squatted there in 1971. By 1979 there were around 30 households and the settlement had been named. By 1999 there was a vibrant squatter settlement, with some 70 households on approximately 30 acres of captured land, and the government was surveying and subdividing (in square metres) their Land of Law for retrieval, sales, registration and taxation.

The first settlers of Zion who appropriated the plantation-land, creating house-yards immediately behind a 'No Squatting' sign, are ancestor-heroes and ancestress-heroines in the making; and it is likely that their house-yards, as well as those of other settlers, will be transmitted as family lands or Lands of Myth. Meanwhile, the squatter settlement provides a foothold for Revival-Zion ritual and a 'Zion' for Rastafarians in 'Babylon'. The Rastafarian movement, which like the Jamaican peasantry itself originated in the proto-peasant adaptation (Besson 1995a), also interweaves with family land in the free villages of Trelawny and with common land in St Elizabeth's Accompong maroon society, as migrant Rastas return from urban areas to root themselves in Caribbean land despite their Ethiopian ideology.[13]

COMPARATIVE AND CROSS-CULTURAL PERSPECTIVES

The articulation of Law and Myth is both dichotomous and more complex in relation to the lands of the eight communities, questioning the plural society thesis of Caribbean land tenure systems (M.G. Smith 1965a; Lowenthal 1972). For example, legal elements such as burial regulations and taxation are imposed on family lands; while free-villagers sometimes draw on the legal code to reinforce, adjust or challenge customary family-land principles. In addition, some aspects of the Law indirectly reinforce the customary system (Besson 1988, 1995e). However, the dominant theme in all communities is the transformation of Lands of Law by Lands of Myth.

As seen in the preceding sections, this appropriation is historically rooted in colonial plantation slavery when proto-peasants established customary cognatic land-transmission systems which became consolidated, reinforcd by ritual, in the maroon polity and in the post-emancipation villages. This cultural creativity overturned the colonial institution of primogeniture on which the plantation system, or Land of Law, was based. The ethos of these Lands of Myth has also since transformed the Law itself, which put an end to primogeniture in 1953 and abolished the Eurocentric status of 'illegitimacy' with the Status of Children Act in 1976 (Besson 1988). As seen above, this process of appropriating the Lands of Law reaches back to the Leeward Maroon Treaty of 1739 and was still ongoing among the squatter-peasantry of Zion in 1999.

Similar appropriations of Lands of Law by Lands of Myth can be widely identified in Caribbean peasant communities, where common lands and family lands articulate with unrestricted cognatic descent systems originating in proto-peasant adaptations (Besson 1987, 1992, 1995d). For example, in the Greater Antilles in the northern Caribbean, an unrestricted cognatic descent system persists at the heart of the *lakou* or landholding kin group in Haiti (Larose 1975), as well as being widespread in family land throughout Jamaica (Davenport 1961; Edwards 1961; Clarke 1966; Carnegie 1987; McKay 1987; Espeut 1992). In the Lesser Antilles of the eastern Caribbean, family land, rooted in unrestricted cognatic descent lines, is likewise found in the British and American Virgin Islands of Tortola, Virgin

Gorda and St John; the Commonwealth Leeward Islands of Antigua, Nevis, and now-erupting Montserrat; Dutch St Eustatius; French Martinique; the Commonwealth Windward Islands of Dominica, St Lucia, St Vincent and Grenada; Carriacou and Bequia in the Grenadines; Trinidad and Tobago; and Barbados.[14] Family land is also found in Providencia in the western Caribbean Sea (Wilson 1995).

In the more northern Bahamas chain similar Lands of Myth, known as 'generation property' and transmitted through cognation, articulate with common land (Otterbein 1964; Craton 1987). On the coastlands of Guyana and Suriname, which form the southern frontier of the Caribbean region (socio-culturally defined), cognatic land transmission likewise co-exists with common land (Despres 1970; R.T. Smith 1971; Besson 1995d). Among the Garifuna or Black Caribs of the Central American Caribbean Coast, which forms the western border of the Caribbean Sea, a cognatic system also co-exists with common land (Solien 1959; Richardson 1992: 165), as on the Carib reservations of the Windward Islands of Dominica[15] and St Vincent (Gullick 1985; Honychurch 1991). As outlined earlier, a similar situation typifies the wilderness reservation of the Jamaican Leeward Maroon polity. A parallel pattern can likewise be identified among the Windward maroons, in the eastern mountains of Jamaica (Bilby 1996; Besson 1997).

In the isolated Leeward Island of Barbuda, cognatic land transmission interweaves with common land in the context of house-yards and provision-grounds, as in Jamaica's Accompong maroon society (Berleant-Schiller 1977, 1987; Besson 1987, 1992, 1995d, 1997). The Barbudan commons, which oral history states were willed to the descendants of the Barbudan proto-peasant slaves (who bordered on marronage) by the Codrington planter family, are in fact an appropriation of Crown land. This land was only leased by the British colonial government to the Codringtons, who had plantations in Barbados and Antigua, to serve as backlands to their Antiguan sugar-estates. The commons have since devolved to the Antiguan-Barbudan state and are claimed as Lands of Law by dominant Antigua, which wishes to develop Barbuda's land and pink-sand beaches for tourism. In the 1990s this legal claim is being contested in the courts, as Barbudans assert their customary rights to these Lands of Myth.

These conclusions both modify and develop Sidney Mintz and Richard Price's (1992) creolisation thesis. Mintz and Price assert that the birth of African-American culture was effected by slaves creating institutions '*within* the parameters of the masters' monopoly of power, but *separate from* the masters' institutions' (1992: 39). The transformation of Lands of Law by Lands of Myth, in the Caribbean plantation heartlands, reflects instead the *appropriation and overturning* of European institutions by the African-American slaves and their descendants – and by the few surviving indigenous inhabitants. Mintz and Price (1992: 68–70) also contend that, in contrast to unrestricted ancestral ritual groups among the slaves in Surinam, such non-exclusive systems could not function for landholding in the Caribbean after slavery. That such unrestricted cognatic descent groups (which anthropologists once thought were unworkable and even now consider rare) are widespread in relation to Caribbean Lands of Myth questions this conclusion. However this cultural creativity – which reversed European slave-plantation systems, transformed West and Central African unilineal kin groups, and maximised scarce land rights and descent lines among the descendants of New World chattel slaves – advances Mintz's (1996) thesis that the Caribbean region reflects the most remarkable drama of culture-building in modernity.

Moreover these unrestricted cognatic landholding kin groups, which have not previously been recognised in the Caribbean region, reveal paradoxical perceptions of land as both economic and symbolic, scarce and unlimited (Besson 1987, 1988). In the context of Euro-American land monopoly, land is perceived by Caribbean peasantries as a scarce economic good. However, within the unrestricted landholding corporation, land serves a long-term symbolic role and even a minuscule plot is perceived as an unlimited resource among ever-increasing numbers of descendants.

Several interrelated features reinforce the perception of such family lands as unlimited and facilitate the functioning of the unrestricted cognatic descent system: the enduring quality of the land; its origin with ancestresses and ancestors; its transmission through oral tradition and intestacy; its long-term role of providing freehold land rights, enabled through voluntary non-use by kin with other options such as migration; its tenure as an undivided joint estate; and its role as a family burial ground. This symbolism of these Lands of Myth is reflected in the language of the peasantries: while humanity and individual members of the kin group are referred to as 'expiring', 'dying', 'ending', the land 'carries continuously' 'serving generations' and the enduring descent line persists 'forever'.[16] These contrasts are further reflected in statements which indicate the timelessness of the land, such as 'I born come see the land'.

Elsewhere cognatic descent systems, which particularly characterise island societies with land scarcity, likewise reveal especially clearly paradoxical perceptions of land as both a scarce economic good and a symbolic resource unlimited through its permanence and immortality: as in the Gilbert Islands, Mafia Island, Tory Island and Rapa in Polynesia; and among the Merina of Madagascar, the Maori of New Zealand and the Nduindui of New Hebrides.[17] However, this dual role of land as economic and symbolic can likewise be identified in unilineal contexts: as among the Trobriand Islanders, the Polynesian Tikopia, the Tallensi of Ghana, Native Americans, Australian Aborigines and the Greek mountain peasantry.[18] This paradox of land as an enduring link between ancestors and descendants and a symbol of the regeneration of life (compare Bloch and Parry 1982), as well as being a source of livelihood, is also found among the Aluku and Saramaka maroons who fled from colonial plantation-slavery and appropriated the South American interiors of French Guiana and Suriname to

retain or forge anew African-type matrilineal systems (Price 1975; Bilby
1989), and may universally exist at the interface of Lands of Law and the
immortal Lands of Myth.

NOTES

My recurrent fieldwork in Trelawny and St Elizabeth in Jamaica over the period 1968–99,
drawn on in this chapter, was funded by the Ministry of Education, Jamaica; the Social
Science Research Council (UK); the Carnegie Trust for the Universities of Scotland; the
University of Aberdeen; and the Nuffield Foundation. My research in the eastern Caribbean
(during the period 1992–4) was funded in part by the British Council; the St Augustine
Campus of the University of the West Indies, Trinidad and Tobago; and Goldsmiths College,
University of London. I am grateful to the participants in the workshop held at University
College London, 25 October 1997, for their stimulating comments on an earlier draft of
this chapter.

1. In the Caribbean context, I use the concept of 'Lands of Law' to refer to the land tenure
   systems imposed through European colonially derived legal systems, and perpetuated
   by Euro-American neo-colonialism and by the Jamaican postcolonial state.
2. In my usage of the concept 'Lands of Myth', I use 'myth' in an anthropological sense
   to refer to issues of origin and creation in a social context, rather than in the popular
   sense of a false belief. In the Caribbean region, Lands of Myth are therefore
   synonymous with creole (and generally customary) land tenure systems, which
   articulate with history, oral traditions, rituals and symbols in relation to social groups
   such as peasant communities and kin groups (cf. Seymour-Smith 1987: 203–5). Such
   customary land tenures, however, may themselves have transformed legal land
   rights, as in the case of maroon treaty land and land purchased in post-emancipation
   villages.
3. Mintz defines a peasantry as 'a class (or classes) of rural landowners producing a large
   part of the products they consume, but also selling to (and buying from) wider
   markets, and dependent in various ways upon wider political and economic spheres
   of control' (1989: 132). He goes on to argue, convincingly, that 'Caribbean
   peasantries are, in this view, *reconstituted* peasantries, having begun other than as
   peasants – in slavery, as deserters or runaways, as plantation laborers, or whatever
   – and becoming peasants in some kind of resistant response to an externally imposed
   regime' (1989: 132). Elsewhere, Mintz qualifies 'landowners', referring instead to
   'small-scale cultivators who own or have access to land' (1989: 141). My use of the
   concept of peasantry draws on Mintz (1989: 131–250), but also develops his analysis
   of modes of peasantisation.
4. The concept of 'proto-peasants' derives from Mintz, who in his definition of the 'proto-
   peasantry' refers to 'a peasant style of life ... worked out by people while they were
   still enslaved' (1989: 151).
5. For a more in-depth analysis of Jamaican Revivalist and Rastafarian religions than is
   possible in this chapter, see Besson (1995a), Chevannes (1994, 1995), and Besson
   and Chevannes (1996).
6. The 1,500 acres of land granted to the Leeward maroons in the treaty were subsequently increased to 2,559 acres (see Campbell 1990: 127, 181–83).
7. Unrestricted cognatic descent is traced through both genders and includes absentees
   (for example, migrants and their descendants) as well as those resident on the land.
   Such dispersed groups therefore overlap and rapidly augment in size. It is tempting
   to view Caribbean cognatic descent groups and house-yards within the analytical
   contexts of 'house-societies' and 'cognatic societies' or 'cognatic systems' (see e.g.
   Carsten and Hugh-Jones 1995). However, not only do the categories of 'cognatic

societies' and 'cognatic systems' need to be unpacked, but also a significant dimension of Caribbean unrestricted descent is the *non-residence* of many members of the landholding corporation on family land and common land (see e.g. Besson 1979, 1987, and note 8 below). The symbolic significance of the *land*, rather than the *house*, is therefore the primary focus. Nevertheless, the impermanent moveable chattel houses that are often shifted onto and off family land by individual members of the descent group do reflect processual social relations within the dispersed landholding corporation; while tombs symbolise landholding kin groups and communities. The architectural changes in relation to both houses (an increase in concrete houses resulting from migrant remittances) and graves (a shift from cairns to concrete tombs and vaults) on the enduring land also reflect the processual movement/passing of generations within landholding descent corporations and communities.

8. In contrast to the cognatic descent groups, which are ancestor-oriented (see note 7 above), the bilateral kinship networks are ego-focused – surrounding each individual on both parental sides. The maroon family system, based on descent, kinship, marriage and affinity, reinforces the maroon polity, which is an autonomous state (based on a corporate landholding community) within the wider national Jamaican state.

9. The Windward Maroon polity was consolidated by a treaty with the British colonial government in June 1739.

10. See note 7 above on changing burial patterns and architecture.

11. In British West Indian primogeniture, among legitimate children males had precedence and the eldest son had primacy. In contrast, the unrestricted cognatic descent system created by Afro-Caribbean slaves includes all children and descendants regardless of legitimacy, birth order and gender.

12. A square chain is one-tenth of an acre.

13. Africa, the continent of origin of the slaves brought to Jamaica, may be seen in the contemporary context to symbolise a Land of Myth whose land space contrasts favourably with the intense land scarcity of the post-conquest Antilles – including the Lands of Myth created in Jamaican peasant communities.

14. On family land in the Lesser Antilles see Maurer (1996, 1997), Olwig (1995, 1997a, 1997b), Philpott (1973), Van Den Bor (1979), Horowitz (1992), Tomich (1991), Trouillot (1988), Honychurch (1991), Acosta and Casimir (1985), Barrow (1992), Crichlow (1994), Rubenstein (1987), Brierley (1974), M.G. Smith (1965b), Price (1988), Littlewood (1993), Greenfield (1960), Besson (1992, 1995d).

15. In addition to my own observations on the Carib reserve in Dominica, Lennox Honychurch has described a situation whereby the boundaries of the reservation imposed on the cognatically transmitted family lands of the Dominican Caribs by the British in 1903 still remain unsettled in the eyes of the Caribs – since all of Dominica belonged to them prior to colonisation (Honychurch 1991: 18–19; 1997).

16. These anglophone illustrations are paralleled by the French creole concept, in relation to the unrestricted cognatic transmission of family lands among both Creoles and Caribs in Dominica, of such land being 'pour mes enfants, et ses enfants, pour tout les générations'. I am grateful to Dr Lennox Honychurch for this information from his DPhil thesis (1997), and for permission to cite his dissertation.

17. See Goodenough (1955), Caplan (1969), Fox (1978), Hanson (1971), Bloch (1971), Webster (1975), Allen (1971), Holy (1996: 120). Allen (1971) claims to reconcile the classic Goodenough–Meggitt (1965) controversy as to whether land scarcity generates cognatic or unilineal descent groups (cf. Holy 1996: 120), but his conclusion reinforces Goodenough's (1955) hypothesis linking population pressure to more flexible cognatic descent systems. Nevertheless, as I argue elsewhere (Besson, in preparation) the role of culture as well as ecology needs to be considered.

18. See Firth (1963: 331), Young (1979), Fortes (1945), Worsley (1956), Feher-Elston (1988), Burt (1977), du Boulay (1974), du Boulay and Williams (1987). This interpretation of the dual role of land illuminates the classic Fortes–Worsley debate as to the primacy of the morality of kinship or economic factors in Tale life.

REFERENCES

Acosta, Yvonne and Casimir, Jean. 1985. 'Social origins of the counter-plantation system in St Lucia', in P.I. Gomes (ed.) *Rural Development in the Caribbean*. London: Hurst, pp. 34–59.

Allen, M. 1971. 'Descent groups and ecology amongst the Nduindui, New Hebrides', in L.R. Hiatt and C. Jayawardena (eds) *Anthropology in Oceania*. Sydney: Angus & Robertson.

Austin-Broos, Diane J. 1997. *Jamaica Genesis: Religion and the Politics of Moral Orders*. Chicago: University of Chicago Press.

Barrow, Christine. 1992. *Family Land and Development in St Lucia*. Cave Hill, Barbados: Institute of Social and Economic Research (Eastern Caribbean), University of the West Indies.

Berleant-Schiller, Riva. 1977. 'Production and division of labor in a West Indian peasant community', *American Ethnologist* 4: 253–72.

—— 1987. 'Ecology and politics in Barbudan land tenure', in J. Besson and J. Momsen (eds) *Land and Development in the Caribbean*. London: Macmillan, pp. 116–31.

Besson, Jean. 1979. 'Symbolic aspects of land in the Caribbean: the tenure and transmission of land rights among Caribbean peasantries', in M. Cross and A. Marks (eds) *Peasants, Plantations and Rural Communities in the Caribbean*. Guildford: University of Surrey, and Leiden: Royal Institute of Linguistics and Anthropology, pp. 86–116.

—— 1984. 'Land tenure in the free villages of Trelawny, Jamaica: a case study in the Caribbean peasant response to emancipation', *Slavery and Abolition* 5(1): 3–23.

—— 1987. 'A paradox in Caribbean attitudes to land', in J. Besson and J. Momsen (eds) *Land and Development in the Caribbean*. London: Macmillan, pp. 13–45.

—— 1988. 'Agrarian relations and perceptions of land in a Jamaican peasant village', in J.S. Brierley and H. Rubenstein (eds) *Small Farming and Peasant Resources in the Caribbean*. Winnipeg: University of Manitoba, pp. 39–61.

—— 1992. 'Freedom and community: The British West Indies', in F. McGlynn and S. Drescher (eds) *The Meaning of Freedom*. Pittsburgh: University of Pittsburgh Press, pp. 183–219.

—— 1995a. 'Religion as resistance in Jamaican peasant life', in B. Chevannes (ed.) *Rastafari and Other African-Caribbean Worldviews*. London: Macmillan, pp. 43–76.

—— 1995b. 'Free villagers, Rastafarians and modern maroons: from resistance to identity', in W. Hoogbergen (ed.) *Born Out of Resistance*. Utrecht: ISOR Press, pp. 301–14.

—— 1995c. 'The creolization of African-American slave kinship in Jamaican free village and maroon communities', in S. Palmié (ed.) *Slave Cultures and the Cultures of Slavery*. Knoxville: University of Tennessee Press, pp. 187–209.

—— 1995d. 'Land, kinship and community in the post-emancipation Caribbean', in K.F. Olwig (ed.) *Small Islands, Large Questions*. London: Frank Cass, pp. 73–99.

—— 1995e. 'Consensus in the family land controversy', *New West Indian Guide* 69(3–4): 299–304.

—— 1997. 'Caribbean common tenures and capitalism: the Accompong maroons of Jamaica', in B. Maurer (ed.) *Common Land in the Caribbean and Mesoamerica*, Special Issue, *Plantation Society in the Americas* 4 (2–3): 201–32.

—— in preparation. *Martha Brae's Two Histories: European Expansion and Caribbean Culture-Building*.

Besson, Jean and Chevannes, Barry. 1996. 'The continuity–creativity debate: the case of Revival', *New West Indian Guide*, 70(3–4): 209–28.

Bilby, Kenneth M. 1989. 'Divided loyalties: local politics and the play of states among the Aluku', *Nieuwe West-Indische Gids* 63 (3–4): 143–73.

—— 1996. 'Ethnogenesis in the Guianas and Jamaica: two maroon cases', in J.D. Hill (ed.) *History, Power, and Identity*. Iowa City: University of Iowa Press, pp. 119–41.

Bloch, Maurice. 1971. *Placing the Dead: Tombs, Ancestral Villages and Kinship Organization in Madagascar*. London: Seminar Press.

Bloch, Maurice and Parry, Jonathan. (eds.) 1982. *Death and the Regeneration of Life*. Cambridge: Cambridge University Press.

Brierley, John S. 1974. *Small Farming in Grenada, West Indies*. Winnipeg: University of Manitoba.

Burt, Ben. 1977. *Aborigines*. London: British Museum.

Campbell, Mavis C. 1990. *The Maroons of Jamaica 1655–1796*. Trenton, NJ: Africa World Press.

Caplan, Patricia. 1969. 'Cognatic descent groups on Mafia Island, Tanzania', *Man* 4(3): 419–31.

Carnegie, Charles V. 1987. 'Is family land an institution?', in C.V. Carnegie (ed.) *Afro-Caribbean Villages in Historical Perspective*. Kingston: African-Caribbean Institute of Jamaica, pp. 83–99.

Carsten, Janet and Hugh-Jones, Stephen. 1995. 'Introduction', in J. Carsten and S. Hugh-Jones (eds) *About the House: Lévi-Strauss and Beyond*. Cambridge: Cambridge University Press, pp. 1–46.

Chevannes, Barry. 1994. *Rastafari: Roots and Ideology*. Syracuse: Syracuse University Press.

——— (ed.) 1995. *Rastafari and Other African-Caribbean Worldviews*. London: Macmillan.

Clarke, Edith. 1966. *My Mother Who Fathered Me: A Study of the Family in Three Selected Communities in Jamaica*, 2nd edn. London: Allen & Unwin. (Orig. 1957.)

Craton, Michael. 1987. 'White law and black custom: the evolution of Bahamian land tenures', in J. Besson and J. Momsen (eds) *Land and Development in the Caribbean*. London: Macmillan, pp. 88–114.

Crichlow, Michaeline A. 1994. 'An alternate approach to family land tenure in the Anglophone Caribbean: the case of St Lucia', *Nieuwe West-Indische Gids* 68(1–2): 77–99.

Davenport, William. 1961. 'Introduction', *Social and Economic Studies* 10(4): 380–5.

Despres, Leo A. 1970. 'Differential adaptations and micro-cultural evolution in Guyana', in N.E. Whitten and J.F. Szwed (eds) *Afro-American Anthropology*. New York: Free Press, pp. 263–87.

du Boulay, Juliet. 1974. *Portrait of a Greek Mountain Village*. Oxford: Oxford University Press.

du Boulay, Juliet and Williams, Rory. 1987. 'Amoral familism and the image of limited good: a critique from a European perspective', *Anthropological Quarterly* 60(1): 12–24.

Echevarría, Roberto González. 1980. '*Biografía de un Cimarrón* and the novel of the Cuban Revolution', *Novel* 13(3).

Edwards, Bryan. 1793. *The History, Civil and Commercial, of the British Colonies in the West Indies*, 2 vols. London: John Stockdale.

Edwards, David. 1961. *An Economic Study of Small Farming in Jamaica*. Mona, Jamaica: Institute of Social and Economic Research.

Espeut, Peter. 1992. 'Land reform and the family land debate', in C. Stolberg and S. Wilmot (eds) *Plantation Economy, Land Reform and the Peasantry in a Historical Perspective: Jamaica 1838–1980*. Kingston: Friedrich Ebert Stiftung, pp. 69–84.

Feher-Elston, Catherine. 1988. *Children of the Sacred Ground*. Flagstaff, Az: Northland.

Firth, Raymond. 1963. *We, the Tikopia*, 2nd edn. Boston: Beacon Press. (Orig. 1936.)

Fortes, Meyer. 1945. *The Dynamics of Clanship among the Tallensi*. London: Oxford University Press.

Fox, Robin. 1978. *The Tory Islanders*. Cambridge: Cambridge University Press.

Goodenough, Ward. 1955. 'A problem in Malayo-Polynesian social organization', *American Anthropologist* 57(1): 71–83.

Greenfield, Sidney M. 1960. 'Land tenure and transmission in rural Barbados', *Anthropological Quarterly* 33: 165–76.

Gullick, C.J.M.R. 1985. *Myths of a Minority: The Changing Traditions of the Vincentian Caribs*. Assen: Van Gorcum.

Hanson, F. Allan. 1971. 'Nonexclusive cognatic descent systems', in A. Howard (ed.) *Polynesia: Readings on a Culture Area*. Scranton, PA: Chandler, pp. 109–32.

Hennessy, Alistair. 1993. 'Introduction', in E. Montejo and M. Barnet, *The Autobiography of a Runaway Slave*. London: Macmillan, pp. 1–12.

Holy, Ladislav. 1996. *Anthropological Perspectives on Kinship*. London: Pluto Press.

Honychurch, Lennox. 1991. *Dominica*. London: Macmillan.

—— 1997. 'Carib to Creole: contact and culture exchange in Dominica', DPhil thesis, University of Oxford.

Horowitz, Michael M. 1992. *Morne-Paysan: Peasant Village in Martinique*. Prospect Heights, Illinois: Waveland Press. (Orig. 1967.)

Kopytoff, Barbara Klamon. 1976. 'The development of Jamaican maroon ethnicity', *Caribbean Quarterly* 22(2–3): 33–50.

—— 1979. 'Colonial treaty as sacred charter of the Jamaican maroons', *Ethnohistory* 26(1): 45–64.

—— 1987. 'Religious change among the Jamaican maroons: the ascendance of the Christian God within a traditional cosmology', *Journal of Social History* 20(3): 463–84.

Larose, Serge. 1975. 'The Haitian *Lakou*: land, family and ritual', in A.F. Marks and R.A. Römer (eds) *Family and Kinship in Middle America and the Caribbean*. Curaçao: Institute of Higher Studies in Curaçao, and Leiden: Royal Institute of Linguistics and Anthropology, pp. 482–512.

Littlewood, Roland. 1993. *Pathology and Identity: The Work of Mother Earth in Trinidad*. Cambridge: Cambridge University Press.

Lowenthal, David. 1972. *West Indian Societies*. Oxford: Oxford University Press.

Maurer, Bill. 1996. 'The land, the law and legitimate children: thinking through gender, kinship and nation in the British Virgin Islands', in M.J. Maynes et al. (eds) *Gender, Kinship, Power: A Comparative and Interdisciplinary History*. New York: Routledge, pp. 351–63.

—— 1997. *Recharting the Caribbean: Land, Law, and Citizenship in the British Virgin Islands*. Ann Arbor: University of Michigan Press.

McKay, Lesley. 1987. 'Tourism and changing attitudes to land in Negril, Jamaica', in J. Besson and J. Momsen (eds) *Land and Development in the Caribbean*. London: Macmillan, pp. 132–52.

Meggitt, M.J. 1965. *The Lineage System of the Mae-Enga of New Guinea*. London: Oliver & Boyd.

Mintz, Sidney W. 1989. *Caribbean Transformations*. New York: Columbia University Press.

—— 1996. 'Enduring substances, trying theories: the Caribbean region as *oikoumenê*', *Journal of the Royal Anthropological Institute* 2(2): 289–311.

Mintz, Sidney W. and Price, Richard. 1992. *The Birth of African-American Culture*. Boston, MA: Beacon Press.

Olwig, Karen Fog. 1995. 'Cultural complexity after freedom: Nevis and beyond', in K.F. Olwig (ed.) *Small Islands, Large Questions: Society, Culture and Resistance in the Post-Emancipation Caribbean*. London: Frank Cass, pp. 100–20.

—— 1997a. 'Caribbean family land: a modern commons', in B. Maurer (ed.) *Common Land in the Caribbean and Mesoamerica*, Special Issue, *Plantation Society in the Americas* 4 (2–3): 135–58.

—— 1997b. 'Cultural sites: sustaining a home in a deterritorialized world', in K.F. Olwig and K. Hastrup (eds) *Siting Culture: The Shifting Anthropological Object*. London: Routledge, pp. 17–38.

Otterbein, Keith F. 1964. 'A comparison of the land tenure systems of the Bahamas, Jamaica, and Barbados: the implications it has for the study of social systems shifting from bilateral to ambilineal descent', *International Archives of Ethnography* 50: 31–42.

Patterson, Orlando. 1973. *The Sociology of Slavery*. London: MacGibbon & Kee. (Orig. 1967.)

Philpott, Stuart B. 1973. *West Indian Migration: The Montserrat Case*. London: Athlone Press.

Price, Neil. 1988. *Behind the Planter's Back: Lower Class Responses to Marginality in Bequia Island, St Vincent.* London: Macmillan.

Price, Richard. 1975. *Saramaka Social Structure.* Rio Piedras: University of Puerto Rico.

—— 1996. *Maroon Societies*, 3rd edn. Baltimore, MD: Johns Hopkins University Press. (Orig. 1973.)

Richardson, Bonham C. 1992. *The Caribbean in the Wider World, 1492–1992.* Cambridge: Cambridge University Press.

Robotham, Don 1977. 'Agrarian relations in Jamaica', in C. Stone and A. Brown (eds) *Essays on Power and Change in Jamaica.* Kingston: Jamaica Publishing House, pp. 45–57.

Rubenstein, Hymie. 1987. 'Folk and mainstream systems of land tenure and use in St Vincent', in J. Besson and J. Momsen (eds) *Land and Development in the Caribbean.* London: Macmillan, pp. 70–87.

Schuler, Monica. 1980. *'Alas, Alas, Kongo': A Social History of Indentured African Immigration into Jamaica, 1841–1865.* Baltimore, MD: Johns Hopkins University Press.

Seymour-Smith, Charlotte. 1987. *Macmillan Dictionary of Anthropology.* London: Macmillan.

Smith, M.G. 1965a. *The Plural Society in the British West Indies.* Berkeley: University of California Press.

Smith, M.G. 1965b. 'The transformation of land rights by transmission in Carriacou', in M.G. Smith, *The Plural Society in the British West Indies.* Berkeley: University of California Press, pp. 221–61.

Smith, Raymond T. 1971. 'Land tenure in three negro villages in British Guiana', in M.M. Horowitz (ed.) *Peoples and Cultures of the Caribbean.* Garden City: Natural History Press, pp. 243–66. (Orig. 1955.)

Solien, Nancie L. 1959. 'The nonunilineal descent group in the Caribbean and Central America', *American Anthropologist* 61: 578–83.

Stewart, John. 1823. *A View of the Past and Present State of the Island of Jamaica.* Edinburgh: Oliver & Boyd.

Tomich, Dale 1991. 'Une petite Guinée: provision ground and plantation in Martinique, 1830–1848', in I. Berlin and P.D. Morgan (eds) *The Slaves' Economy*, Special Issue, *Slavery and Abolition* 12(1): 68–91.

Trouillot, Michel-Rolph. 1988. *Peasants and Capital: Dominica in the World Economy.* Baltimore, MD: Johns Hopkins University Press.

Van Den Bor, Wout 1979. 'Peasantry in isolation: the agrarian development of St Eustatius and Saba', in M. Cross and A. Marks (eds) *Peasants, Plantations and Rural Communities in the Caribbean.* Guildford: University of Surrey, and Leiden: Royal Institute of Linguistics and Anthropology, pp. 117–41.

Walvin, James. 1983. *Slavery and the Slave Trade: A Short Illustrated History.* London: Macmillan.

Webster, Steven. 1975. 'Cognatic descent groups and the contemporary Maori: a preliminary reassessment', *Journal of the Polynesian Society* 84(2): 121–52.

Williams, Eric 1970. *From Columbus to Castro: The History of the Caribbean 1492–1969.* London: André Deutsch.

Wilson, Peter J. 1995. *Crab Antics: A Caribbean Case Study of the Conflict Between Reputation and Respectability.* Prospect Heights, IL: Waveland Press. (Orig. 1973.)

Worsley, Peter M. 1956. 'The kinship system of the Tallensi: a revaluation', *Journal of the Royal Anthropological Institute* 86: 37–75.

Young, Michael W. 1979. *The Ethnography of Malinowski.* London: Routledge & Kegan Paul.

7 MYTHIC RITES AND LAND RIGHTS IN NORTHERN INDIA

Kusum Gopal

In the Indian subcontinent, the introduction of the 'black letter law' tradition[1] provided the bedrock for the establishment and fortification of colonial rule for nearly 200 years. In the process, mythic understandings of land–body and land–person relations came to be replaced by an inflexible adherence to legalism.

This chapter analyses the annihilation of mythic lands brought about by the colonisation of the trans-Rapti belt of Uttar Pradesh, where I conducted my fieldwork among *kisan* communities between 1991 and 1993.[2] Prior to the establishment of legal proclamations that defined landownership on the basis of caste identities, both the cultivation and the ownership of land by the *kisans* had been regarded as an inalienable right, regardless of caste or any other identity.[3] Even today, the *kisans* do not primarily distinguish themselves as belonging to a distinct ethnic group or groups, and prefer to be regarded essentially as cultivators of the land with the right to own it.[4] They continue to firmly believe that they have no other possibility of survival apart from living by the land and working on it. Indeed, agriculture constitutes their principal source of livelihood, so much so that Bourdieu's description of the Algerian peasantry could be applied to the *kisans*:

> [Land] haunts these people's thinking, governs their conduct, orients their opinions, inspires their emotions. And yet, often escapes explicit consciousness and systematic statement. It is the invisible centre around which social behaviour revolves, the virtual vanishing point of the sub-proletarian view of the world. (Bourdieu 1979: 56–7)

This ethnographic account examines how the administration of land tenure and agricultural practice under colonial rule disrupted the habitus of the *kisans* (Bourdieu 1971). Its argument is that too much anthropological research on south Asia has focused on symbolic cultural formations – such as caste, mysticism, rituals, religions and material culture – and has overlooked the extent to which expressions of cognition and symbolic power are linked to people's everyday practical land-based struggle for livelihood and human dignity. Building on Felix Padel's pioneering ethnography (1995), and Johannes Fabian's critique of time and 'the self' in modes of rep-

136

resenting 'the other' without regard to coevality, I explore the externally imposed patterns of land legislation, agricultural practice and inscription among the *kisans*, as a way of disclosing how both colonial administration and ethnographic discourse imply 'bad epistemology which advance cognitive interests without regard for their ideological presuppositions' (Fabian 1983: 33).

The first section of this chapter contrasts the different perceptions of landscape arising out of autochthonous mythical rites and colonial law from the late 19th century to the mid-20th century. The colonial government regarded the domination of the physical world as legitimate: 'the environment was a protagonist to be attacked, tamed and worked upon: the purpose being to maximise its output by employing the language of predation and exploitation' (Croll and Parkin 1992: 32). Through the written word, promulgated by the 'master narratives' of men-in-power, legal boundaries systematically subjugated mythical realms by means of 'collective works of euphemisation', a process by which a dominant group teaches itself and masters its own truth (Bourdieu 1992: 41). In this way, the dominant group binds itself together by tacitly defining the limits of the thinkable and the unthinkable, and thereby demonstrates its power.

Further, biological and physiological differences based on tribal, caste and religious affinities were judged to be the principles of politics. The 'natives' were categorised into distinct racial phenotypes, and set apart in the interests of order, rationality, standardisation and profit for the empire. From caste or tribal identities to religious and sectarian affiliations, the objectification of a subject people was complete: all traditions of politics were seen as group identities and essentially bodily differences. Moreover, the gendered terms of reference indicate how hierarchy and difference were employed to separate and selectively define society thus, effectively, obliterating 'feminine' local categories and distinctions by giving a higher status to colonial 'masculine' representations. Thus, through the formal introduction of the 'black letter law' tradition, the indigenous people, their practices and their customs were directly deduced and reconstituted through arbitrary, legally sanctioned rules (cf. Galanter 1989).

In the last section of this chapter I will demonstrate how the widespread indigenous disenchantment against land legislation gave rise to violent movements of resistance, which mounted an opposition against established legal boundaries. These boundaries were contested by mythic orders, which were seeking to overthrow the legitimacy and power of the legislation and to restore the old order. The demand for *haq i-milkiyat*, or ownership rights over the land, for all castes led to mass movements for land reform and the restoration of human dignity in the 20th century. The subjects of the mythic domains sought to reclaim what had been theirs for centuries by appropriating the signs, axioms and aesthetics of the lands under British rule (*angreezi hukumat*).

ANGREEZI HUKUMAT AND THE LANDS OF MYTH

Until the late 19th century, the trans-Rapti region formed a heavily forested, flat and extensive plain in the north-eastern reaches of the province. Nearly all the rivers flow through Nepal to the region providing it with an abundant and continuous supply of water. Following the annexation of the territory by the British during the early 19th century, most of the lands, which had been covered with dense forests, were forcibly cleared, particularly in the north. Further, the colonial authorities abolished customary tenures, such as the pre-existing system of landownership. During the late 19th century, communities of smallholders were replaced by *zamindaris* or proprietors (Baden-Powell 1892: 441). With the rapid clearance of the forests and the concentration of extremely large estates in the trans-Rapti tract by the end of the century, the region acquired a definitive topography, a pattern of land use and a distinct sense of place.

Thus, the creation by the colonial government of a social and physical terrain in its own image and for its own requirements, tended to undermine, oppose and destroy the landscape as it had been perceived by the indigenous people, the *kisans*, who defined their identity primarily in relation to the land. Further, the exclusive consideration of land legislation with the 'rationalisation of economic conduct' undermined the local temporal and moral consciousness in the measurement of time (Bourdieu 1979: 7). In accordance with the Judaeo-Christian tradition, colonial legislation introduced a linear, irreversible calibration of time, which contradicted indigenous perceptions of time. The *kisans* were predominantly influenced by a subjective, cyclical understanding of time, which was interwoven, recurring, but rarely overlapping. To the *kisans*, the experience of time was 'habitual' and tied to their agricultural world and its 'natural' cycles; movements in space inevitably meant movements in time: days and nights, seasons, the human pattern of reproduction, its life-cycles, senescence, death and rebirth.

Within this immanent tradition, the *kisans* believed that an individual's life begins by imbibing the environment as the immediate source of nourishment. Eventually, this process becomes the basis of a philosophy, the very conditioning of the spirit. The kinship terms used by my informants illustrate how people orient themselves to the land, inspired as they are by a heritage of intuitive wisdom gained from living on the land and drawing strength from it. The *kisans* defined their belonging to the soil and the land as an extension of the body and the human spirit whose paths were connected with the essential divine being: the earth was divine, their mother, sister and child – *mai*. The common *kisan* practice is to grasp intuitively the whole process of life and accumulate experience that constitutes tradition (*parampara*). The renewal and regeneration of the earth (and all forms of life on earth) could only be possible by submitting the body and the mind to the cues offered by nature. The *kisans* moved among these surroundings, not as trespassers, but as participants in a steadily directed life which was theirs by habitual right: a life which went forward day after day, allowing them to partake in its process of renewal, affirming their sense of time and space. Similarly, plants, trees, animals – and their own human interactions – are perceived as part of a single spiritual, physical and moral regenerative system.

CASTE AND LAND

With the annexation of Awadh during 1860s, the identification of land as the chief criterion in the availability and collection of revenue led to determining, first, who had the right to own land and, second, how much wealth the land could produce, or how it was to be collected. Further, officialdom engendered certain perspectives, whereby 'caste' became the primary referent (cf. Cohn 1984; Inden 1990: 49) and dominated the landscape of power upon which was inscribed and enacted the narratives of the powerful and the powerless: only the upper castes were deemed fit to own land.

Whilst conceptualising relationships, legislation worked actively to differentiate persons from one another, separating spheres of community activities, thus entrenching caste status as the basis of identity and individual rights. Caste was interpreted more as a tightly knit hierarchy, a functional fit. Such interpretations have been reinforced by Dumont's thesis of an all-encompassing Brahmanical view of society where the traditional values of the hierachical East made it essential to regard these principles in opposition to the egalitarianism and individualism of the West (Dumont 1966). According to the same author, such holistic traditional values in caste relationships of consanguinity, affinity and contiguity were based on an implicit understanding of reciprocity whereby each caste's social and ritual status was determined a priori by principles of purity and impurity. For Dumont, such a social structure remained undisturbed by colonialism, as these values were everlasting in an eternal, static East.

A study of the official writings further reveals the racial prejudices of such attitudes.[5] In representing caste, the preoccupation with ethnicity and ethnic differences makes the work of physical anthropologists significant. Through extensive anthropometric studies of the physical body, it was argued that ethnicity could be equated with caste identity; a collective sameness which was bounded, enduring and essential. For example, H.H. Risley, the influential Census Commissioner of India, noted in 1891 that, 'within certain geographical boundaries, it may be laid down at least by law, that the social position of caste varies inversely as its nasal index'. (Risley 1891: 36 quoted in Pedersen 1984: 15). The Brahmans and the Rajputs were by their physical light-skinned appearance and perceived upper-class status in the caste hierarchy, 'the natural leaders of society', while the common terms used for dark-skinned lower castes (and tribes) were depraved, 'criminal', deceitful and ignorant (Mill 1858). To quote from the journal of an administrative official (John Fitzroy) writing about the Chamars in 1895, 'the disposition of that caste partakes much more of animal suspicion and cunning borne out of lustful practices' (United Provinces Report 1895: 67). This is why individuals from lower castes were not allowed to bid for landownership. In such administrative documents, the 'natives' were normally regarded as 'things', unchanging objects whose history and society were to be comprehended through separate biological attributes, measured with callipers, thus indicating how these natives were to be judged and psychologically understood as subjects by the wider process of institutionalisation (Risley 1909).

Principles of caste 'purity' and 'impurity' became further translated into the land equation, to determine who could, and who could not cultivate the land and partake of its resources. In addition to the lower castes, there were the 'clean' castes among the untouchables such as the Ahirs, Kurmis and the Koeris who were allowed a marginal tenurial status to cultivate the land, while those designated as 'unclean' such as the Chamars were expressly forbidden to do so. Although the Chamars accounted for the majority of the population in the entire division of Gorakhpur, they were allowed to own a total of only 26 acres of land. Although there were disagreements about the a priori existence of data as essentially knowable aspects of reality, it can be argued that official knowledge was not constructed from reality or even directly about reality. Practical classifications were subordinated to practical functions and oriented towards the production of social effects: the monopoly of power, the making and unmaking of groups (Bourdieu 1991: 220–8). For example, it was deemed by the administrators of the 1870s, known as 'the Oudh men', that the solution to landownership lay in locating the traditional political authority (Reeves 1991: 44). They argued that 'the Kshatriya not the Brahman' was to be regarded as a 'national king'.[6] The *kisan*s, like other strata within society, were perceived within the mental space of cognition and representation. Only the Brahmans and the Kshatriyas and higher-strata Muslims were seen as the natural leaders of society. The power of the dominant model allowed these ways of seeing constantly to produce and reproduce themselves, and to impose their own principles in their construction of reality. By delineating differences of caste, religion and rights of people with reference to the land, the perception of social disadvantage was used to discriminate between different groups and enforce selective disadvantage.[7]

The 'black letter law' tradition exclusively privileged the upper castes and consolidated their position in society. I was told that various social groups, depending on the circumstances, went against allegedly fixed structures of caste in matters of endogamy and commensality, during colonial times. For example, in the Dhawai village, 'caste status' did not necessarily determine marriageability. Among the Kurmis of Basti, there had been a practice of girls marrying Jats in the Punjab and this tradition was commonplace. However, Medhiya Kurmi, an elderly *kisan* woman noted that her great-aunt and a group of other women, were arrested in the 1930s 'for making themselves out to belong to better castes than they really were', and were discouraged from engaging in such practices by threat of punishment. In the construction of identity, hierarchy exists and individuals and groups construct differences both within and outside their castes and communities; cultural identities are represented, reiterated or negotiated according to political and social relations. According to the law, any challenge to official representations of caste identity could be deemed a punishable offence.

Thus, the upper castes were seen to represent the economic wherewithal so they became the 'lords of the land', and controlled most of the land and its resources. From the 1870s onwards, tenancy laws became instrumental in establishing the ownership and land was exclusively concentrated in the hands of the upper castes. These were further given *de facto* and *de jure* powers, and became responsible for the administration and collection of revenue. It was no accident that two-thirds of the land came to be held in perpetuity by the upper castes such as the Kshatriyas, Brahmans, Bhumihars and, among the Muslims, the Sheikhs and the Sayyids. As Table 7.1 indicates, the politics of social exclusion and alienation led to the concentration of extensive estates among the upper castes. The following statistics are based on the Census report taken in 1919 for one district in this region, and can be used as a model for the entire region. Indeed, they serve as a good example of how land rights came to be fixed in perpetuity:

Table 7.1 Distribution of land in one district

Caste land	(million hectares)
Kshatriyas	368,074
Brahmans	298,200
Bhumihar	231,130
Saithwas	185,125
Kayasth	54,642
Vaishya	49,240
Halwais	31,955
Muslims	24,056
Atiths	13,074
Ahirs	8,214
Koeris	6,283
Government	5,407
Total	1,329,66,412

(E.A. Phelps 1919, Final Report of the Revision of Settlement in Gorakhpur district, Allahabad, Appendix 3, p. 41.)

As a consequence, the officially perceived subordinate castes were deemed ineligible, and excluded from the land equation. Almost inevitably, this led to the majority of the population being dispossessed (Bagchi 1992).

In precolonial times, notions of social hierarchy were recognised but the boundaries varied in spatial and temporal terms: caste was primarily a process and a performance.[8] Difference and asymmetry within relationships could not be perceived as hierarchy and inequality. While hierarchy existed, its nature and form varied. Individuals and groups constructed differences within and outside their communities in terms other than caste hierarchy. Often, gender differences according to age, status and stage in the life-cycle were more important. Indigenous economic and social arrangements determined an individual's identity. Although there was also a deep consciousness of what caste meant, which was defined by birth signifying certain privileges based on rituals and duties, it was usually tempered by considerations of relative power and social location. Existing social and economic arrangements were based not simply on the way relatives interacted with one another, but also on how relationships between communities were constituted; they were also based on the passage of time, or relations between generations, and about the future. Such boundaries and distinctions were not clear or irrevocable. Gender, age and non-kin social relationships were in many instances of greater import in evaluating social relationships than a colonial view of caste based on lineal and sub-lineal descent.

What also occurred was forced extensive socio-economic and geographical migration. *Kisans* spoke about having left families behind in the south to seek a livelihood. Such displacement and movement of peoples caused further changes in kinship systems and family structures. Also, changes that occurred in the social structure between men and women displaced local, customary or lower-caste forms of family organisation, and access to property creating institutionalised patrilineal forms of inheritance under what was deemed to be Hindu and Muslim Law. This brought about an extension of the power of men over women in a number of crucial fields. Even if a woman owned property it was to be managed by a male member in the family. Neither status, lineal descent, age, nor the caste status of a woman guaranteed her rights as it had in the past.

In the experience of individuals such official social identities ultimately determined their fate, irreversibly altering the political and social determinants of representation. The tribes, with their desire to live outside society, were forced to move out of the jungles, to assimilate and to integrate within the lower levels of caste society. Representative examples of this are the Doms and the Musahars who regarded the forests as their home and had subsisted on its produce. Bholu Dom, an elderly resident of Kota village who had lived as a child with his family in the forests, said that he had been beaten for resisting moving into the village in 1933, and sent to a rehabilitation school, set up specifically for this purpose, whence he ran away to the city as a small boy. It was much more difficult for his kinsfolk to live in the village; they were averse to cultivation, maintaining as they did a powerful cosmological relationship with the spirits of the forest, and they suffered immeasurably. As elsewhere in British India, the tribes and other hill dwellers were allowed only restricted use of the forest by legislation and resisted. These acts were promulgated for the registration, the surveillance and the control of 'those destined by the usages of caste to commit crime' (Yang 1985: 108). On account of official 'measurements' of ethnic characteristics, and their refusal to abide by the new rules, they came to be categorised as a lower caste group and were defined as such by the Criminal Tribes and Castes Act.[9]

The distinctive divide between tribe and caste is a very powerful one and some ethnographers fail to investigate the rich cosmological traditions that continue to be undermined by enduring colonial laws in the production of knowledge and practice (cf. K.S. Singh 1994; Unnithan-Kumar 1997).[10] The cultivators and the tribal peoples have been forced to accept such identities, unable as they were to argue against fixed and imposed representations in their legal statuses.[11] The administrators were perplexed by the *populi ignoti* and their unwillingness to conform to the classificatory methods established by law. Senior Uttar Pradesh civil servants were perplexed during the 1931 Census, and one of them, E.A.H. Blunt, noted that:

the mere act of labelling persons as belonging to a caste tends to perpetuate the system... It is striking that any Hindu should hold that opinion and what is even more striking is that nearly two million of them should agree with it in so far as to state that they had no caste at all. (Blunt 1938: 60)

The officials threatened to jail the *kisans* and penalised them unless they recorded their 'alleged' caste status. Pabbar Ram noted that he was ordered to pay Rs 4, a large sum in those days, which he, like many other *kisans*, simply could not afford; he thus opted to spend six months in jail.

A similar situation existed with respect to the classification of people's 'religion'. By registering the social order into different religious categories, and by giving consequently, new meanings to religions, official divisions were created which were inimical and foreign to the deeply syncretic, philosophical tradition of the subcontinent. Thus, Indian languages do not possess a noun for 'religion' as signifying a single uniform and centralised community of believers. A supra-local Hindu religious community of believers, for example, has been regarded by scholars as a modern colonial creation (Lipner 1994; Oberoi 1994: 11).

In the colonial context the formalisation of these principles of social organisation, land tenure and religion was legitimated as the imposition of a Cartesian mindset of logical order over an unruly world of incorrigible indeterminacy. The resulting 'regimes of truth' (Foucault 1979) operated like self-fulfilling prophecies. Indeed, ways of thinking about caste, religion, language and identity fused with institutional practices to produce bewildered self-conscious subjects who were forced to experience and regard themselves in such foreign terms. Positioned, as they were, in relation to the omniscient state, the truth about themselves and their situations thus appeared to be self-validating.

THE *ZAMINDARI* SYSTEM OF LANDOWNERSHIP

The administrative reports which record the debates between men-in-power provide a perceptive insight into the workings of the colonial state which reversed, both in spirit and in structures, the centuries of rule by precolonial regimes. Mughal administrative treatises, which are representative of pre-colonial times, describe the ruler as the traditional guarantor of land rights. For the people themselves, their place in the landscape is depicted in medieval oral traditions. It had been customary that rights to, and responsibilities for looking after the land were allocated, but they could not be embodied into a fixed model in mythic conceptualisations of the land. Nor could they be translated into what was perceived by the *kisans* as perplexing Western proprietary concepts. To them land rights, like personhood, were understood to be inalienable.

By contrast, colonial, legal pronouncements illustrate how people's affil-iations on the land question ought to be determined: perceived caste status and religion were taken as common points of reference. From the mid-18th century, albeit more trenchantly during the 19th, defining measures were introduced that wrenched existing forms of social relations and cultural practices from their precolonial structures. The consequences of these measures came to be regarded as *ankreech hukmaa* (as spoken in Bhojpuri) or British Rule. Such representations of the land and translations into legal rights exclusively privileged 'the upper castes' in both religious groups. Legal definitions of who could own land were defined by official interpretations in terms of caste and religion; each group was hierarchically marked out as separate. A detailed classification of individual proprietary rights was compiled through a succession of legislative acts by the colonial state. The revenue acts had a tendency to create new forms of tenure that served to secure and strengthen the *zamindari* system. Nearly all the land came to be owned by *zamindars*, the landed gentry responsible for annual revenue payments, and they were given *de facto* and *de jure* authority to govern on behalf of the government. Through a maze of clauses and sub-clauses, greater differentiation was introduced within the nature of landownership. The colonial body, thus reproduced the legal landscape in its own image and for its own requirements.

Through the continuous interaction of a system of centralised colonial law and the officialdom of the district collectors with rural social networks, the *zamindari* system supplemented formal power. As lords of the land, the dominant social class in rural society, *zamindars* were portrayed in official sources as epitomising the imperial presence, harbingers of progress in rural development. They would cooperate with the collector and the district bureaucracy and they were expected to render any kind of assistance. The most powerful landowner was the Raja of Bansi who, by a conservative estimate, owned 310,000 acres of land. This estimate did not include land occupied by forests, lakes or the numerous villages in Nepal. He also had, and continues to exercise, revenue rights over fishing, village markets and other local institutions. The Raja of Shorhatgarh, Shivapati Singh, and the Raja of Tejgarh were regarded as major *zamindars* although, in size, their lands were a fraction of the Bansi estate.

These large *zamindaris*, also known as *taluqdaris*, functioned principally through the institution of the *thekedari*. Each *theka* (revenue contract) consisted of a village, or part of it, which was leased by the *zamindar* to the highest bidder from among his kinsmen; women were excluded. The *thekedar* (bailiff) paid the *zamindar* a *nazarana* (premium) and took charge of rent collection. He, in turn, leased out small plots of land to the cultivators for a fixed term in return for rent in cash or kind. Below these *thekedars*, depending on the length of the time the cultivator worked on a holding, there were provisions made for gradual advancement: to gain an occupancy tenancy after having been a non-occupancy tenant for seven years, and from being a cultivator-at-will. The obfuscating nature of the law however, denied the cultivator such a right. These terms were not adhered to as the *thekedar* could, on the slightest pretext, evict the *kisan* and lease the land to another *kisan.*

In addition to rents, extra-legal payments were extremely high and debt bondage often prevented the *kisans* or their descendants from acquiring any form of security of tenure. Thus, capitalist practices in the form of rentier landlordism came into existence: land became a commodity. Through the tacit cooperation of local officials such as the headman (*patwari, sarpanch*), policeman (*thanedar)* or *daroga*, and the village-guard (*chowkidar*) the *zamindars* were surrounded by an informal court of retainers whom they rewarded for their services. Although these local officials were appointed as public servants, they acted in a private capacity. Stories narrated to me by Ram Kurmi and Bhairathi, two *kisans* in their 80s, who had lived with the *zamindari* system reveal how these officials often exploited their positions of influence during the collection of rent from the cultivators. For example, the *patwar*i was responsible for the land registers and had considerable opportunities for extortion; he removed their names from plots of land, forcing them to migrate to the city. A large proportion of legal disputes occurred on account of incorrect entries with regard to the ownership of plots in the revenue records. The *patwaris* and other local officials actively colluded with the *zamindaris* to undermine the *kisans'* position.

Further, the *kisans'* activities were closely monitored, and the fact that they were constantly visible reinforced their subjection (Foucault 1979: 87). The village crime-monitoring notebooks maintained by the *chowkidars* were sent by the *thanedars* to the district HQ in the form of police weekly intelligence reports. The villagers lived in dread of the *lal pagrees* (red-turbaned police), and the *daroga* and his subordinates were regarded with deep distrust. Their frequent abuse of power, familiarity with the personnel of the admin- istration, and knowledge of government agencies made them appear as evil-doers, to the lower castes in particular. Men in uniform were as deeply feared as the petty government officials; the *kisans* regarded this as a cumbersome and ruthless bureaucratic structure. By establishing a culture of terror, domination by the bailiffs, *thanedars, chowkidars* was built into the culture and life of the *kisans*. The *kisans* described this as *zamindari julum* or tyranny of the *zamindars*. One elderly *kisan* leader, Balbadrinath, who spoke Urdu, quoted a popular couplet: *'Watan ke patan ki jadi bimariyan, Buri un sab mey sey zamindariyan.'* (There are many illnesses the land suffers from, the worst of them all is the *zamindari*.)

LANDS, LAW AND CULTIVATION

The rapid transformation of the physical landscape into extensive estates by the *zamindari* led to a profound shortage of land that could be held as a freeholding; the sentiment echoed by many *kisans* was: 'to be even able to cultivate a piece of land was fulfilment, indeed'. Almost all the land in every village in the trans-Rapti tract was owned by the *zamindars*. Dikhu, another *kisan* who lived through those times, said it was like a permanent famine where many starving people gather for a few cobs of corn. Those with the cobs of corn offer it but when the hand reaches the cob, they withdraw giving the cob to another: everybody was pitted against each other, brothers and sisters turned against each other and were prepared to die for a grain of corn. Most of the holdings were on an average less than half an acre. From a study of the land maps in Sonpara village, dated 1936, it was difficult to estimate the number of *kisans* who owned plots measuring 0.39 to 0.45 of a *bigha* (officially measured as three-twentieths of an acre) but almost all the 30 *kisan* households had less than a *bigha* of land.

The entire *kisan* household was expected to serve the *zamindar* and the extended structure of *zamindari*. The 'patriarchal' system entailed that marriages were exogamous, residence was virilocal. New inheritance laws on land formulated that the sons of the *kisan* would inherit his property based on lineal descent. Often the *kisan* had to work on fields leased by the *thekedar* which were far away from their homes in the village. Both men and women worked in the fields, and children learnt from watching their parents and other elders. Generally, a *kisan* household consisted of extended family, the husband and wife and three children on an average (deaths during childbirth and infancy were frequent), the parents and younger siblings of the man.

Further, only part of the estate was leased out and fertile land was under the direct control of the *zamindar*'s family. This was called '*sir* land'. For example, the Choudhary of Dhekhari, the *zamindar* of Barhni, owned 600 *bighas* of which the cultivation of a fertile 300 *bighas* was directly controlled by the *zamindar*. The smallholdings were often less than an acre, and forced double-cropping patterns reduced the fertility in the soil and led to low yields. Based on several *kisan* households among the lower castes, it was evident that the cost of cultivation kept them in a state of indebtedness. Of the total income earned (both in cash and in kind) based on a study of ten households in Sonpara village, *a kisan*'s household spent 74 per cent on rent, 17 per cent on plough and cattle purchases, 5 per cent repayment of earlier debt, 7.5 per cent on subsistence payments to the *zamindar* for various social functions, 5.5 per cent on seed, 3 per cent on trade, hiring of the cart, 17 per cent bribes demanded by local officials, and 2 per cent on litigation. This works out to 136 per cent, thus their expenses far outweighed the cost of cultivation. There was never enough to eat and many found it hard to manage even a square meal, so they ate *sattu*, baked wheat that killed the appetite and kept them alive.

Human dignity and sense of being was put seriously to the test as *zamindari* and *julum* began to be synonymous. Furthermore, beside paying rent, the *kisans* of Barhni village, as elsewhere, were expected to till the *zamindar*'s lands unpaid, and carry their own plough and drive their oxen to the *zamindar*'s fields. For three continuous days each week, the *kisans* were forced to plough, sow and reap the crops by day, and to winnow the crop by night. After that, they were given two or three days' leave before returning to these tasks. In addition, whenever the *zamindar*'s coal supply arrived at the station they had to unload it and distribute it as required. This form of forced labour was also undertaken during rainy season: those *kisans* whose clothes were dry were whipped for not working; only those with wet clothes were paid. These incidents had been experienced by my informants who later joined the Communist Party and began to fight, like many thousands of *kisans*, for the abolition of the institution of the *zamindari*.

Also, in addition to performing free labour and supplying provisions, extra payments from every *kisan* household were demanded by the *zamindars* called *abwabs* (exactions). These exactions – described by some *kisans* as 'feudal' privileges and duties – were of an arbitrary nature, and had to be paid whenever the *zamindar* or his family engaged in any form of social or family activity that incurred personal expenditure. The amount charged to each cultivator varied from 2 *annas* to Rs 4 or more. The commonly found levies were *ghorawan* (purchase of a horse), *hathiana* (purchase of an elephant), *motorowan* (purchase of a car), *tehbazaari* (for a village fair), *pujahi* (for conducting a religious ceremony), *baagawan* (to plant an orchard), *purohiti* (to pay the *pandit*), if the *zamindar* had a stomach ache he charged *peetpirawan*, for a daughter's engagement *biahu*. These exactions varied in each *zamindari*, being more numerous in some than in others, but the enormous disparity of power between the rural elite and the cultivators prevented the latter from seeking any redress.

TIME AND SPATIAL CATEGORIES

Colonial attitudes towards time, calculation and forecasting introduced new schedules and calendars into socio-economic life, which were at odds with the *kisan* practice of waiting for natural cues for action. As a result the *kisans* experienced difficulties in adapting to the time requirements of the capitalist economy. Land legislation regarded cultivation in terms of the economic profit it would bring. All land was to be tilled and exploited to its maximum potential; cash-crop cultivation was actively encouraged. The use of hybrid seeds and chemical fertilisers was advocated for maximum yields. The *kisans* maintained that chemical fertilisers heated the soil very quickly and made the crops grow unnaturally, changing the taste. To them, the earth could only regain its strength through cow dung and horse manure. The produce was renewable within the space of a year so *kisans* usually aimed for the foreseeable future, and were suspicious of a mediated, abstract future based on rational or scientific calculations: the tendency was to value foresight rather than forecasting.

The administrative practices introduced conflicted with the fundamental tenets of local wisdom. For example, the rent of the field was determined by the nature of the soil as gauged by official estimates. The constitutive elements in the soil content were also subject to official scrutiny. The soil classifiers, or *chaktarashes*, were instructed to divide the villages into soil tracts and the classification of each field was checked by the settlement officer. In some cases there were found to be 12 to 14 different kinds of soils inside a village (Chevenix-Trench 1938). The *kisans* found these practices repellent and described it as prostituting mother earth. There was also to them a deep correlation between the land and the female/male bodily union which had been tampered with by such practices. Customarily, they judged the degree of fertility according to the feel of the soil, the crop or succession of crops to be planted that would nourish the soil, the season and the soil's potency according to cyclical time. Thus the appraisal of revenue of the villages (generally taken as a group) was based on arbitrarily calculated yields based upon the soil classifications, and the possible price of crops. Such estimates could not be changed, and made no allowances for floods, famine or a poor harvest. These were definitive categories that did not accommodate local practices.

The cropping pattern of cultivation was changed by colonial land legislation. Cash-crop cultivation such as opium and, later, sugar-cane cultivation, were enforced over the preferred choice of the *kisans* for food grains.[12] The sugar mills that were established were owned by the *zamindars* and their retainers often cheated while weighing the cane, paying a nominal sum to the *kisans* whilst reaping huge profits. These practices disrupted the agricultural calendar and introduced new time schedules and work ethics. Some *kisans* defined time as a goddess who moved through seasons, guiding cultivation patterns: she was imperishable and disobedience to her could bring about destruction. Some *kisans* remember that couplets were recited in the evenings such as:

Dukhiya kisan ham hai, Bharat ke rehene wale, be dam hai na dam hai, be mauth marne wale, insan ban ke aye, go pak uus zamin par, hamse accha hai ye accha, ghas charne wale. (We are the dispirited *kisans*, inhabitants of India; we are without any energy and no energy left to revive us; alive yet dead. We were born as humans, but even the cows are better off than us, as there is some grass for them to chew.)

EPILOGUE: RECLAIMING THE LAND

Despite mythic lands being jurally subjugated, the colonial transformation of topography, environment and the perception of time were never totally accepted by the *kisans*. For them, freedom and salvation meant an escape from a transcendent tradition which had destroyed their sense of being. Growing disenchantment in the villages was tapped into by the Congress movement, and later by the Communists and other left-wing parties. Following the politicisation of the *kisans*, movements for land rights took root in the late 1930s. During this time the *zamindari* tried to incite communal tensions between the Muslim and Hindu *kisans*. There was a widespread demand for the abolition of *zamindars* and granting of *haq-i-milkiyat* or inalienable land rights, and many *kisan* movements spread over rural India.

The *kisans* remember that period as a rather disquieting time caused by extreme political repression. It was inevitable that the mounting opposition would be stirred by the demand for the abolition of *zamindari*. The character of the movements was inspired by beliefs and rituals drawn from mythic understandings of the land through which the *kisans* negotiated their own space, which encouraged resistance and validated self-worth. Due to recurring protests from the *kisan* movements and the passing of Tenancy Acts, the institution of *zamindari* was formally annulled by the Bill for *Zamindari* Abolition in the 1950s.[13]

In the fight for landownership and rights over cultivation, the struggle for women's rights simply did not exist. The exploitation of women, both upper caste and lower caste, remained an uncontested issue. As Bourdieu has pointed out, the potentially contestable issues of gender – particularly the implications of gender equality – were often consigned into the realm of *doxa*. *Doxa* is precisely the incontestable, that which is taken for granted (Bourdieu 1984: 471); gender issues remained submerged while other political issues were being addressed (Hart 1991). These struggles tended to utilise traditional orientations so long as they did not conflict with their major priorities. Although sexual exploitation of lower-caste women was regarded as *julum* (tyranny), in general the position of women remained an uncontested issue because gender was not the object of the struggle against *julum*. The main ideological thrust of these struggles was against the everyday experiences of material and social inequalities, such as differential access to resources. These could be achieved politically without touching upon women's subordination. So although caste and religion came to acquire distinctly new meanings, popular politics made no change in gender relations: it merely took on the shape of the gender relations that were already in existence.

The *kisans* contested the colonial claims through their persuasive impact on the Congress movement, and the ideology of nationalism brought the land rights question into national focus. From the 1920s, the Congress espoused the *kisans'* campaign for landownership rights. That was the time of the 'All India Non-Cooperation' movement where every self-respecting Indian was expected not to cooperate with the British government. Gandhi's presence galvanised the movement, which developed a strong network at the grassroots level. Most of the rank and file were from the lower castes: Ahirs, Kurmis, Koeris Pasis and Chamars who became committed activists and mobilised a phenomenal grassroots following for the Congress. In Uttar Pradesh, land reform movements developed a powerful network in the countryside. The stress was on their collective identity and the need for *sangathan* (unity) by their leaders, who were frequently addressed as '*kisan bhaiya and bahina*' (*kisan* brothers and sisters) at their political meetings. The watchwords were not to fear the jail or the police; women began to court arrest. A popular chorus in a song echoes a woman who urges her companions and mother to court arrest:

> *Chaalu chaalu sakiya, jaile javaiya gey,*
> *Chaalu Chaalu matari, jail jehal key javaiya rey.*
> (Let us go, let us go sisters, let us go to jail;
> let us go, let us go mother, let us go to jail.)

What was particularly liberating from the *kisans'* point of view was that the struggle for land rights would touch upon wider issues of oppression, the breaking of social taboos and overthrowing all ties with the past. Customary taboos were everywhere being openly questioned: not only were hierarchies of caste being challenged, but also existing caste practices were being re-examined. Marriages of lower-caste women to upper-caste men occurred. Everyone had the right to wear the *janeo* (or sacred thread) and recite the *Gayatri mantra*, (once solely the prerogative of the *dwija* or Brahman). Lower castes were encouraged to educate their children. They were taught to spin, and weave *khadi* (cloth). It is apparent that such movements for caste reform, removal of untouchability and the re-assertion of religious identity, need to be understood in the context of the politics of dignity and social justice. The right to own land, inalienable rights or *haq-i-milkiyat* (legal ownership rights), was for many *kisans* the beginning of freedom and salvation.

With the transfer of power, the Congress government failed to fulfil its promises. In Uttar Pradesh, the pressure from below forced the Congress government to change its conservative tactics. It finally agreed to draw up the *Zamindari* Abolition Bill. However, the delay in passing it gave the *zamindars* plenty of time to make multiple registrations of their property in the names of their children, family members and even elephants.[12] Although the structure of landholdings was no longer *zamindari*, they still enjoyed ten times the income. Today, capital-intensive agriculture through fertilisers and tractors, as well as the control over grain stores, groves, ponds, fairs and bazaars, allows the landowners to retain their spatial network of power. Further, the Bill stated that *zamindars* had to be compensated Rs 140 million (Rs 140 crores). Thus the landless *kisans* were expected to pay for their land. This was not accepted by the left-wing parties. What was particularly galling to the *kisans* was that some *zamindars* had even proposed that they would assist the government in collecting compensation money. Some *kisans* maintained:

Muawza mangney wale dhurth hain, aur muawza dene wale murkh hain.
(Those who ask for compensation are cunning and those who pay it are fools.)

As the ethnography presented in this chapter has illustrated, autochthonous resistance to colonial and postcolonial praxis in northern India has involved a protracted and agonising process of negotiation. The *kisans* succeeded in establishing that an individual belonging to any caste has the legal right to own land. By upholding the underlying theodicy of the black letter law in the modern Indian state, the 'cosmologies of the powerful' continue to dominate, and to re-affirm the inflexible adherence to a legalism that is implicit in the discourse of power that pain is equal to punishment, in that the powerless *kisans* were condemned to experience suffering indefinitely in their unattainable quest to create a just moral order.

Evoking Foucault, Veena Das notes, 'that pain and suffering are not simply individual experiences which arise out of the circumstances which threaten to disrupt the social order, they are actively created and distributed by the social order itself' (Das 1995: 154). Since these experiences 'are located in individual bodies they bear the stamp of the authority of society upon the powerless' (Das 1995: 154). Thus, what the land protest and other movements were to symbolise was the irreversible efficacy of the colonial transformation of mythic subjectivities – not their return.

NOTES

1. The 'black letter law' is defined within the Anglo-Saxon legal tradition as the principles of law which are generally known, free from doubt or dispute.
2. The geographical focus of the trans-Rapti tract comprises the *tahsils* of Bansi, Dummariaganj and Maharajganj situated in the districts of Basti and Gorakhpur adjacent to the border of Nepal. Prior to independence, this region had been officially designated as the United Provinces of Agra and Awadh.
3. The term *kisan* contains culturally specific connotations which are not conveyed by the sociological term peasant and more importantly, overlooks its preferred usage by the *kisans* themselves.

4. Prior to colonisation, in both the oral and written traditions, it was implicit that rights to, and responsibilities for looking after the land could be held in perpetuity by all groups. It was customary in the subcontinent to take relationships for granted as vital supports for all living beings. Habib (1999) has insightfully treated the Mughal land records as a good example that demonstrates how ownership of land was regarded as an inalienable right. This was also true of other parts of the subcontinent. For example, Ludden (1985) states that in pre-British times ownership of land did not exist in the Tamil regions. Property was embodied in *pattam* and *pangu* or shares: legally owned land, *sondam*, is a construct of British law (Ludden 1985: 165). Dirks (1992) has made similar observations in his examination of south Indian kingdoms.
5. Home Department Files and Settlement Reports. See also, Risley (1909).
6. Such debates still persist in the writing of ethnography. In recent years, Quigley has maintained that 'caste is a form of political structure where kinship and kingship pull against each other and the priests are the mediators of the tension' (1993: 165). Also quoted in Sharma (1998: 25).
7. Dirks observed that 'under colonialism caste became a specifically Indian form of civil society, the most crucial site for the textualisation of social identity but also for the specification of public and private domains, the rights and responsibilities of the colonial state, the legitimating conceits of social freedom of societal control, and the development of the documentation and certification regimes of the bureaucratic state' (1992: 76).
8. Sharma's (1998) compendium on caste has not discussed these issues in detail but she has looked at the ethnography on caste and her arguments challenge the immutable status it has received in several ethnographies.
9. Even today, official subsidies, concessions and welfare schemes continue to rely upon such colonial distinctions, and do not account for the degree of fluidity in status and authority within and between various castes, religions and sects. Colonial laws formalised discrimination and enforced social control. See also Whitehead (1992) and Dirks (1992).
10. Singh (1994: 12) notes that, in the 1981 census, 87.1 per cent of the Scheduled Tribes had been recorded as Hindu and regarded as followers of the Hindu faith.
11. Padel (1995) notes that critics of British Indian rule have examined the bodies of theory that have shaped both British rule and its consequences in some depth. He quotes Edward Said:

> Imperialism has been defined and studied almost exclusively as a social, political or economic formation. There has hardly been any work on what role culture plays in sustaining imperialism, or for that matter in initiating it ... we need closer attention to the verbal, imaginative and the ideological overlapping between narrative on the one hand and on the other, ethnographic reports, travel accounts, political treatises and the like. (Said 1984, in Padel 1995: 27)

12. Amin (1984) points out how traditional methods of crushing sugar-cane or unrefined sugar (*gur*) by wooden crushers (*kolhus*) were formally discouraged; the *kolhus* were seized and *kisans* were forced to supply their sugar-cane crops to the sugar mill at low prices, resulting in yet another form of injustice.
13. Baljit Singh and Sridhar Mishra (1964) have pointed out how the *Zamindari* Abolition Bill was withheld in 1952, 1954 and 1956 for further amendments, so that it was not finally passed until November 1959.

REFERENCES

Amin, S. 1984. *Sugarcane and Sugar in Gorakhpur: An Inquiry into Peasant Production for Capitalist Enterprise in Colonial India*. Delhi: Oxford University Press.

Baden-Powell, B.H. 1892 (1974). *Land Systems in British India*. Delhi: Manohar Press.
Baden-Powell, B.H. 1899 (1991). *The Origin and Growth of Village Communities in India*. Delhi: Manohar Press.
Bagchi, A.K. 1992. 'Land laws, property rights and peasant insecurity in colonial India', *Journal of Peasant Studies* 20(1): 1–49.
Blunt, E.A.H. 1938. 'The structure of the Indian people', in E.A.H. Blunt (ed.) *Some of the Social and Economic Problems of the Indian People*. Cambridge: Cambridge University Library, pp. 41–77.
Bourdieu, P. 1979. *Algeria 1960*. Cambridge: Cambridge University Press.
——. *Distinction: A Social Critique of the Judgement of Taste*. London: Routledge.
—— 1991. *Language and Symbolic Power*. Cambridge: Polity Press.
—— 1992. *The Logic of Practice*. Cambridge: Cambridge University Press.
—— 1999. *The Weight of the World: Social Suffering in Contemporary Society*. Cambridge: Polity Press.
Chevenix-Trench, C.G. 1938. 'The rural community', in E.A.H. Blunt (ed.) *Social Service in India: Some of the Social and Economic Problems of the Indian People*, pp. 78–111.
Cohn, B.1984. 'Census, social structure and object in South Asia', *Folk, the Journal of the Danish Ethnographic Society* 26: 25–49.
Croll, E. and Parkin. D. 1992. 'Cultural understandings of the environment', in E. Croll and D. Parkin (eds) *Bush Base, Forest Farm: Culture, Environment and Development*. London: Routledge.
Das, V. 1995. *Critical Events: An Anthropological Perspective on Contemporary India*. Delhi: Oxford University Press.
Dirks, N.B. 1992. 'From little king to landlord: colonial discourse and colonial rule', in N.B. Dirks (ed.) *Colonialism and Culture*. Michigan: University of Michigan Press.
Dumont, L. 1966: *Homo Hierarchichus*. Chicago: University of Chicago Press.
Fabian, J. 1983. *Time and the Other: How Anthropology Makes its Object*. New York: Cambridge University Press.
Foucault, M. 1979. *Discipline and Punish: The Birth of the Prison*, trans. by Alan Sheridan. Harmondsworth: Penguin Books.
Galanter, M. 1989. *Law and Society in Modern India*. Oxford: Oxford University Press.
Gopal, K. 'No Fixed Abode: Wanderings and Reminiscences among the *kisans*'. Manuscript in progress.
Guha, R. 1982. 'On some aspects of the historiography in colonial India', in R. Guha (ed.) *Subaltern Studies I*. Delhi: Oxford University Press.
Habib, I. 1999. *The Agrarian System of Mughal India, 1556–1707*. New Delhi: Oxford University Press.
Hart, G. 1991. 'Engendering everyday resistance: gender patronage and production politics in rural Malaysia', *Journal of Peasant Studies* 19(1): 93–121.
Inden, R. 1990. *Imagining India*. Oxford: Blackwell.
Lipner, J. 1984. *Hindus, their Religious Beliefs and Practices*. London: Routledge.
Ludden, D. 1985. *Peasant History in South India*. Princeton, NJ: Princeton University Press.
Mill, J. 1858. *The History of British India*. London: Madden, Puper, Stephenson & Spencer.
Oberoi, H. 1994. *The Construction of Religious Boundaries: Culture, Identity, and Diversity in the Sikh Tradition*. Delhi: Oxford University Press
Padel, F. 1995. *The Sacrifice of Human Being: British Rule and the Konds of Orissa*. Delhi: Oxford University Press.
Pedersen, P. 1984. 'The racial trap of India: reflections on the history of a regional ethnography', *Folk, the Journal of the Danish Ethnographic Society* 28: 5–24.
—— 1986. 'Khatri, Vaishya or Kshatriya: an essay on colonial administration and cultural identity', *Folk, the Journal of the Danish Ethnographic Society* 28: 19–30
Quigley, D. 1993. *The Interpretation of Caste*. Oxford: Blackwell
Quigley, D. and Gellner, D. 1995. *Contested Hierarchies: A Collaborative Ethnography of Caste among the Newars of the Kathmandu Valley*. Oxford: Clarendon Press

Reeves, P. 1991. *Landlords and Government in U.P.: A Study of their Relations until Zamindari Abolition, 1920–1950*. Delhi: Oxford University.

Risley, H.H. 1891. 'The study of ethnicity', *Journal of the Royal Anthropology Institute* 20.

—— 1909. *The People of India*. Calcutta: Government of India Press.

—— 1924. *The Ethnology, Languages, Literature and Religions of India*. Oxford: Clarendon Press.

Said, E. 1984. 'A review of Benita Parry's *Conrad and Imperialism*', *Times Literary Supplement* 12 October: p. 1149.

Sharma, U. 1983. *Women, Work and Property in North-West India*. London: Tavistock.

—— 1998. *Caste*. Buckingham: Open University Press.

Singh, B. and Mishra, S. 1964. *A Study of Land Reforms in Uttar Pradesh*. Calcutta: Gupta Press.

Singh, K.S. 1994. *The Scheduled Tribes*. Delhi: Oxford University Press.

Unnithan-Kumar, M. 1997. *Identity, Gender and Poverty: New Perspectives on Caste and Tribe in Rajasthan*. Oxford: Berghahn Books.

Whitehead, J. 1992. 'Images of nature and culture in British and French representations of caste', *Journal of Historical Sociology* 5(4): 410–30.

Yang, A. 1985. 'Dangerous castes and tribes, the Criminal Tribes Act and the Maghaiya Doms of North-East India', in A. Yang (ed.) *Crime and Criminality in British India*. Phoenix: Tuscon Press.

OFFICIAL DOCUMENTATION

Unpublished Typed Records

Sessions Trials 1940–46, Azamgarh, District court.
Land revenue records (hand written with field-maps), Azamgarh Collectorate.
Bansi tahsil court records 1920–65, Basti District.
Village Crime notebooks, Tarwa *thana*, Lalganj *tahsil* Azamgarh.

Published Official Records (all printed at The Government of India Press, Agra, unless otherwise indicated).

Administrative Reports for the United Provinces of Agra and Oudh, 1875–1945.
Report on the Administration of Revenue for the United Provinces of Oudh, 1900–1946.
Report on the Administration of Justice for the United Provinces of Oudh, 1900–1945.
Police Abstracts of Intelligence, 1921–1949.
Home Department Records, 1921–47.
Judicial Department Records, 1921–47.
Report of the Administration of the Police for the United Provinces of Agra and Oudh, 1900–1945.
Report on the Land records for the United Provinces of Agra and Oudh, 1900–1945.
Report of the Collector of Azimgurh on the Settlement of the Ceded portion of the District commonly called Chuklah Azimgurh by John Thomason, Agra, December 1837.
Final Report of the Settlement for Gorakhpur District , by A.W. Cruickshank, Vols I and II, Allahabad, 1893.
Final Report for the Settlement of Gorakhpur District, E.A. Phelps, Allahabad, 1909.
Final Report for the Settlement of Gorakhpur District, E.A. Phelps, Allahabad, 1919.
Azamgarh, A Gazetteer, volume XXXIII, Allahabad, 1911 D.L. Drake Brockman.
Basti, A Gazetteer, volume XXXII, by H.R. Nevill, Allahabad, 1907.

Gorakhpur, A Gazetteer, XXXII, Allahabad, 1907 and 1922, H.R. Nevill.

Final Report of the Settlement Report for Basti District, by A.G. Clow, Allahabad, 1919.

Census of India: North-Western Provinces of Agra and Oudh, XVI, 1871.

Census of India: North-Western Provinces of Agra and Oudh, XVI, Calcutta, 1891.

Imperial Gazetteers, volumes XXXI and XXXII by H.R.Neville, Allahabad, 1909.

Minutes from the Royal Commission of Agriculture for the United Provinces, VII, London, 1928.

United Provinces Report, 1895.

Uttar Pradesh Zamindari Abolition Committee Reports, I and II, Lucknow, 1950.

Congress Records (Lucknow Archives)

UPPCC, Agrarian Distress in the United Provinces: Being the Report of the Committee Appointed by the Council of the United Provinces Provincial Congress Committee to Enquire into the Agrarian Situation in the Province, 1931.

UPPCC, Congress Agrarian Enquiry Committee Report: Being the Report of the Committee Appointed by the Council of the United Provinces Provincial Congress Committee to Enquire into the Agrarian Situation in the Province, 1936.

Private Papers and Diaries

Richard Kreber, Personal Diary of a Jesuit Priest, 1924 – The Commisioner's office, Varanasi.

8 POLITICS, CONFUSION AND PRACTICE: LANDOWNERSHIP AND DE-COLLECTIVISATION IN UKRAINE

Louise Perrotta

In this chapter I will suggest that framing theoretical descriptions of land relations in terms of binary oppositions between the 'mythical' and the 'juridical' obscures the complex, processual, contextualised and often contradictory nature of people–land relations in a situation of dramatic political, social and economic change. By concentrating on the processual nature of land reform and the formation of land relations in the former Soviet Republic of Ukraine, I hope to demonstrate that emerging land relations are the product of diverse and unstable political, economic and practical interests. The very uncertainty and instability of these interests preclude identification of emerging land relations with either the traditionally mythical or the rationally juridical. In comparison to the measure of certainty, consensus and cohesion that attend both myth and juridical rationality, land relations in Ukraine exhibit uncertainty and contention in a complex relation with established practice. The chapter will describe both the formal processes of land reform and the diverse ways in which social actors attach meaning(s) to those processes. I concentrate on rural/agricultural land reform, and base my interpretation on experience of advising international aid agencies' land reform and farm restructuring projects, and on research conducted among the rural population in 1998–9.

Current juridical changes in the people–land relation in Ukraine do as much to confuse as to clarify or rationalise the relationship between people and land, as privatisation is plagued by competing political and economic interests, and by the absence of legislative expertise. This results in confusion over who is the subject of the new 'private' ownership relation (individuals, or the collective enterprise with which they are associated), and over the object of the new 'private' ownership relation (as this usually relates to un-demarcated shares in collectively occupied land, rather than to clearly defined land parcels). Similarly, we shall see that there is no ritual or mythical attachment to the land, as these relations are commonly understood. Instead we find a diversity of relationships to land. This diversity is linked to the different interests of different groups of people, engaged in or affected by changes in land relations. This diversity is also associated with the ways in which people relate to land of different categories (household plots versus land shares). We shall see that the closest relation between people and land is located at the level of the family and their household plot. This relation is one of intimate interdependence, where the labour invested in the land produces food, the means of subsistence, and the fuel for further investment of labour in land. Understanding the role of labour in people–land relations goes some way towards clarifying both the absence of a mythical relationship to land and the failure of attempts to introduce rational, juridical people–land relations.

PRIVATISATION AND THE DEVELOPMENT OF JURIDICAL LAND RELATIONS

In the most general sense, rural land reform in Ukraine (as in much of the former Soviet Union) is based on a commitment to privatisation, i.e. to the creation of private property rights in land and the allocation of those property rights to those that till the land. In Ukrainian law, there are three 'forms of ownership': state, collective and private. Land reform is described as a two-stage process: the first stage involves the transfer of landownership from the state to 'the collective'; the second phase entails the distribution of land shares to individual members of 'the collective'. The vast majority of former *kolkhoz* (collective farms) and a significant proportion of former *sovkhoz* (state farms) have changed their status to that of a Collective Agricultural Enterprise (CAE). The most significant differences between a CAE and a *kolkhoz* or *sovkhoz* are their right to own land and their independence, i.e. their right to decide how to manage their own economic affairs, what to produce and how, and how to dispose of their produce. Most CAEs have applied for and many have received title to all or some of the land they occupied as a *kolkhoz* or *sovkhoz*: the State Act for Collective Ownership. A significantly smaller proportion has undertaken implementation of the second stage – the distribution of individual land shares to CAE members.

This process is regulated by a large number of opaque and contradictory laws, Presidential Decrees, Resolutions from the Cabinet of Ministers, and Regulations and Recommendations issued by government departments and ministries charged with the design and implementation of privatisation policy. Although there is almost universal acceptance of the general principle of land privatisation, this process is fraught with uncertainty and inconsistencies. On the one hand, legislation frequently confuses the definition of the ownership relation with lists of either the subjects or the objects of the ownership relation. Long lists of 'types of land' (agricultural land, bogs, land under roads, land under water courses, etc.), compete with long lists of 'types of owners' (citizens of Ukraine, citizens of other countries, people without citizenship, cooperatives, joint stock companies, etc.). Yet legislation often fails to indicate whether some or all of these different entities should be treated differently in law. There are three critical absences which impinge on the efficacy of land reform: the definition of the subject of 'collective ownership', the definition of the object of land share ownership, and definition of the rights and responsibilities which attach to the ownership of a land share.

There is considerable confusion as to the identity of the subject of the ownership relation, once ownership of land has passed from the state to the 'collective'. In the first instance a Collective Agricultural Enterprise (CAE) applies for and is granted legal title, a State Act for Collective Ownership of all or a portion of the land it occupied and used as a *kolkhoz* or *sovkhoz*. This legal document names the CAE as the subject of ownership, but necessarily includes the legally verified list of names of the members of that CAE. Membership of a CAE is based on current and/or past employment: it includes all workers not on temporary employment contracts and all pensioners who retired from the former *kolkhoz/sovkhoz* but who are still resident on its territory. In the second stage these individuals have the right to receive an equal share of this collectively owned land; they are entitled to receive a legal document – a land share certificate – which attests their ownership of x no. of 'point hectares'.[1] Land is rarely demarcated into individually owned parcels. Thus, although each member may receive a certificate which entitles him or her to x 'point hectares', they cannot point to a parcel of land and say 'that is mine' (see Wegren 1994b for an analysis of the prototype for land reform in Nizhni Novgorod, Russia). Although there are good practical reasons for not demarcating land into individual parcels, this creates both a sense of confusion as to what it is that is owned and contributes to the cynical but common conviction that 'nothing has changed'. The apparently unanswerable question is, who owns the land? Is it the abstract 'collective' or is it a collection of named individuals? Is it the juridical entity Mayak CAE who is the subject of the land relation, or is it the list of persons who are the legally defined members of Mayak CAE? Is there a distinction between the CAE as a juridical entity and the individuals who constitute its membership? Do they have different rights and obligations with regard to the land? There are as many answers to this question as there are interests.

Throughout Ukraine, as in other parts of the former Soviet Union (FSU), there are local authorities charged with the implementation of policies which emanate from the centre, in this case from Kiev. Each *oblast* and *raion*[2] will have a Department of Agriculture, and a Land Resource Committee, which are closely involved in the land reform process. The personalities and interests of the powerful individuals in these departments exercise considerable influence on the ways in which reform policy is interpreted and implemented. (See Van Atta 1993; Perrotta 1995, 1998; Wegren 1996a for further discussion of rural politics and land reform in the FSU.) For example, in one *oblast* with which I am familiar, the head of the Department of

Agriculture claims to be an active supporter of reform, proof being that he has dedicated staff to the implementation of the reforms. He even claims to have set up a 'centre' to assist CAEs in acquiring their State Acts and in determining and distributing land shares. In reality, he has delegated responsibility for the implementation of complex reforms to one person, to whom he has allocated no resources, and whom he constantly directs to undertake tasks wholly disconnected from the reform process. When asked as to the progress of distribution of land share certificates, he invariably asserts that 'almost all land share certificates have been distributed in the *oblast*'. In reality less than 20 per cent of CAEs have distributed land share certificates, either because they themselves have failed to undertake the necessary steps, or because the *oblast* Department of Agriculture or the Land Resource Committee has placed a stream of obstacles in their path, or because of the nationwide shortage of printed certificates. To the extent that land reform is a technical bureaucratic process of issuing title to land, the ability of bureaucrats to hinder or help the process is enormous. Their interests in hindering the process are sometimes political (simple opposition to privatisation), but more often economic. As official wages are low and often paid late, bureaucrats increasingly rely on 'presents' from the supplicants trying to get the necessary paperwork done.

When asked who is the subject of ownership on a Collective Agricultural Enterprise (CAE) which has received its State Act for Collective Ownership, representatives of both the Department of Agriculture and the Land Resource Committee at *oblast*-level usually insist that it is the CAE as a juridical entity, emphasising that the State Act bears the name of the CAE. When pressed for an explanation as to the rights and responsibilities that attend ownership of an individual land share certificate, both explain that 'yes, the people own the land,' but 'they own it collectively'. Frequently they add that, 'we must avoid fragmentation at all costs'. 'Fragmentation' refers to the much-feared process of land share certificate holders deciding en masse to withdraw from the large collectives and to farm their land as small Private Peasant Farms;[3] this is seen to be an undesirable outcome by all but the most vociferous advocates of land privatisation. The Department of Agriculture is in favour of land privatisation if ownership of the land by the tillers will improve productivity by improving 'labour discipline' through better economic stimuli. They are not in favour of land privatisation that will seriously change the pattern of land holdings and production. This is partly linked to a genuine fear of plummeting production and attendant risks to food security. It is partly linked to a straightforward resistance to change in any shape or form; this resistance is in itself the product of the profound cynicism resulting from endless and irrational changes in Soviet policy. More significantly, it is linked to the threat to their own power base.

During the Soviet period, these officials enjoyed absolute control over the movement of resources, allocating (perennially scarce) inputs to farms and distributing the products. Ambitious farm directors had to 'establish relations' with these powerful players, in order to ensure that they received inputs of the right quality and quantity and at the right time. 'Good relations' with officials also ensured timely payment for deliveries. In turn the *kolkhoz* or *sovkhoz* could acquire a reputation from being 'a strong farm', which would, in turn, boost the power and prestige of the farm as a whole and, more specifically, that of the farm director. Further, 'a strong farm' was able to produce a surplus above 'plan', which was distributed to farm members, who thus also benefited from the relation. It is clear that in the course of land reform, bureaucrats risk the loss of long-established and fruitful relationships with small numbers of farm directors, relationships which yielded both material and immaterial benefits. It would be impossible to re-establish these relations with thousands of small, unknown newcomers, unwilling to maintain the special relationship between bureaucracy and primary producers.

Similarly, representatives of the state Land Resource Committee favour interpretation which indicates that the subject of ownership of a State Act is the juridical entity of a CAE and not the hundreds of individuals with entitlement to a land share, whose names are appended. Again, they have less of a problem with an interpretation of land privatisation which shifts control of land use from their sole control to that of small numbers of farm directors, than they do with a process which creates uncontrollable numbers of new owners, with all the options normally associated with private ownership. They are paralysed with fear at the loss of control presented by land reform and are convinced that the new owners of land will most certainly abuse the land in the absence of effective state controls. They have considerable power to obstruct and delay, as each stage of the process must be implemented and approved by them. Again, their resistance is a combination of genuine fear about degradation of the land, cynical inertia and a fear of loss of power. In the case of the Land Resource Committee, there remains a scientistic desire to collect all possible information about the land, including who has the right to a land share, their education and capacity for agriculture. They will then produce a 'plan', which will direct each land owner as to what he or she will produce, on what kind of rotation, using what agri-chemicals. They would like to retain control of all land transactions both leasehold and freehold, including the determination of all terms and conditions, including price. When I suggested that the collection of this information would take us well into the next millennium, even if resources were available (which they aren't), the response was a resigned shrug, whose interpretation eludes me still.

Conversely, and often at the smaller, more local administrative level of the *raion*, bureaucrats sometimes facilitate the process of reform with unusual alacrity. There are a number of reasons for this. At a very simplistic level, officials at *raion* level are likely to be younger than their superiors at *oblast* level. They are 'on their way up' rather than 'already arrived'. It is clear that throughout the FSU, age is one of the most critical factors correlated with attitudes to and engagement with reform. Second, as a *raion* Department of

Agriculture is more closely involved with the day-to-day difficulties of production and marketing, many recognise that effective reform is necessary to halt the decline. They recognise that their interests and ambitions will not readily be satisfied by the exercise of power and influence over failing enterprises. With less to lose from the demise of the old system, some are making pragmatic attempts to achieve their ambitions through engagement with the new opportunities presented by a re-vitalised local economy. Thus in the same *oblast*, a small number of *raions* may have pushed through the distribution of land shares and may actively encourage land share certificate holders to see themselves as the 'owners' of the land. Finally, even if some *raion* officials might ideally prefer to exercise traditional Soviet-type power over the land in their jurisdiction, they simply no longer have the means to do so. They no longer effectively control access to the resources necessary for agriculture (inputs, markets), and cannot therefore effectively control those in charge of production (CAE directors and their workers). Because of the greater intimacy between *raion* officials and primary agricultural producers, there is much less inconsistency between what they say and what they do. If this contradiction is easily sustained at the level of the *oblast*, it is more difficult when the evidence is literally on your doorstep.

At the level of the farms themselves, participation in the land reform process varies hugely. In a single *raion* with which I am familiar, two (out of 20) Collective Agricultural Enterprises (CAEs) distributed land shares as early as 1994 whilst others have not yet taken the first steps towards defining entitlements. However, on one farm, which claimed to have distributed its land shares, it was discovered that they had not in fact been distributed at all, but were kept in the office safe. The farm director argued that he had not distributed the land share certificates, because he was worried about people losing them and so was 'keeping them safe'. In different conversations however, he invariably railed against the dangers of 'fragmentation' and would frequently refer to the CAE as 'my' farm. Significantly, this farm is located on the outskirts of a major city. Although everyone knows there are strict controls on land use, everybody also knows that it is possible to circumvent these rules if the profits are high enough. The land occupied by this CAE has a very high potential value for non-agricultural use. Further, the farm director on this particular CAE was busy reducing staff, and therefore the number of people entitled to receive land share certificates. None of the members of this farm were aware that 'their' land share certificates were sitting in the farm director's office.

Not surprisingly, the majority of farm directors insist that it is the Collective Agricultural Enterprise (CAE) as a juridical entity which owns the land. Given the concentration of power and responsibility in the hands of CAE directors, ownership of the land 'by the CAE' is in practice indistinguishable from control of the land 'by the CAE director'. Even where land share certificates have been distributed, CAE directors are often reluctant to inform the entitlement holders of their rights, opportunities and obligations.

At best they inform their populations that the land share certificate entitles them to a share of the 'profits' from the land. As there are almost never any 'profits' to speak of, it is naturally deemed to be a fairly worthless 'right'. Some try and encourage their populations to think of the land as their own in order to improve fast deteriorating 'labour discipline'. However, in the absence of a discernible link between ownership and improved living standards, most farm members receive these exhortations with practised indifference. I know of only one case where a CAE director has not only distributed land share certificates, but has actively encouraged the entitlement holders to acknowledge and exercise their ownership rights, including the right to make alternative choices about occupation and use. Not surprisingly, this CAE had been the recipient of intensive support from one of the major aid agencies.

LANDOWNERS AND LANDOWNERSHIP: CONFUSION AND DIVERSITY

Exploring the relationship between the new 'juridical' owners of land (farm members) and the land they now own is, of course, most critical (see Chmatko 1994; Brooks 1996; for descriptions of rural populations' attitudes to land reform in Russia). There are a number of factors to take into account. First is the distinction between Collective Agricultural Enterprises (CAEs) themselves: some CAEs have, just, changed their status from *kolkhoz* to CAE but have progressed no further; others have applied for and some of these have received their State Act for Collective Ownership, with its appended list of names; of these, some have applied for and received their individual land share certificates and of these some will have distributed the land share certificates to entitlement holders. Of these, some land share certificate holders are the bewildered recipients of a piece of paper which accords them uncertain rights and obligations whilst a very few are aware of the opportunities and constraints that attend their realisation of these rights and obligations. Needless to say, where individual farm members have nothing more than a theoretical right to receive, sometime in the future, a land share certificate, about which they know little and understand less, discussions over who owns the land are premature. They continue to identify themselves as 'members' of the farm (usually as members of the *kolkhoz* rather than of the CAE), and maintain that the criteria for membership is a combination of labour and local residence. At the opposite and much narrower end of the spectrum, some farm members acknowledge the apparent truth that they now exercise something called 'landownership'. Some can quote some of the rights and obligations that attend landownership. Fewer still express any desire or intention to exercise those rights, particularly the right to withdraw, demarcate one's land on the ground, acquire private ownership of this land, and establish a 'genuinely' Private Peasant Farm.

Here it is extremely important to note whence the resistance to 'genuinely' Private Farming. This is not, as is sometimes suggested, evidence that Slavic people have an historical and cultural preference for 'collectivism'. Nor does it necessarily indicate nothing more than farm directors' and others' fear of 'fragmentation' and attendant loss of power; although these are important factors, it is important not to ignore farm members' own perceptions and understandings. In fact, new land share holders make sensible assessments of the risks which attend withdrawal from the collective for the purposes of Private Farming. These include both assessments of risks of Private Farming in the absence of a supportive infrastructure for small farms, and assessments of the benefits which attend remaining within the collective fold, if only for the time being. These latter include (official and unofficial) access to forage and pasture for household livestock, as well as access to transport and to periodic distributions of 'in-kind' payments in lieu of wages. On many CAEs, there is little risk of disciplinary action against theft or absenteeism, both of which are necessary for sustaining the household subsistence economies on which most families depend. As most farm members see only two alternatives – staying within the CAE or small-scale Private Peasant Farming – and as the latter is deemed high-risk in current conditions, few choose to exercise the right to individualised 'private ownership' of a demarcated parcel of land (see Wegren 1992a and 1996b for a discussion of the development of Private Farming in other parts of the FSU).

It is not, perhaps, surprising if the diverse attitudes and understandings of the participants in the process reflect their diverse interests. However, it is surprising that this diversity is repeated and reflected in the professional interpretations of lawyers and policy makers. The lack of clarity in the written laws pertaining to land reform in fact forbids any coherent interpretation. Although frustrating, the lack of clarity reflects legislators' attempts to square the circle and to achieve mutually exclusive aims. Their overall objective is to improve the performance of the agricultural sector. On the basis of evidence from abroad and from the well-documented efficiency of rural populations' 'private plots',[4] they concur that private ownership seems to be directly related to improved performance. So they have embarked on a country-wide programme of privatisation. Simultaneously, they feel obliged to observe a basic principal of social justice and to distribute landownership fairly and equally between all those who labour or have laboured on the land. These two factors effectively create literally millions of owners of small land shares (average *c*. 5 ha). As policy makers fear the fragmentation of agricultural land into uneconomically small units, they invented the notion of 'collective ownership', which was intended to reconcile these competing aims. Although 'collective ownership' reflects the attempt to achieve the perceived benefits of private ownership whilst avoiding the dangers of fragmentation, it has created confusions which seriously retard and impede progress and improvement. The result is that no one actually knows who owns land in 'collective ownership'.

Questioned about the identity of the subject of collective ownership, lawyers, both local and foreign, sometimes assert that it is the legal entity, the Collective Agricultural Enterprise (CAE), that owns the land because the official land title bears the name of the CAE. *Sometimes* they add that the CAE is no more and no less than the list of individuals whose names are appended to the State Act; they suggest that the term 'CAE Mayak' stands for the named individuals as a kind of convenient shorthand, which fits on one line, but which clearly refers to the appended list of names. One lawyer has suggested that the land belongs to both the juridical entity and to the named individuals, so that if there are 500 names on the list, there are 501 owners of the land, with the CAE participating as a juridical person.

The confusion as to who is the subject and what is the object of ownership is hardly clarified when we investigate the nature of individual land share ownership. All members of a CAE have the right to receive a land share certificate, which attests to their right of ownership of an equal share of the land, within the boundaries of the land represented on the State Act for Collective Ownership. These land shares are rarely demarcated into individual parcels. However, each land share certificate holder clearly enjoys the legal right to withdraw from the CAE, and to demand the demarcation of their land share in kind, on the ground. If a CAE member decides to withdraw with their land, they will exchange their land share certificate for a State Act for Private Ownership of their demarcated land parcel. Some argue that as ownership of a land share certificate implies the right to exchange a land share certificate for a State Act for Private Ownership, that the owners of land share certificates are therefore the (private) owners of the land. They argue that collective occupation and use of the land is fully consistent with private ownership of undivided shares in the land. Others find this concept difficult to comprehend and insist that collective occupation and use is only consistent with collective ownership, to the same extent that private occupation and use is only consistent with individualised private ownership.

If the lawyers have been unable to agree on the identity of the subject of landownership which is attested by a State Act for Collective Ownership, the problem has more recently been exacerbated by the absence of any mention of 'collective ownership' in the Ukrainian Constitution. As the Constitution stands above other laws and as 'collective ownership' is not mentioned as a legal form of ownership, many argue that it is no longer a legal form of ownership. In a strictly legal sense, it could be argued that land reform is back to square one, as the thousands of State Acts for Collective Ownership which have been issued are no longer legal title to land. Unbelievably, some lawyers actually (and not a little sadistically) argue that this is so and that it will be necessary to re-visit the entire process. Luckily, to date pragmatism seems to have prevailed and most participants are carrying on as if this new problem had not arisen.

THE RIGHTS AND WRONGS OF THE OWNERSHIP RELATION

We have discussed the ways in which the confusion between 'collective ownership' and individual land share certificates precludes definition of who exactly owns the land. This confusion is evinced by the competing and contradictory interpretations of lawyers, *oblast* and *raion* bureaucrats, farm directors and farm members. We have explained the roots of this confusion by referring to the contradictory aims of policy makers, and to the struggles to maintain or acquire power at various levels of the bureaucracy. We have indicated that farm directors often want to retain control over their large land-holdings and that farm members themselves often prefer to remain within the 'collective', in the absence of a viable practical alternative. In this section, I want to discuss the nature of the ownership relation as this is conceptualised in Ukraine. This will involve a discussion of the nature of the rights and obligations that attend landownership.

There is considerable confusion as to the complex of rights and obligations that attend land (share) ownership. Some rights are a matter of consensus. These include first, the right to receive an income from the land. Second, land share owners enjoy the right to bequeath the land share to an heir. Third, they enjoy the right to withdraw their land share 'in kind': those who have a land share certificate may in theory exchange this certificate for a Title of Private Ownership of a demarcated land parcel. Some argue that this process is only allowed if the withdrawing CAE member wishes to set up an official Private Peasant Farm. Others argue that this is not a necessary condition, but can see no other reason for withdrawal and demarcation.

Other rights are subject to dispute. These include the right to sell or to lease a land share. Although the land share certificate states that rights include the right to sell, many argue that as there is a six-year moratorium on the sale of land received for free from the state, land share certificate holders cannot sell their land share certificates for six years; some argue that you can sell a land share certificate, but not land; others argue that you cannot sell a land share certificate but only land (i.e. you can sell the land after six years only *if* you exchange your 'abstract' land share for private ownership of a demarcated parcel. The Law on CAEs states that land share certificates can be sold, but that 'co-owners' have the right of first refusal (whether this refers to the CAE as a juridical entity or to other individual land share holders is also subject to confusion).

Similarly, although the land share certificate states that it might be leased, this is also subject to dispute. Some argue that you can't lease a land share certificate, only land, i.e. you can only lease land that has been withdrawn, demarcated on the ground, and for which an individual Title to Private Ownership has been issued. The recently published 'Presidential Decree on Leasing Land' is noticeably silent on this issue. Significantly, one pilot project attempting to promote land leasing avoided collision with this confusion by developing a 'forbearance agreement' in lieu of a leasing contract. The land share certificate holder agrees to forego his or her right to demand withdrawal and demarcation of their land share in kind for a certain period in return for the fulfilment of certain conditions. In fact this is a lease agreement, by another name. Another pilot project promotes the use of 'joint production agreements', where the land shareholder invests the land and the occupier/user donates labour and other inputs.

What seems relatively clear from the above is the nature of the distinction between rights which are contested and rights which are a matter of relative consensus. The right to own, occupy and receive an income from land are generally agreed. This is linked to the belief that the right to own, occupy and receive an income will increase agricultural efficiency as the rewards for efficient use will accrue to the producer. There is also a general agreement that land shares should be the object of inheritance. The high proportion of elderly land shareholders (on average about 50 per cent of land share holders on any CAE are pensioners), means that there is a relative consensus that they should have the right to bequeath this recently acquired asset to their heirs. What is less clear is whether one may bequeath a land share to someone who is neither 'kin', nor a member of the CAE. Similarly, the right to exchange a land share of collectively owned land for a Title of Private Ownership of land for the purposes of Private Peasant Farming is accepted, again because it retains a connection between ownership, occupation, labour and income.

There *is* dispute about the exchange rights that attend ownership of a land share in particular as regards leasing and sale. This nervousness has two roots: opposition to commodification of land and the desire to maintain control of land and its owners. First, there is a critical opposition to the commodification of land and to the disconnection of economic gain from labour. Resistance to both leasing and to the sale and purchase of land are firmly linked to a continued opposition to all forms of economic gain, which are not based on labour. Leasing would allow those who do not work the land to acquire an income from that land. This is felt by many to be morally unacceptable. It is sometimes argued that as up to 50 per cent of land shareholders are not of working age, they ought to be able to receive an income from their land through leasing. Although the rights of pensioners to receive an income from leasing is less contentious than the rights of the able-bodied to do the same, some workers (who are also CAE members and co-land shareholders), refuse to contemplate any payment to pensioners for the use of their land, even though pensioners may be excluded from the distribution of in-kind goods produced on their land. There is also much disagreement about the rights and wrongs of sale and purchase of land. If it is morally acceptable to receive an income from the combination of ownership, occupation and labour, it remains morally reprehensible to make money from speculation – buying and selling. This opposition is strengthened rather than weakened by observation of the fortunes being made by traders in other parts of the economy. If the trade in non-land commodities is reprehensible, the trade in land is deemed speculation of the worst sort, to be avoided at all costs (see Wegren 1995 for a discussion of market relations in land in Russia). There is also a somewhat suspect paternalism which is used to justify the suppression of land sales. Policy makers are convinced (or appear to be convinced) that the moratorium on land sales is designed to protect the recipients of land both from being pressurised into selling their land and from their own ignorance. It is frequently asserted that the moratorium is designed to avoid the possibility of selling the family's land share for a bottle of vodka. If the protectiveness of this justification is perhaps admirable, it is nevertheless based on the assumption that the powerful urban bureaucrat inevitably knows what is best for the poor uneducated peasantry. The same bureaucrats are rarely concerned with improving the ability of the peasantry to look after their own interests.

The second and more subtle thread of the opposition to the lease, sale and purchase of land follows close on the heels of this suspect paternalism. The lease, sale and purchase of land would entail change in the identity of those in control of the land, temporarily in the case of lease and permanently in the case of sale. As long as the 'landowners' are an ill-informed peasantry, confused as to the meaning of their ownership rights and subjugated to the whims of the farm management, they and the land they own remain firmly under the practical control of the farm directors and their political masters. As noted above, the latter have old ties of interdependence which sustain their mutually vested interests. Exchange rights would enable the ownership and control of land to pass to newcomers, who may choose to exercise a more muscular form of ownership, ignoring the political and economic demands of those who continue to enjoy *de facto* monopoly control over land. It seems likely that the moratorium is intended to prevent change, specifically the concentration of landownership in hands over which they have no effective control.

On the other hand, there is a strong argument (supported by some very senior policy makers) that one of the chief mechanisms for increasing efficiency through private ownership is the possibility of concentrating landownership in the hands of the few, in order to enable an unfettered landowner to take responsibility, take risks and attract investment. It is certainly true that one of the critical benefits of private landownership is the facilitation of movement of resource use from the less efficient to the more efficient. In order for this movement to occur, ownership must include exchange rights. More recently, proposals for effecting exchange rights in land are being developed, as the exchange rights of private ownership are increasingly acknowledged as necessary for increased efficiency. However, again, legislators and policy makers continue to evince their belief in a value system based in production. Draft laws inevitably include formula for assessing the (cash) value of land for sale or lease.[5] This assessment is inevitably based on evaluation of the productivity of the land concerned, i.e. on the value of the average yield for land of this type and quality. The notion that land is worth the price agreed between a willing buyer and a willing seller, or between a willing lessor and a willing lessee, is a novel one. Although policy makers are becoming more aware of the need to accord exchange rights to landowners, their insistence on controlling exchanges evinces their fear of 'free exchange rights' and attendant loss of control.

Thus far we have discussed the confusion over the identity of the landowner(s) and the confusion over the definition of the rights and responsibilities which attend landownership. I want to continue with a discussion of the relation between labour and landownership, and conclude with a discussion of the importance of 'practice' for establishing the nature of people: land relations.

LAND AND LABOUR

As noted above, landownership in Ukraine (as in other parts of the FSU) is firmly linked to labour, i.e. the right to own land is based on evidence that one is currently employed in labour on the land or on evidence that one was employed on the land prior to retirement. This is hardly surprising as the entire concept of citizenship in the FSU was linked to labour. Both juridical and practical rights to housing, education, health care were securely linked not just to employment in general, but to officially registered employment in a given enterprise. Indeed the 1936 Constitution declared:

Work in the USSR is a duty, a matter of honour for every able-bodied citizen – He who does not work, shall not eat. (quoted in Lane 1987: 14)

As the ideological basis for citizenship was based on labour, it is not surprising that the definition of entitlement to new rights (e.g. landownership) has also been based on labour. What is interesting is the way in which the definition of those rights themselves continues to be based on labour. As noted above, when landownership is linked to occupation, use and labour, there is a general consensus about the rights of the landowners (as individuals or as a collective) to retain the profits which accrue from their landownership *and* their labour. The right of landowners to retain the profits which accrue from the sale or lease of, or from trade in land, are subject to considerable dispute. Indeed both the Land Code and the Law on Private Peasant Farms specify that a Private Peasant Farmer may lease his or her land, only when he or she is incapacitated, and/or when he or she is called away on official duties (e.g. to serve in the army or in a government office to which they have been appointed or elected). These laws specify to whom the land may be leased, and define the terms of the lease. Similarly a Collective Agricultural Enterprise (CAE) may lease *unused* land; in practice a CAE would need to *prove* that they are unable to make productive use of the land, in order to acquire official permission for land leasing.[6] Here, the need to ensure that the land remains productive overrides resistance to leasing as such. As the later Presidential Decree on Land Leasing is more permissive, many officials prefer to quote the more conservative Land Code, in order to maintain control over the exchange and use of land. Thus, by giving ownership of the land to those who labour on the land and by restricting the exchange of land (by sale or lease), the connection between labour and ownership is maintained. As noted above, this reflects a continuation of the ideological commitments of Soviet policy; it is sustained by the support of bureaucrats and farm directors in defence of mutually vested interests. It is also supported by the new landowners themselves.

Here it is useful to examine the distinction between the relations people have with their small household plots (individual subsidiary holdings), and the relations they have with the land occupied and/or owned by the collective of which they are a member. Private household plots are usually located around the house, or at a short distance. People grow fruit and vegetables, and often rear livestock. These small plots of land have always been 'their own', even though they have only recently received legally ratified 'ownership' of these plots. The produce has traditionally been theirs to consume or to sell at the *kolkhoz* markets. The produce/income generated by these private plots has always been important to the household economy, supplementing the meagre incomes derived from employment on the collective farm. At present, with the large CAEs struggling to survive in market conditions, these household plots have acquired enormous significance, often making the difference between a reasonable subsistence and utter destitution.

Research conducted in Ukraine[7] at the end of 1998 shows that:

- 97.4 per cent of the rural population have some land for their private use;
- the average size of household plots is 0.44 ha;
- 42 per cent have one plot of land, of which 65% are owned by householders;
- 37 per cent have two plots of land, of which 40% own only one plot; 27% own both plots;
- 21 per cent have three plots of land, of which 21% own one plot; 34% own all three plots.

Production in this sector is greater than would be imagined from the overall quantity of land under private plots.

Agricultural land in Ukraine amounts to 34,890,500 ha, of which land under private plots amounts to 5,604,400 ha. Produce from private plots accounted for the following percentages of national production in 1997:

- 97 per cent of national production of potatoes;
- 82 per cent of national production of vegetables;
- 76 per cent of national production of fruit and berries;
- 65 per cent of national production of meat;

- 63 per cent of national production of eggs;
- 61 per cent of national production of milk and dairy products;
- 44 per cent of national production of wool.

The survey shows that over 90 per cent of rural households depend almost wholly on the produce from their household plots for their own consumption needs. Further, 66 per cent of rural households acquire some part of their cash incomes from sales from private plots. The proportion of rural household incomes derived from sales of surplus from household plots ranges from 3 per cent to 100 per cent with a median 56 per cent. Cash incomes range from 1 to 650 Ukrainian *hryvna* (UAH)[8] per household per month (median 62.50 UAH per month).

During the course of the survey, it became crystal clear that the maintenance of the household plot has shifted from a peripheral activity to the main activity of most of the rural population, including senior farm managers and administrators. Table 8.1 shows the time invested in household plots.

Table 8.1 Time spent working on household plots

	Hours per week							
	Winter period				Summer period			
	Min.	Max.	Average	Median	Min.	Max.	Average	Median
Household – all	2	300	47	40	4	380	88	80
Women	1	105	29	25	2	210	54	50
Men	1	210	26	21	2	220	46	42
Per capita	1	90	21	20	2	112	38	37

As we can see from Table 8.1, household plots occupy a substantial proportion of people's time and are the most significant source of both food and cash incomes. It is also significant that household plots are invariably tidy, free of weeds and evince the care and attention that is lavished upon them. Household livestock look healthy and well-fed. Indeed almost all statistical analyses (including Soviet-era analyses), which compare the productivity of household plots and livestock to productivity in the collective sector, indicate that the former are more productive by a wide margin. It is, however, frequently argued that that the greater productivity of the household plots is intimately linked to the opportunity for 'free' inputs and is therefore dependent on continued association with the collective. This is indeed the case and continued formal employment on disintegrating CAEs continues to be valued as the sole mechanism for maintaining household plots. The CAEs may not pay wages, but they do distribute grain and other produce to members, which are necessary for feeding household livestock. Where quantities distributed are insufficient, theft is rife. Indeed in current circumstances, most farm directors turn a blind eye to theft, recognising that household plots and livestock are the sole means of subsistence for most of the local population.

The 'meaning' of the household plot can only be fully appreciated in comparison with the overall air and appearance of collectively owned/occupied land and livestock. Once outside the private plot, weeds and rubbish compete in unhappy profusion everywhere and anywhere. Similarly, labour on 'collective land' (and there is little practical difference whether this land is 'owned' by the collective or whether land share certificates have been distributed), is haphazard and profoundly careless. Workers watch idly as a combine sprays grain back into the field, causing huge harvest losses. They shrug helplessly as they shovel worthless straw into the feeding troughs of skinny cattle. They toss rubbish outside their front gate, inside of which all is neatly stacked and conserved.

It seems clear that the confused, abstract juridical relation between people and land which emerges in the course of 'land reform' is in fact of little practical interest to those who are on the receiving end. This lack of interest is linked partly to lack of knowledge and understanding of the rights and obligations that attend this new form of land–people relations. This lack of understanding is firmly linked to the contradictory and confused nature of the legislation and to the inconsistent and competing interpretations of that legislation. It is also linked to the cynical certainty that any change is bound to be for the worse and/or that any potential benefits will accrue not to the new owners of land but to the traditionally powerful echelons of farm directors and local authority bureaucrats. Even if the recipients know that 'share ownership' gives them a right to a share of profits from that land, they also know that either there will be no profits, or that, if there are any profits, they'll never know there were. The rights of ownership may well include the right to a share of profits, but as those profits are contingent on so many factors out of their control, the possibility is simply irrelevant. These factors range from the arbitrary decisions of the state (to forbid sale of grain outside the *oblast*, to withhold payments for delivery of grain on state orders, to increase taxes), to the dishonesty of the farm management (distorting the books), to the lack of faith in co-workers to pull their weight in collective productive endeavour.

The lack of active interest in 'land reform' is also linked to the reasoned assessment of the poor chances of successful small-scale Private Peasant Farming on individualised, privately owned plots. During my own early work on former *kolkhoz* and *sovkhoz*, I was surprised by the lack of enthusiasm for land reform or for the new opportunities for rural enterprise. Farm members frequently said that they 'didn't want a land share', because it is impossible to be productive on 5–20 ha in the absence of a supportive infrastructure (i.e. adequate access to credit, inputs, transport or markets). Thus, without the real possibility of occupying and managing privately owned land successfully, the potential right to do so remains irrelevant. For any individual, these factors combine to preclude not just realisation of private ownership rights and obligations, but to preclude any desire to engage in a hopeful relation.

From a policy-making standpoint, it is difficult to see how the inherent contradictions of the land reform process can be resolved. The socially just distribution of landownership creates many owners of small quantities of land. There is reasoned resistance to the fragmentation of large-scale land holdings and production, by almost all participants from top to bottom. Yet the attempt to resolve the contradiction with the invention of 'collective share ownership' has been unsuccessful both because it is inadequately conceptualised, and because it fails to stimulate necessary change. And so the large-scale collective enterprises continue to operate, but with decreasing success, caught in a downward spiral of inefficiency, debt and looming collapse. This downward spiral further alienates already alienated workers, who withdraw their time, their labour and their attention, steal what's left and concentrate on their household plots. In the effort to avoid universal 'fragmentation' into thousands of 5–20 ha Private Peasant Farms, policy makers have created the conditions in which fragmentation is not only occurring anyway, but is occurring at the micro-scale of the tiny household plot. (See Shlapentokh 1989 on the process of atomisation in general in the FSU.)

CONCLUSION

This book explores and expands on the dichotomy between the imagined, mythical attachment to land of 'pre-industrial', 'pre-modern', 'pre-capitalist' societies and the rational, juridical relation to land of the industrial, modern, capitalist self/other. This examination of changing land relations in the Ukraine is intended to shed light on the assumed universality of these opposing forces. The absence of rational juridical relations to land does not necessarily imply the existence of mythical attachments to land. The reader will have noted the absence of any reference to mythical attachments to land, based in myths of origin, or in animation of the landscape. The closest we can find to a mythical attachment to land is reflected in the concept of *rodina*. *Rodina* means one's native land, and usually refers to one's native village, or, more occasionally, to the Ukraine as a whole (as the native land of the Ukrainian people). This concept is sometimes used ideally, as an expressive attachment of people to a socially meaningful space ('I am happy to be home in my *rodina*'). These references to '*rodina*' are expressions of affection, for one's native soil, one's family and for the security of a known space. They are not however underpinned by anything approaching the usual anthropological understandings of the mythical or the ritual. I have been working with rural populations in Russia and Ukraine for six years and have never encountered an understanding of land as anything mystical. In fact the concept of '*rodina*' is more often used in a more overtly political way, for example, to denounce private ownership or, more specifically, land sales

('How can one buy and sell one's *rodina?*'). Many a Communist Party agitator will refer to '*rodina*', to justify opposition to land reform, thinly masking mundane self-interest in things staying as they are, with all the ongoing opportunities for corruption and control.

We have discussed in detail the confused and confusing efforts to create or avoid the creation of new juridical land relations. We have seen that juridical does not necessarily mean rational, as laws are passed which defy logical interpretation. Juridical rationality is regularly undermined by political interests. We have also seen that the development of juridical land relations is not necessarily associated with rational economic exploitation, as the imagined benefits of privatisation are regularly undermined by failure to accord owners all the rights normally associated with private ownership, or adequately to define the subject or the object of the ownership relation. Commodification of land is avoided, further reducing its economic potential.

In Ukraine, and indeed throughout the former Soviet Union, it is the combination of human labour and land, which feeds and sustains, which is the central pivot on which people–land relations are constructed. Occasional references to 'ownership by God' pale into insignificance when compared to the overwhelming importance of human labour in the formation of meaningful land. The labour–land conjunction is sustained on the one hand by the ideological valuation of labour during the 70 years of the Soviet period, complemented by a deeper history of labouring peasantry. If we refer back to the rights associated with landownership, we note that the right to receive a return on land is uncontested as long as the ownership of the land is accompanied by labour on the land. There is virtually no opposition to the notion that the worker/owner should receive a return. There is only sporadic opposition to the notion that a pensioner should receive a return on their land, as long as the pensioner has contributed labour to the farm in the past. There is, however, considerable opposition to the receipt of a return on landownership, dissociated from labour. The reluctance on the part of the authorities to accord exchange rights to landowners is complemented by the population's own opposition to returns dissociated from labour (rent or sale income). This historical/ideological foundation for the land–labour conjunction is animated and enlivened by the real, practical, physical engagement of body and soil on the household plot, for 40 hours each week, 52 weeks a year – an engagement which provides food and a future.

It could theoretically be argued that the labour–land conjunction approaches the mythico-ritual in opposition to rational commodification, by attributing mythico-ritual status to the moral justification for the land–labour conjunction. For example, it is morally acceptable to labour on land and receive a return, but morally unacceptable to receive a return on land disconnected from any labour input, present or past. Even here however, moral justification for the land–labour relation varies from the non-existent to the politically expedient to the genuinely felt, depending on subject and on context. As the indigenous perception of the labour–land relation is intensely physical, practical and indeed rational in the context of uncertain alternatives, and as the relation is not associated with a consistent discursive 'explanation', much less with a traditionally mythical 'explanation', I cannot stretch my own understanding of the mythico-ritual to encompass Ukrainian people–land relations.

I would suggest that this absence of a consistent mythico-ritual attachment to land is, like the absence of a rational juridical relation to land, the product of a history of change, of violent upheavals and of the ongoing collision between rhetorical political aims and the confusions of real-world practice. Ukraine is a society in the throes of dramatic change. It cannot easily be categorised as either 'modern' or 'pre-modern'. It has been industrialised, but much of its industry has collapsed leaving the majority of the population engaged in subsistence agriculture. It is neither 'pre-capitalist', 'capitalist' nor 'developed capitalist'. It is post-Soviet and definitely 'transitional', although its 'transitional' status threatens to become a permanent classifi-cation, in spite of transitory connotations. As such, it is not easily classifiable. It is a society which exhibits a complex range of contradictions, in which people–land relations cannot be categorised as either mythico-ritual or rational-juridical. The closest representation we can offer on present evidence is a practical, 'sweat and bread' relation where sweat and labour are invested in the land, which in turn produces the bread that enables further investment of sweat and labour. If there is a resistance to commodification of land, this is not related to its mythico-ritual status, but to the ability of the land to feed and sustain. Land may be classically a 'means of production', but it is more meaningfully the essential 'means of reproduction'.

NOTES

1. 'Point hectares' are used to ensure that individuals acquire ownership of land of equal value, taking into account soil quality and sometimes also location. Thus although each land share will be equal in 'point hectares', this might translate into 5 hectares of high-quality land for one individual and 5.5 hectares of poorer-quality land for another, should the land ever be demarcated into individually owned parcels.
2. Ukraine is divided into administrative units called *oblasts* (comparable to county or province), which are further subdivided into *raions* (comparable to districts).
3. Private Peasant Farms are officially registered enterprises, usually family owned and managed. They are treated as juridical entities and are subject to the payment of taxes, budgetary contributions, etc.
4. Even during Soviet times, most collective farm workers enjoyed the use of a small (average *c.* 0.04 ha) 'private plot', on which they could grow food for household consumption, selling any surplus in the '*kolkhoz* markets'. Even Soviet statistics generally showed that these private plots were far more efficiently managed than the collectively worked land holdings.
5. In fact, although the draft Law on Land Leasing did include such formulae, the Presi-dential Decree on Land Leasing (23 April 1997) does *not* stipulate the value of land rents except for lands owned by the state or municipal agencies.

6. In practice however, CAEs often lease small quantities of land for a season to highly productive itinerants, often Koreans.
7. This research included interviews with over 700 members of the rural population on 20 CAEs in five *oblasts* (see Perrotta 1999a, 1999b).
8. At the time of fieldwork (Oct. and Nov. 1998), the exchange rate was 3.50 UAH/US$1.

REFERENCES

Brooks, K. (ed.) 1996. *Agricultural Reform in Russia: A View from the Farm Level.* World Bank Discussion Papers No. 327. Washington, DC: World Bank.
Chmatko, N. 1994. 'Les agriculteurs Russes faces aux changements economiques', *Information sur les Sciences Sociales* 33(2).
Lane, D. 1987. *Soviet Labour and the Ethic of Communism: Full Employment and the Labour Process in the USSR.* Brighton: Wheatsheaf.
Perrotta, L. 1995. 'Aid agencies, bureaucrats and farmers: divergent perceptions of rural development in Russia', *Cambridge Anthropology* 18(2).
—— 1998. 'Divergent responses to land reform and agricultural restructuring in the Russian federation', in S. Bridger and F. Pine (eds) *Local and Regional Responses to Transition in Eastern Europe.* London: Routledge.
—— 1999a. 'The size and structure of rural household incomes in Ukraine', USAID funded Center for Privatization and Economic Reform in Agriculture, Kiev, Ukraine.
—— 1999b. 'Individual subsidiary holdings – the micro-economics of subsistence in Ukraine', USAID funded Center for Privatization and Economic Reform in Agriculture, Kiev, Ukraine.
Shlapentokh, V. 1989. *Public and Private Life of the Soviet People: Changing Values in Post-Stalinist Russia.* New York and Oxford: Oxford University Press.
Van Atta, D. 1993. *The Farmer Threat: The Political Economy of Agrarian Reform in Post-Soviet Russia.* Boulder, CO: Westview Press.
Wegren, S. 1992. 'Two steps forward, one step back: the politics of an emerging new rural social policy in Russia', *Soviet and Post-Soviet Review* 19(1–3).
—— 1994. 'Farm privatisation in Nizhnii Novgorod: the model for Russia?', *RFE/RL Research Report* 3(21).
—— 1995. 'The development of market relations in agricultural land: the case of Kostroma Oblast', *Post Soviet Geography* 36(8).
—— 1996a. 'Rural politics and agrarian reform in Russia', *Problems of Post-Communism* 43(1).
—— 1996b. 'The politics of private farming in Russia', *Journal of Peasant Studies* 23(4).
Wegren, S. with Durgin, F.A. 1995. 'Why agrarian reform is failing', in *Transition* 1(19).

9 THE RE-APPROPRIATION OF SAKAI LAND: THE CASE OF A SHRINE IN RIAU (INDONESIA)

Nathan Porath

Recent writers on land have taken up the notion of landscape as something which has meaning for the identity of local populations (Bender 1993; Tilley 1994; Hirsch and O'Hanlon 1995; Fox 1997). These writings try to pull the notion of landscape away from its ideological European meanings of an aestheticised natural scene presented to the senses, to be looked at, its air imbibed and image fantasised (Hirsch and O'Hanlon 1995; Schama 1995). Bender takes this position one step further by placing cultural meanings and symbols within historical moments of contestations between rival social factions (1993: 3). Landscape, she argues, is always re-negotiable. Bender also posits two general categories of discourse about space (land). One is of the power-holders; the other is of the local population to whom the discourse of the powerful is directed. Although these discourses of space are distinct, she points out that they share the same 'edges' (1993: 248). It is these 'edges' of discourses which are of interest in this chapter, since, for local populations, contesting claims to land may very well be couched not only in local mythical and legendary discourses (local landscapes), but also within the dominant discourses and their supporting legal apparatuses.

Writers on landscape suggest that there are many ways of experiencing landscapes. If so, we can also speak of the experiences of landscapes of dispossession. I understand landscapes of dispossession as areas of land which, although fraught with meaning for its inhabitants, have been expropriated and transformed by another politically defined group. The dispossesed are confined, settled in specific designated areas and prohibited from entering other areas. They are left only with a mental image of the land, a memory of what it once was like before the others had transformed it. Many indigenous landscapes which anthropologists work with are landscapes associated with some form of dispossession.

This chapter is concerned with the Sakai, a Malay-speaking indigenous people of Riau (Sumatra, Indonesia) who have had much of their traditional land legally (and on occasions, illegally) taken away from them. It must be noted, however, that the Sakai can be held partly accountable for their own

176

loss of land, since some Sakai families sell land in the ideological context of state development. I describe the general legal and developmental context in which Sakai dispossession was made possible, and go on to provide an example of a Sakai attempt at re-appropriating ancestral land on a traditional sacred site, the shrine of Grandfather White-Blood. The group of Sakai families attempting to re-appropriate the shrine and the surrounding land not only express their arguments and position in traditional discourses, but also within the very legal and developmental discourses, which originally dispossessed them in earlier years.

A LANDSCAPE OF DISPOSSESSION

The *Orang Sakai* (Sakai people) live in, and are indigenous to, an area between the recently constructed market village of Minas and the small market town of Duri. Historically, Malays called them Sakai. The exonym Sakai in the past had derogatory connotations of slavery and debt bondage. It was a term used by Malays for non-Muslim forest people. In Malaysia the term is not officially used anymore as the people it is applied to consider it an insult. Today the Sakai of Riau have come to accept the name Sakai and are ethnically identified as such by Indonesians. The people of Riau are descendants of once-autonomous Malay kingdoms. The Siak kingdom (*Kerajaan Siak*) was located on and around the great Siak River which flows east to the Malacca straits. Its political centre, the town of Siak Indrapura, was situated close to the mouth of the river. The Sakai ancestors lived on the periphery of the Siak kingdom as a semi-forest dwelling people. They represented part of the non-Muslim Malay population of the kingdom. Their area was the border region between the Siak kingdom and rival sister kingdom of the Rokan region, which are also part of Riau province. Today the province of Riau is claimed by the Indonesian Malay descendants of the inhabitants of these historical kingdoms. Also included in this ethno-political claim are the various peripheral ethnic groups, referred to in the Riau area as *Orang Asli* (indigenous peoples). One of these *Orang Asli* groups is the Sakai.

Historical accounts describe the forest-dwelling Sakai as living in administrative areas called *pebatin*, some of which were named after the rivers they flanked. The name of a *pebatin* was also the name given to its non-Muslim Malay inhabitants. The *pebatin*'s headman was officially referred to as *batin*. He was one of the local inhabitants and was officially appointed by the Sultan. Each *batin* (headman) was the representative of the *pebatin* population to the Sultan. There were 13 *pebatins*, which for historical reasons, were divided into two groups – *Batin limo* (the five batins) and *Batin selapan* (the eight batins). Malays called all these *pebatin* populations Sakai. The peoples themselves eschewed the word, however, and preferred instead to be known as *Orang Batin* (people of the *batin*). Although today they have more or less come to accept the exonym Sakai they still prefer to be called *Orang Asli* (indigenous people).

In a general sense the landscape of the Sakai is a landscape of dispossession lost in a landscape of development. The *pebatin* organisation hardly exists any more. When I first went to the area, I took out a turn-of-the-century map. People crowded to look at it. They fingered the map, following the lines representing the rivers trying to locate their traditional territories. It was a very emotional moment and I noticed that the eyes of some even began to glisten. Somebody – I think a non-Sakai Indonesian who was present at the time – sympathetically re-confirmed that their territory had certainly been large before the roads were built. The next day, this moment of landscape nostalgia, was put aside, and the people continued with their daily activities within the landscape of development that surrounds them. It is in this landscape of development that Sakai families have to work today, to make a living and re-appropriate the land. This is a type of landscape that anthropologists and indigenous people alike have to come to terms with.

A LANDSCAPE OF DEVELOPMENT IN RIAU

Starting out from Pekanbaru (the provincial capital) and running across the main rivers to cut right through the Sakai area is the 'Pekanbaru-Duri-Dumai' highway. An oil pipe which ends at the coastal town of Dumai accompanies the road. It is a common sight to see people's washing spread out along the pipe, left to dry in the sun. Pacing on the pipe can be the safest means of walking on the side of the busy highway.

The highway passes through a number of local market settlements, tin-roofed shops, eating-houses and food stalls managed by migrant vendors and traders selling vegetables, fish, meat, cosmetics, manufactured clothing and 'as advertised on TV' medicines. Also along the road are eating-houses that cater for passing inter-city bus travellers. Travelling along this road, there is a point where hilly remnants of forest territory can be seen, but the view quickly reverts to the more common scenery of oil pipes and stretches of cleared sand-dirt territory. Visible further away are the rising heads of Caltex oil rigs, shaped like bowing heads of pick-axes, which dot parts of the landscape in certain areas. Elsewhere along the road are stretches of palm-oil plantations and patches of rubber plantations owned by private shareholding companies. The Sakai population was forced to settle along this highway in the late 1960s and early 1970s when it was nothing more than a dirt road. Today it carries heavy logging trucks and Caltex oil-container trucks, buses, local village transport, minibuses, motorbikes and, if you like, bicycles too.

Dotting the edge of the highway are small, tin-roofed houses which accommodate tired and hungry truck drivers. Here, the truck drivers can break their journey eat drink and sleep. Some of these houses accommodate women who offer sexual services for a few rupiahs. The highway road also passes the notorious *komplek*: a settlement of tin-roofed timber houses lined in rows housing young Javanese prostitutes who service the local rural male population. Heavy music is sometimes played in the *komplek* on Saturday nights and local men visit to dance freely (*joget*) with the women, drink and indulge in other pleasures that a few rupiahs can buy. Well cut dirt roads, sometimes slippery with oil, extend eastwards and westwards off the main road into inner areas. These roads wind their way through forests of palm-oil and rubber plantations. They pass oil stations and lead up to settlements of tin-roofed box houses inhabited by plantation labourers and migrant settlers. They also lead up to the few inner Sakai settlements.

As a province of the modern state of Indonesia, Riau has come to host diverse ethnic groups from other parts of Sumatra, Indonesia and even further afield. In the Sakai area there is a large North Sumatran population, the Bataks, many of whom are Christian. There are also growing numbers of rural Sumatran-Javanese, rural Minang folk and a small population from the island of Nias, all of whom have come to the area in search of work and cheap available land. Further, small settlements of temporary plantation wage labourers have been brought to Riau for a few years to work on share-holding companies' (rubber, palm oil) plantations. An Indonesian middle class (Javanese, Malay, Batak, etc.) consisting of mobile professionals and white-collar office workers is also prominent. Akin to them and the models who, in many respects, culturally define their modernity (Petras 1997: 187), are Western expatriates who work on contracts for the area's two state-owned oil companies (Caltex-Oil-Pacific and Pertamina). Members of these classes are often seen driving through the Sakai area. They sometimes follow a tradition going back to the 1970s of paying visits to the Sakai living on the edge of the main road and paying them for exotic photographs.

The Sakai live amidst all this in clusters of houses scattered between the area of Minas and Duri and the areas east and west of the road. Many of the Sakai settlements are on or near the edge of the road. Some are at the end of the dirt roads. Some live in ethnically mixed villages. Others live in large government-sponsored settlements of tin-roofed houses where large numbers are concentrated. Other settlements are break-away settlements consisting of a few raised thatched houses on the edge of the road or river. Clearly then, although the Sakai settlements extend between Minas and Duri, this territory today is not 'theirs'. Rather, they have become an indigenous minority population in what used to be a vast forest area which has been claimed and parcelled out among other Indonesians, ranging from the Indonesian state-owned oil companies, to various shareholding companies and Indonesian migrants. In their traditional territory, the Sakai have become a minority population, living in clusters of houses forming pocket settlements amidst a large migrant population throughout this area. This landscape of development is the Sakai landscape of dispossession.

LAND AND SMOKING MONEY

The Sakai are shifting cultivators, and also traditionally forest resource collectors. As in the past, today they make their living by gathering the produce of the forest to supply merchant demand. Individuals and families collect timber, rattan, bark, aloe wood, dammar and other forest products. The Sakai also use land to build houses, and for shifting cultivation. In the past, they did not really live in village settlements, but rather in scattered houses surrounded by their swidden fields and a patch of unfelled wild growth. Beyond these settlements, further houses dotted the felled landscape.

The Sakai cultivated cassava and, at times, rice, a practice they still engage in today. They practise shifting agriculture, using the land for a few years, then they move on to another location, leaving the land to fallow. They sometimes leave the unharvested crops and return for them at a later date. Fruit trees are also planted. The fruit trees are the property of the person who planted them. Fruit trees can mark ownership of land if the person who planted them is also the person who reclaimed the land. However, people who once squatted on another person's land and who planted fruit trees there, will still return to pick fruit from these trees even though they may have moved elsewhere. The tree is still their property although the land is not. Thus, conceptually, ownership of fruit trees is seen as distinct from the ownership of the land that the trees are planted on. In a time when land was more abundant, fruit trees were clear signs of who originally *worked* the land.

In Sakai customary land tenure, each family which works unclaimed land for their immediate usage is considered its current owner. After the death of the original owners who reclaimed it, the land can pass to the children, and the eldest sibling is placed in charge of it. Beyond the second generation the land returns to the pool of communal land reserve. Families have the right to reclaim it, if they are of the community and/or descendants of the previous occupiers (*hak ulayat*). They also had to receive the permission of the community's elders. To claim new land from primary forest, the interested Sakai party used to notify the *batin* (headmen) who would ask the permission of the Sultan of Siak.[1] The Sultan would then send a letter of permission granting the newly acquired land to the *pebatin* population. Today, Malays and educated 'town' Sakai who are concerned about the indigenous population's land plight may show historical and more recent governmental documents granting land to a group of people for their own use or settlement. Shareholding company representatives present their HGU (right to clear land for exploitation) and retort, 'This is now Indonesia'.

Writing on a similar indigenous people of southern Riau, Turner (1997) and Effendy (1997) reveal that the Patalangan see themselves as the gatekeepers of the local forests. During my fieldwork there were hints from the Sakai that they also regarded themselves as such. Thus, the wild produce of the forests is not really seen today as anyone's property unless claimed. Once there is a demand for a product, the people who invest their time in harvesting and delivering it are its owners until it is passed on for payment. In this manner Sakai individuals and families make a living and obtain money, which they call *uang rokok* (smoking money) in Indonesian. The term implies a small amount of money to be spent immediately for the purchase and consumption of commodities from the local shop, particularly clove cigarettes, as well as food and commodities for the coming days. In logging young Sakai men make even larger amounts of money. People with money thus earned can buy more expensive goods such as televisions, stereos, cassettes, clothes and gold jewellery.

One money-producing commodity for which there is a major demand is land. Just as consumer goods are in demand by Sakai, land is in demand by other Indonesians. Land which in the past would have lain fallow only to be reclaimed by a descendant's household can today become a major source of income for those Sakai families who want to move elsewhere. Since there is no prohibition against selling land, male heads of households can sell land for their households' benefit. The money increases families' purchasing power. They can buy motorbikes, chainsaws, sofas, wall units, and they may even build a corrugated tin-roofed house without waiting for the government to give them one. All these goods are considered *lebih maju* (more 'progressed').

Batak migrants who invest their money in land, young palm-oil plants and opening commodity shops, ridicule the Sakai consumption of modern goods. They consider the Sakai ethnic group as a *bodoh* ('stupid', 'backward') people who sell their land to purchase commodities and returning to the forest with the goods. In actuality Sakai families may simply move to another settlement down the road. Some migrants who cannot afford commodities explain the Sakai rate of consumption of modern goods in terms of what they see as their 'lazy backwardness', which makes them live beyond their means.

Sakai do sell their land to obtain money to buy commodities, yet they also leave an area because of ethnic pressures and stigmatisation by migrants, especially by the North Sumatran Bataks. Based on experience, they have a general model of how the migrants from North Sumatra take over their land. First, an incoming Batak befriends them so succesfully that they adopt him as a sibling. He then purchases a stretch of land and invites some of his family to come over. Later, he begins to expand by purchasing more land. Finally, the migrant, thinking that Sakai are too stupid to notice, starts working unused Sakai land adjacent to his plot. The Sakai owner tries to claim it back. However, the Batak, supported by his kin and others of his ethnic group, turns around and claims that the land did not belong to anybody and that he has legitimately claimed it. Not wanting a confrontation, the Sakai shy away and the land becomes Batak land. Rising tensions then lead other Sakai families to sell their land, take the money and move elsewhere. Nevertheless, Sakai families are still receptive to friendly overtures by migrants to the area. Classificatory and affinal kinship ties are still established with newcomers and not all these relationships necessarily turn sour.

IDEOLOGIES OF LAND USE AND LAND LAW

Nationally, current Indonesian land law evolved from the Dutch Agrarian Act of 1870 (Colchester 1986: 104). The colonial government promulgated two systems of rights to ownership of land. For non-locals, ownership had to be determined in accordance with civil law, which demanded survey, registration and land-titling following European principles (MacAndrews 1986: 19). For locals, the colonial government believed that it recognised claims to ownership of land in accordance with the local customary (*adat*) laws of each specific region (1989: 20). In both systems landowners had to show some proof of ownership, either through use, occupation or a verbal or written account. The colonial government and its various representatives, however, misconstrued customary ownership of land. They built their theories of landownership on European landholding ideas. Land tenure practices which involved leaving cultivated land to lie fallow for many years was ultimately understood in terms of relinquishment. Such land was considered vacant (*terra nullius*). This led colonial legal theorists to treat the land of shifting cultivators as flexible and falling short of full ownership (Wong 1975: 13). The Dutch Agrarian Land Act thus legally dispossessed shifting cultivators of much of their land reserve. The only land that was considered theirs was the land they lived on or showed signs of using continuously (Colchester 1986: 105; Haverfield 1999: 53).

The Agrarian Land Act was kept after Indonesia's independence in 1945, but was abolished in 1960. The new law recognised that local customary land tenure practices should prevail as long as they did not interfere with the interests of the nation-state. Wherever customary law did not correspond to the national laws and regulations, then custom was to be adjusted. Moreover, all exploitation of natural resources was to be regulated by the state (MacAndrews 1986: 22), which saw itself as representing and defending the rights and interests of the total (Indonesian) population living within its national boundaries. The Land Act reserves the right for the state to dismiss customary laws and practices if it sees them unfit or threatening in accordance with the interests of the nation-state and its ideologies (Colchester 1986: 105; Haverfield 1999: 51; Lindsey 1999: 15).

State ideologies and policies perceive shifting-cultivators' customary use of land to be inefficient and primitive (Dove 1985) and to hamper more productive commercial exploitation. Shifting cultivation is blamed for forest fires, land erosion and other natural calamities (1985: 3). Dove has called this official government view a 'Javanese agroecological myth' that serves the political economy of the Indonesian state. According to the same author, this negative attitude towards shifting cultivation is rooted in the traditional Javanese political attitude towards agriculture which favoured wet-rice cultivation and from which the territorially large Indic Javanese kingdoms extracted large proportions of the produce.

Shifting-cultivators however cultivate for their own subsistence and their mobility made them ungovernable. They could evade taxation and state coercion by escaping to the forest subsisting on hunting and gathering as well as shifting agriculture. This evasion was seen as a form of resistance and protest against the power of the state, or even as a challenge to it. Usurpers could mobilise the frustrated population from within the forests against the political centre. In the Javanese kingdoms, wet-rice cultivation was associated with the rise and development of the Javanese state, order, culture and civilisation. In contrast, the forests were associated with the wild, the uncontrolled and ungovernable. Shifting-cultivators suggested an alternative subsistence economy without the presence of the state order. From the Javanese political centre's point of view, swidden fields were still considered as jungle (Dove 1985: 20, n.77). According to Dove, the present state of Indonesia retains this prejudice against shifting-cultivators and acts towards them accordingly (1985: 21). Ownership rights of land lying fallow can be declared null if the land is not legally registered. It is then repossessed by the state (*Tanah negara*) and can be legally claimed for exploitation by interested parties.

Evolutionary models drawn from European 'travelling' theories (Said 1983) about human diversity underlie the official Indonesian understanding of tribal communities. Such communities are not understood as cultural populations in their own right; they are evaluated in terms of their alleged primitiveness (Colchester 1986: 94). The diverse populations have been officially lumped under the term *masyarakat terrasing*, which means 'isolated' or 'alien' or 'outsider' society (Persoon 1990). They are considered to possess a pre-village form of social organisation, which verges from the main course of Indonesian cultural development. Consequently, they have become targets of development policies that try to coerce them into conforming through assimilation and integration within the nation state of Indonesia (Colchester 1986: 89).

During Indonesia's New Order period under President Suharto (1966–98) resistance to state policies provoked disparaging comments and risked people being defined as anti-Indonesian. Resistance even called forth military intervention. Concerned scholars writing during the 1980s noted that, over time, military intervention and bureaucratic stigmatisation of local people can create a sense of cultural inferiority, and lead to the destruction of self-respect and of cultural values (Apell 1985: 9, 89; Colchester 1986: 95). With respect to the Sakai, populations were 'persuaded' to leave the forest interior in order to claim land at the edge of the highway and be closer to the development intended for the area. This is how their areas in the forest interior became vacant. By the 1990s, much of the original Sakai lands of the forest interior – the lands they had been 'persuaded' to leave vacant – had been legally parcelled up. Moreover, the traditional *pebatin* system has been totally smashed and no longer really exists. Instead, the Sakai are well incorporated into the modern developing rurality of the area and the main road gives them their orientation. Inland secondary-growth forest areas, which were convenient for settlements when traffic was river focused, are nowadays seen as not very appropriate places to live. Sakai will claim that these areas are too far, there are no roads and no transport to them.

A MYSTICAL LANDSCAPE OF SPIRITS AND DEVELOPMENT

When the Sakai left the forest to live on the edge of the road, they also left behind them their spiritual-mystical landscape. For the Sakai the natural environment hosts another reality of beings called *antu* (*hantu*) or spirits. Spirits are located at certain places within the natural topography of the area. They usually live in dense forest, a thicket in the woods, a large spectacular tree or a natural hole in the ground.

Spiritual-mystical landscapes should be understood as more than landscapes imbued with local meaning and belief. For the Sakai, some spirits are associated with the natural topographies of the land which are alleged to have effected or still have the power to effect the unconscious and conscious experience of people. For instance, a person (Sakai or non-Sakai) walks by a tree, and for the next few days he or she suffers from disturbed sleep, lucid dreams, obsessive longings to return to the site, hallucinations and experiences of an altered state of consciousness. Although spirits are associated with natural formations of the landscape, they move in different dimensions (*alam lain*). Their space is like the space experienced by people in dreams: a space in which they can move like a flash from one location to another. In fact, the distance between 'spirit countries' (*nego'i antu*) associated with dense forest thickets in the woods or riverine locations, and a Sakai settlement, wherever this may be, is very small.

Many of these spiritual-mystical locations which the Sakai associate with spirits have been interfered with or uprooted during the development process of the area. They form part of the Sakai landscape of dispossession. Natural locations which harboured 'spirit countries' today have a plantation or a human settlement built on them. Nevertheless, for Sakai, since spirits live in another dimension, the destruction of the physical landscape does not effect the ontological existence of spirits. The latter can simply move to another place and cause havoc elsewhere.

The Sakai say that spirits, like people, sometimes stand their ground and fight against the development process. A large tree at the entrance to one of the earlier Sakai settlements set up by the government was not cut down, as it was purported to be the abode of a spirit. People began to fall ill and the various afflictions were attributed to the malevolence of the tree-dwelling spirit. A local Muslim mystic (*kalipa*) was called to perform a ritual in which he circumambulated the tree seven times while reciting passages from the Koran. The confrontation of the spirit with Islam forced the spirit to move to another location and the afflictions of the spirit abated. This is further elucidated by the story of a Javanese logger. This man was told by the locals that a particular large tree housed a spirit. He did not believe them. The night before he intended to cut the tree down, he suffered from disturbing dreams which he understood to be the spirit inhabiting the tree warning him not to cut it down. The Javanese logger left the tree standing.

As part of the Sakai spiritual-mystical environment, shrines, ancestral graveyards and other legendary sites contain Spiritual presences. Sakai and Malays categorise these sites as sacred or *keramat*. *Keramat* (an Arabic-derived term) is a magical quality attributed to an object like a grave, or natural formations, such as trees, rocks or hills (cf. Winstedt 1924, Skeat 1965 [1900]). The greater inter-regional Malay cultural area is dotted with places that are attributed with magical-mystical *keramat* qualities. Unlike locations associated with spirits who can be a nuisance to people, *keramat* places usually contribute to the well-being of the local population. However, to do so, they have to be looked after.

... AND A SHRINE ...

Lying on the bank of the Penaso River, is the sacred burial shrine (*mokam keramat*) of (Old Man) Grandfather White-Blood (*Datuk Bu'da'a Putih*). The shrine is the burial place of a highly revered and influential man of the *pebatin* people who today would be called a Sakai. According to the Sakai, Grandfather White-Blood was born in the *pebatin Penaso*, but moved to *pebatin Paoh* after marriage. His body magically floated back to the Penaso area after his death and naturally buried itself at the site where it now lies. The white blood running through Grandfather White-Blood's veins was evidence of his uniqueness. In the Malayo/Indonesian world, only people with special powers like the Sultan and his family were believed to have white blood (Errington 1987). According to Sakai lore, Grandfather White-Blood served the Sultan of Siak as a high court-guard (*hulubalang*). He was assigned to protect the king's daughter on her travels within the kingdom. When they reached the river of his own *pebatin* of birth (*Sungai Penaso*), according to one account, Grandfather White-Blood 'married' the princess.[2] Thus, this man of the *Orang Batin* (*batin* people) is believed to embody the ritual substance of kings.

The Sakai belief of Grandfather White-Blood's ancestral shrine is part of the wider Malay belief in specific legendary figures attributed with saint-like qualities.[3] British colonial writers on the Malay peninsula counted 51 *keramat* locations including three graves of magicians, six graves of settlement founders and 12 graves of Muslim saints (Winstedt 1924). In 1900, Skeat noted that one of the graves in the Malaya peninsula was the burial place of an indigenous non-Muslim Sakai from the Malay peninsula (1924: 70). Some Malaysian *keramat* graves are also reputed to have animal guardians. Moreover, although these graves are considered sacred, many had no real distinguishing mark other than the offerings left at them (1924: 61–71). Furthermore, according to Winstedt when the persons buried in the *keramat* graves were alive they 'often [bore] the hallmark of some physical peculiarity ... all [had] mysterious powers and some [could] perform miracles' (1924: 264). In this general Malay perspective, Grandfather White-Blood's grave is a Riau (Sakai) *Keramat* grave and should be understood as part of this greater traditional Malay cultural shrine-complex recognised by these earlier writers on the peninsula, and also found on Java (see Hock Tong 1998, Boomgaard 1995).

To look at, the shrine of Grandfather White-Blood is just a small burial mound surrounded by trees. However, the mound is considered magical ground possessing very strong powers. People visit the shrine to ask Grandfather White-Blood for aid in healing and for other personal requests. They also state what they will give in return if the request is granted. Sometimes, they leave a small offering before leaving the mound. If the offering disappears within three days then Grandfather White-Blood is believed to have consumed it. Even if the offering remains at the shrine it is considered to have been consumed in its refined (spiritual) form, thus rendering it ownerless. The first passer-by to see the offering is then entitled to consume it. Alternatively, an animal may be ritually slaughtered and shared by the community after Grandfather White-Blood has consumed the meat in its refined spiritual form.

There are no pilgrimages to the shrine. Neither are there any cults relating to the shrine or large-scale visits to it. In fact, some people avoid it unless they have a request to make. The shrine is a burial place of a highly respected magic-man of the *pebatin,* who, on his death, returned to it to become a living element of the land, with whom the living can still communicate.

In accordance with the colonial descriptions quoted above, until recently, the mound existed as a patch of raised earth, without any real distinguishing marks other than its presence, its accompanying displays of offerings and a shared consciousness of its living presence. Although a powerful living reality of the land, it was not bounded and physically set apart from it. Sakai believe that animals avoid the mound and even trees felled by the wind are said to fall to its left, or to its right, but not directly upon it. Moreover, the burial mound has its own particular forest guardians in the form of a tiger, elephant and a crocodile. The latter lives in the river, metamorphosing into a white cat when visiting the shrine. These forest guardians are imbued with an awareness of Grandfather White-Blood's shrine and his descendants, who can call on them for help.

RE-APPROPRIATING THE SHRINE AND FENCING IT

During the mid-1990s, one respected old and blind shaman living on the edge of the road had a dream calling him to re-enter the woods and protect the shrine of Grandfather White-Blood (*Datuk Bu'Da'a Putih*). The shrine was lying in a secondary-growth wooded area designated for a shareholder company palm-oil plantation. The blind shaman was once the *batin* (headman) of the area before being allegedly cheated out of the position by thumb-printing an agreement he could not read.[4] The group of families originally brought together by the shaman and his wife for the purpose of protecting the shrine, consisted of two generations of siblings and their spouses who were cognatically descended from him (his children and grand-children). The families claimed to be descended from the historico-legendary magic-man reputed to be buried under the mound. Their aim was to protect the shrine and a nearby abandoned graveyard. They were also trying to reclaim the surrounding land to inhabit and cultivate.

Before their arrival at the shrine, this group of families used to squat on a small area of land by the road where a high concentration of Sakai families lived in a settlement of ethnically mixed migrants opposite the notorious *komplek*. They moved into an area and planted cassava fields, thus taking possession of land that had already been used by their *Orang Batin* forebears. This land is an important investment, since, if the group is ever evicted, they will have to be compensated. A year after their arrival they moved again. At the second location they cleared the woodland, erected their thatched houses alongside a partly abandoned dirt logging-track which led up to the river and the shrine and planted a second cassava field. Then, through networks with Sakai engaged in governmental development work, they managed to achieve official recognition of their settlement as a subdistrict of the admin-istrative village area under which it fell, on the basis of the shrine being a Sakai heritage site needing protection.

Just before the Sakai families re-appropriated this area, an ethnic-Chinese man visited the mound to ask Grandfather White-Blood for success in a business venture. He was successful and, in return, he placed many loaves of bread and biscuits on and around the shrine as an offering. He also placed a written sign next to the mound to mark the spot as a 'Sakai burial shrine'. The Sakai families followed his example. Working together as a group they chopped some wood, and built a small fence and a gate around the mound. The gate was locked and the key was kept by the shaman. The Sakai also erected a white post in front of the mound to mark the burial ground and shrine of Grandfather White-Blood. At the bottom was added the inscription '+ – 250 years' making Grandfather White-Blood's historico-legendary reality a dated historical event. A post was also placed in front of the abandoned graveyard, but it was not fenced. Since the graveyard was not as important as the mound, it was just left without any further markings.

The idea of fencing and creating boundaries has a central role in Sakai cosmological thinking and healing activities. For Sakai, physical objects have an unseen 'spiritual' side, which could potentially merge other objects affecting them beyond their physical boundaries. These permeating rela-tionships are considered as part of the natural process of the unseen world. Consequently, according to the Sakai cosmology, unboundedness leaves room for negative permeations. Hence, creating a fence (*paga'*) around the shrine was a novel attempt at emphasising its presence and protecting it.

The families who have moved into this area today have pulled themselves away from negative influences which development has brought to the region. However, in their attempt to protect the shrine, these families confront a new threat from the shareholder company. The shrine is embedded in land which the shareholder company wants to appropriate and the fence creates boundaries for the shrine to protect it from this encroachment. Keeping the shrine under lock and key (*di kunci*) symbolically expresses the very attempt at keeping and protecting the shrine from the property structures and material forces of development.

The shareholder company that is trying to claim and exploit the land surrounding the shrine put up some resistance to the presence of the Sakai families who have returned there. Company representatives occasionally visited the Sakai with military protection. They remind the Sakai that they are Indonesians and that they cannot simply return to the forest and disperse again.

In fact, the Sakai families are not interested in dispersing into the forests. They are trying to regain their rights, as indigenous Indonesians, to their ancestral land. On the other hand, the shareholder company representatives, who cannot challenge the settlement's official heritage status, nevertheless 'recommended' them not to reclaim further land surrounding the settlement. They have tried to persuade the Sakai families to move to another village, offering to build them houses if they do so. The Sakai families are not persuaded. Instead some of the original families planted their own palm-oil plots and began constructing a small mosque and cleared land for a school and a volley-ball pitch – all signs of a modern Muslim Indonesian village.

During late 1997 and early 1998 the shareholder company began to cut a dirt road through the woods which intersected with the logging track leading up to the shrine. This opened up new opportunities for obtaining land lying on the edge of this new road. More families joined the original group living by the shrine. Most of these families were related to the blind shaman's deceased siblings. These families brought with them two practising shamans (*kemantan*), one ritual drummer (*bidu*), two local representatives of Islam (*kalipa* mystics) and a midwife (*bidan*). Their customary village tasks were made official, on paper, by the headman (*kepala dusun*) of the settlement. One family opened a small shop selling basic food commodities.

In the beginning of 1999 (nine months after President Suharto stepped down from office), the headman (*kepala dusun*), with the help of a well-known local Malay philanthropist, petitioned the newly appointed Riau Governor for the land around the shrine. The last that I have heard is that the Sakai of '*Makam Jiat Keramat, Penaso Asal*' (The sacred shrine of Jiat, the origin of Penaso) were granted 2,000 ha of land surrounding the shrine for their own community use. However, as yet they do not know where the agreed boundaries of the land are.

NOT THE LAST WORD ...

In this chapter I explained the historical context in which a local group of Sakai families are trying to re-appropriate a shrine and its surrounding land. This re-appropriation occurs in a landscape of dispossession, in which Sakai resist encroachment, revitalise the meanings of land and demand legal rights based on those meanings and customary cultural practices. It becomes apparent that, within this historical complexity, the Sakai have basically had their lands legally (and at times illegally) pulled like a rug from under their feet, but they have also been active agents in the commodification of land (Chappell 1995). What makes the Sakai uncomfortable is the realisation that unregistered land that has been left vacant is often legally appropriated from them too.

Whether the Sakai families who reside by the Grandfather White-Blood shrine will fully succeed in preserving the land for local agricultural practices is yet to be seen and really depends on the priorities of the provincial government. Regardless of the final future outcome, this chapter has presented a historical moment in the biography (Kopytoff 1990) of the shrine and the surrounding land. In such moments, mystical landscapes, landscapes of dispossession and landscapes of development re-negotiate the meaning of land and reconstruct it into a contemporary, live-scape.

NOTES

I would like to thank Profesor R. Schefold, F. Colombijn of IIAS, Rob Aitken, Allen Abramson, Dimitrios Theodossopoulos and Sylvia Davis for their stimulating comments and suggestions.

1. In Siak the Sultan was not considered the owner of the land, if the community was Muslim. Non-Muslim communities like the Sakai, however, were officially not considered owners of the land they lived on. This was in accordance with Islamic law that prohibited non-Muslims from owning land. Hence, officially they were granted the right by the Sultan to live on and use the land which in legal theory belonged to the Sultanate, but which in practice was their own.
2. This is a reversal of the actual Sakai experience. In the past, a Malay nobleman had the right to stay in any Sakai house over night and 'marry' the household's daughter.
3. A well-known and famous *keramat* grave in Riau is that of Raja Ali Haji on the island of Tanjung Pinang (see Barnard 1997).
4. The man who took his place was a local indigenous Malay who later sold Sakai land to a shareholder company without communal consent and pocketed the money himself. Some Sakai told me that this man later died from an uncurable illness in which his belly swelled up. They blamed his illness and subsequent death on his greed in making money at the expense of others.

REFERENCES

Appell, G.N. 1985. 'Integration of the periphery to the centre: processes and consequences', in G.N. Appell. (ed.) *Modernization and the Emergence of a Landless Peasantry: Essays on*

Integration of Peripheries to Socioeconomic Centres. Williamsberg: Studies in Third World Societies, publication no. 33.

Barnard, T. 1997. 'Local heroes and national conciousness: the politics of historiography in Riau', *Bijdragen Tot de Taal-, Land- en Volkenkunde* 153: 509–26.

Bender, B. 1993. *Landscape, Politics and Perspectives.* Oxford: Berg.

Boomgaard, P. 1995. 'Sacred trees and haunted forests in Indonesia – particularly Java, Nineteenth and Twentieth centuries' in O. Bruun and A. Kalland (eds) *Asian Perceptions of Nature: A Critical Approach.* London: Curzon Press.

Chappell, D.A. 1995. 'Active agents versus passive victims: decolonised historiography or problematic paradigm?', *Contemporary Pacific* 17: 303–26.

Colchester, M. 1986. 'Unity and diversity: indonesian policy towards tribal people', *The Ecologist* 16(23): 89–98.

Dove, M. 1985. 'The agroecological mythology of the Javanese and the political economy of Indonesia', *Indonesia* 39–40: 1–36.

Effendy, T. 1997. 'Petalangan society and changes in Riau', *Bijdragen Tot de Taal-, Land-en Volkenkunde* 153: 630–47.

Errington, S. 1987. 'Incestous twins and the house societies of insular south-east Asia', *Cultural Anthropology* 1(2): 403–44.

Fox, J.J. (ed.) 1997. *The Poetic Power of Place: Comparative Perspectives on Austronesian Ideas of Locality.* Canberra: Australian National University.

Haverfield, R. 1999. 'Hak ulayat and the state: land reform in Indonesia', in T. Lindsey (ed.) *Indonesia, Law and Society.* Sydney: The Federation Press.

Hirsch, P. and O'Hanlon, M. (eds) 1995 *The Anthropology of Landscape: Perspectives on Place and Space.* Oxford: Oxford University Press.

Hock Tong, C. 1998. 'The sinicization of Malay keramats in Malaysia', *Journal of the Malayan Branch Royal Asiatic Society*, vol. 71, part 2, 1998.

Kopytoff, I. 1990. 'The cultural biography of things: commoditization as process', in A. Appadurai (ed.) *The Social Life of Things: Commodities in Cultural Perspective.* Cambridge: Cambridge University Press.

Lindsey, T. 1999. 'From rule of law to law of rulers – to reformation?', in T. Lindsey (ed.) *Indonesia, Law and Society.* Sydney: The Federation Press.

MacAndrews, C. 1986. *Land Policy in Modern Indonesia: A Study of Land Issues in the New Order Period.* Boston: Lincoln Institute of Law Policy.

Persoon, G. 1990. 'Impacts of development: the changing environment of tribal peoples', in A.A. Saleh and D.F. van Giffen (eds) *Socio-Cultural Impacts of Development: Voice From the Field.* Andalas: University Research Center, Padang.

Petras, J. 1997. 'The New Cultural Domination by the Media', in Majid Rahnema and Victoria Bawtree (eds), *The Post-Development Reader.* London: Zed.

Said, E.W. 1983. *The World, the Text, and the Critic.* Cambridge, MA: Harvard University Press.

Schama, S. 1995. *Landscape and Memory.* New York: A.A. Knopf.

Skeat, W.W. 1965. *Malay Magic: An Introduction to the Folklore and Popular Religion of the Malay Peninsular.* London: Frank Cass & Co. (Orig. 1900.)

Turner, A. 1997. 'Cultural survival, identity and the performing arts of Kampar's Suku Petalangan', *Bijdragen Tot de Taal-, Land- en Volkenkunde* 153: 640–71.

Tilley, C. 1994. *A Phenomenology of Landscape: Places Paths and Monuments.* Oxford: Berg.

Winstedt, R.O. 1924. 'Karamat: sacred places and persons in Malaya', *Journal of the Malayan Branch Royal Asiatic Society* 11.

Wong, D.S.Y. 1975. *Tenure and Land Dealings in the Malay States.* Singapore: Singapore University Press.

10   BOUNDING THE UNBOUNDED: ANCESTRAL LAND AND JURAL RELATIONS IN THE INTERIOR OF EASTERN FIJI

Allen Abramson

What happens to Austronesian land which, inhabited by the ancestors and embodied by their descendants, is bureaucratically subsumed as property? In contrast to ancestral land, propertied land is surveyed, mapped and registered and set up for sale and purchase. The question is: can the bounded ancestors be properly delineated and commoditised. Or, do these same ancestors defy jural laws of property and economic laws of value?

This chapter pursues the theme of the persistence of the ancestors in the former British colony of Fiji. Fiji is a territory where overall stability depends upon the political harmonisation of ethnic relations and where communal harmony between Fiji Indians and ethnic Fijians is almost entirely a function of the political state of land relations. In this context, in spite of the official dominance of a jural definition of traditional land relations, most ethnic Fijians still orient themselves to land in terms of ancestral roots and presences rather than in terms of ownership and capital. Consequently, too, most ethnic Fijians are unwilling to relinquish ancestral land to the market. Ethnic Fijians, moreover, see the preservation of their ancestral land relation as *the* defining feature of their latter-day ethnicity and as a guarantee of their ethnic political strength in capitalist Fiji. In the meantime, many Fiji Indians are denied access to agricultural land. Others fear that leases close to expiry will not be renewed.

The contradiction between the jural status and economic potential of ethnic Fijian land on the one hand, and the continuing cultural grip of the ancestors on the other, lies at the root of most inter-ethnic problems in Fiji today. This chapter probes the juxtaposition of invented property forms and embedded ancestral relations, and does so in the hope that some small measure of anthropological analysis might further the possibility of a harmonisation of land interests in modern Fiji.

The local ethnography referred to in this chapter relates to the ethnic Fijian chiefdom of Serea which is located in the interior of Viti Levu island. This chiefdom is populated by a group of different clans who often collectively refer to themselves as Waimaro people. I have lived and kept contact with the Waimaro people at Serea since the end of the 1970s. Waimaro people have long accepted the official legal subdivision of their territory. However, at the same time, their landscape is also replete with the tracks, traces and sites of ancestral activity, all of which have a strong bearing upon local patterns of land possession and belonging. In effect, Sereans in Waimaro district divide up their land on the basis of law but also on the basis of these primordial points and lines. Given this duality, my aim in this chapter is to show how the advent of land law and the crystallisation of local jural models squeeze and constrict, but do not refuse, the actualisation of the ancestors in contemporary patterns of possession and belonging. So that, rather than contribute to the disenchantment of this landscape by infusing it with jural culture, land law nationally and legal models locally are obliged to operate on enchanted lands.

THE VIOLATIONS OF LAND LAW

The Genesis of Colonial Land Policy

Faced, in the 1870s, with local rebellions caused by the sale of their subjects' lands to white settlers; and facing, anyway, defeat by Tongan armies in the east of the archipelago, the highest chiefs of eastern Fiji pleaded with the new British authority to annex the Fiji Isles, safeguard Fijian lands and, consequently, save their chiefly careers (Derrick 1950; France 1969). Confronted by unwanted armed conflict between British white settlers and ethnic Fijians, and facing the threat of a strategically damaging Tongan–French alliance in Western Polynesia, the British Crown acceded to Fijian requests in 1874. A council of paramount chiefs – a little Oceanic House of Lords, in effect – was quickly established to help transpose native custom and tradition into colonial law.

In the 1870s, the first of several Land Commissions was set up in the colony and commanded to identify the principles of Fijian social organisation and land tenure. Several Commissions later, these principles were established in law. In particular, an entity known as the *mataqali* was recognised as the universal unit of landownership in native Fiji. Conceptualised along evolutionary lines (Fison 1881), the *mataqali* was described as a generic patriclan: viz. as a village-based agnatic group whose members traced descent back through fathers to a single male ancestor. Though the term *mataqali* was not indigenously used in all parts of Fiji, the Executive Council of the colony decreed that equivalent groups did exist everywhere. In essence, it proclaimed that the *mataqali* existed right across Fiji.

By 1914, the *mataqali* in each village chiefdom of Fiji had been identified and registered. Land boundaries were ascertained and codified and land was formally allocated. On the basis of this registration, land considered to have been unfairly or mistakenly alienated to white settlers was returned; whilst, in the other direction, 'vacant land', not claimed by any extant *mataqali*, was appropriated by the British Crown. Crown land was in part set aside for leasing to white settlers but mainly retained as the land-base for the country's expansive sugar industry. At the same time, tempted by the promise of eventual freeholds of their own, landless labourers from India were recruited to work for this industry under initial conditions of indenture. Today, following the abolition of indenture, a small percentage of the Fijian Indian rural population farm on freehold land gifted by the Crown. However, the majority are only able to lease ethnic Fijian land under the paternalistic auspices of the Native Land Trust Board.

Discrepancies

Contrary to the expectations of prevailing ethnological orthodoxy at that time, Fijian informants themselves experienced great difficulty in communicating to Europeans all of what they genuinely wanted to say about land relations. In fact, virtually all historical studies show (especially France 1969; Clammer 1973) that the emergence of the *mataqali* as a specifically legal fact proved enormously problematic. Frequently, the elders were either unable to name their *mataqali* or any equivalent patrilineal group. When asked to outline the boundaries of their land, informants proved to be inexact and, amongst themselves, contradictory.

Consequently, one Land Commission after the other failed to deliver the *mataqali* as the sole unit of Fijian landownership because, even appropriately prompted by anthropological advocates, Fijian elders could not unequivocally make the same identification themselves. Contemporary records report that 'the people are absolutely incapable of classifying themselves without assistance' (Maxwell cited in Clammer 1973: 203). In point of fact, these testimonies also indicated that, for the most part, people were unable to classify themselves *even with assistance*!

In general terms, the problem was that Fijians always seemed to be saying something worryingly surplus to theoretical requirements. Administrators were always left with a disturbing residue of inexplicable testimony that could not be easily mopped up by the powerful discourse on patriliny, patriclans and landed property. Since the procession of Land Commissions each came up with a different system of native land tenure, this surplus testimony had to be politically buried; otherwise, it was clear that Fijian land law would not be workably codified. In 1879, therefore, the Governor of the colony, Sir Arthur Gordon, overruled the Commissioners and bullied the Great Council of Chiefs into unanimously agreeing that 'that all land was vested in the *mataqali* alone ...' (Clammer 1973: 218). At which point, *at the legal level*, the discrepancies were effectively buried alive.

The Efficacy of Invented Tradition

Evidence of this legal burial is found everywhere in the field. In fact, whenever I inquired about land matters, Serean informants would mechanically reel off the official list of their *mataqali*. Queried on inconsistencies between the official account of social organisation given by this catechism and the different model offered me as I enquired about myth, ritual and other understandings of social organisation, I would be testily told: 'So, if you don't believe us, why don't you look at the lists and land maps in the Suva offices of the Native Land Trust Board?' (which, in fact, no ethnographer can do because these files are too secret and sensitive).

Because it has always been a pertinent misrepresentation of local structures, rhetorical compliance with the official model of traditional organisation has always bred a tactical (rather than a principled) relation to land law. Clammer notes that there always had been amongst Fijians some sort of 'willingness ... to present to the Land Commission a neat and tailor-made version of their land tenure system in accord with the preconceptions and desires of the commissioners' (1973: 217). The same is true today when the ethnographer puts the question. In this respect, rural Fijians mirror the invented imagery of their rulers, wilfully contributing to a semi-intelligible dialogue that takes place in the no-man's-land between two cultures and languages. Moreover, right from the beginning, it seems, village elders toyed with their colonial masters, apparently playing the legal imperative as a game in order to preserve as much of their land as possible. Thus, one contemporary commentator reported how, in preparation for the visits of the Land Commissioners, clansmen in some villages instituted rapid planting manoeuvres, extending the area of their land under cultivation in order to prove 'ownership' (Thomson 1908). Today, the persistence of this jural model is critical in determining the practical essence of modern Fijian citizenship. Thus, from a legal standpoint, being ethnically Fijian, and being able to vote nationally on the ethnic Fijian register, means having a name entered into Nai Volavola Kawa (the book of patrilineal ancestries). This can only happen on the strength of a father's registration to an officially named *mataqali*, which means him legally owning a share in the latter's land.

This latter-day political imperative anchors the official *mataqali* model within the doctrinal superstructures of contemporary Fijian society so firmly that, over the years, the model has crystallised into a categorical tradition. Today, reflexively, *mataqali* land orthodoxy is recounted as 'the Fijian way' (*nai sala vakaviti*), 'the way of the chiefs' (*vakaturaga*) or 'the way of the land' (*vakavanua*). In his essay in *Anthropology and the Colonial Encounter*, John Clammer (1973) notes that some anthropologists (Geddes 1959, in particular) have been taken in by this neo-traditionalisation of the jural invention, characteristically overlooking its colonial origins. What many Fijians genuinely intellectualise as quintessential Fijianness is, in historical fact, a mix of ancient custom and colonial invention (Thomas 1991, 1992).

Crucially, Clammer's radicalism indicts the colonial model not for inventing a new form and displacing what was authentic but for iconoclastically replacing a plethora of local systems with a single jural account.

POINTS OF IDENTITY, RITES OF BELONGING: THE ELEMENTS OF
MYTHICAL LAND IN EASTERN FIJI

Land and Identity

Clammer's radicalism is typical of the first attempts to truly historicise social anthropology. Wanting to undermine the essentialism of primitivist discourse, Clammer placed the transformations of colonial hegemony at the heart of his analysis and so deduced the, more or less, wholesale emascula-tion of local Fijian social organisation and land tenure. This position can now be seen to have overestimated the power of the colonial centre and to have correspondingly underplayed the durability of local processes.

In particular, it is not at all obvious that the laws and categories which make up the jural model of tradition in Fiji are so culturally pervasive. Throughout the archipelago, underlying trajectories of ritual practice survive to shape meaningfully a wholly different type of land relation: one that is decisively not one of property. Indeed, Fijians say that they are *taukei na qele* ('together with cultivatable soil') or *taukei ni vanua* ('together with ancestral land') rather than owners of it. In ritual practice, and when kinsmen find themselves without land, Fijians do not relate to land as though it were a propertied object. Thus, whereas property thinking hails subjects who manage the destiny of their land, Fijians express land-relatedness in terms of their submission to ancestors and ancestral histories. In effect, Fijians *belong* to their land (*vanua*) rather than it to them (de Coppet 1985). People are one of land's attributes. This means that, no matter how Fijians relate to their land in the jural terms of property, Fijians firstly relate to their land by a singularly mythical mode of belonging (Leenhardt 1949/1979). Controlling and intimate, this prior mode of belonging determines the forms in which Fijians can also legally own their land.

From personal experience, and with intimate knowledge of the Waimaro peoples assembled on the banks of the Wainimala river, an emminent Fijian social anthropologist, notes of *vanua*:

The *Vanua* ... is an extension of the concept of the individual self, the group self ... To the people of Nakorosule the idea of parting with one's *Vanua* is tantamount to parting with one's life ... The *Vanua* is also the *tamata* (people) or *lewe ni vanua* (flesh of the land or contents of the land) ... The people are the human or social identities of the land ... A land without people is likened to a person without a *yalo* (soul). *The people are the souls of the physical environment.* (Ravuvu 1988: 6–7, my emphasis)

This discourse indicates how ancestral land is felt to be the *fleshy body* of the people, whilst people themselves are portrayed as vital *souls* of the land. The interdependence hinted at recalls Lévy-Bruhl's notion of *participation* (Lévy-Bruhl 1910/1985). Another Fijian scholar writes:

the Fijian's relation to land ... is the nexus of Fijian society. He confers an emotional attachment to the land not for its economic value, but as an inheritance from his ancestors to be handed down for his future descendants. Land is therefore not a 'commodity' to be alienated but something to be possessed for safe-keeping. (Suguta 1986: 186)

Consequently, Aloesi Suguta opines, 'in the Fijian world view there is no such thing as "ownership" in the western sense, only possession' (Suguta 1986: 186).

These telling contributions by Fijian intellectuals might well be read as neo-traditionalist twists to the official ethnic tale. However, romanticisations though they undoubtedly are, these intellectual reflections on ancestral land also resonate with underlying layers of mythical narrative and ritual practice. Aggregate Fijian land relations are anchored to important ritual tranformations of person as well as being anchored in different cultural directions to an expressive politics of ethnic identity. It is these ritual cycles – described below for the Viti Levu chiefdom of Serea – which contain and constrain the unfolding of land as legal property.

The Patriclans of Serea and their Mythical Land Relations

Like all Fijian *koro* or village-chiefdoms, the *koro* Serea is a bounded settlement, surrounded on one side by plantations and, all around, by forest. Over the last 30 years, the lower slopes of the forest have been cleared for dairy farming (Abramson 1999) and small farms, leased by clans to clansmen, have become loosely enclosed. The chiefdom is usually represented by its inhabitants as a unique convergence of named patrilineal groups upon a site previously called Soloira. As locally told in their chronicles (*itukutuku)*, the *koro* was formed through the staggered arrival of these ancestral groups. This occurred sometime after the Fijian Fall from Nakauvadra, a fabulous place of origins, located somewhere in the north-east of Viti Levu island. In Serea, for both ceremonial and legal purposes, these patrilineal groups are termed *mataqali*. In contrast to chiefdoms in different parts of Fiji, there is no evidence that these groups were ever known by any other term. Three kinds of chronicles are told by *mataqali* in the village: those of autocthonous patrilines, those of terrestrial immigrants and those of oceanic chiefs.

Land histories of autochthonous patrilines

Two autochthonous patriclans in the chiefdom of Serea claim to have inhabited Soloira since the aftermath of the Fiji fall. Being autochthonous, these patriclans are said to be *itaukei ni koro* at Serea and, as such, they are said 'to go together with the village site' or be its 'possessors'. They are also known as *na imatai*, 'the first ones' at the site and their burial grounds are referred to as *yavu mata*, 'eyes of foundation'.

Land histories of terrestrial migrants

Members of *mataqali* in other chiefdoms in the area say that their ancestors quarrelled at Serea and emigrated from 'eyes of foundation' in other chiefdoms. Similarly, there are within Serea itself four patriclans which glance upstream to foundation mounds where ancestral brothers are said to have quarrelled long ago. Having arrived overland, these immigrant groups are not thought of as being 'foreign' (viz. as *vulagi*). They are called *bati* ('borderers' and 'teeth'), a double play on words signifying the fact that (a) the land of the *bati* clans are further away from the village greens at Serea than those of the other *mataqali*; and that (b) *bati* act as vicious warriors to the chief. *Bati* are like chiefly incisors, rooted to the edge of a chiefdom, ready to snap at invaders who appear at the margins. On the other hand, *bati* always stress their independence, likening themselves to the detachable chiefly tooth (the *tabua*) whose gift from one man to another carries with it the sacred will of the chief.

Land histories of the Serean chiefs

Chiefly *mataqali* also claim descent from ancestors outside Soloira, but they tell of shark-born ancestral migrations from far-away aristocratic lands, across the sea. Members of these patriclans are called *vulagi*. They are 'strangers': literally 'those with origins in the horizon'. At the heart of chiefly ritual, in the symbolically 'high' zones of public space, the chiefs are always spatially associated with the symbolic 'sea' and 'sky' and, in the Church, with the Judaeo-Christian heavens (Sahlins 1983; Toren 1990).

   These chiefly patriclans never freely admit to possessing 'places of issue' in the forest *yavu mata*. In both their own chronicles and in the chronicles of the common/autochthonous 'possessors of the village site', the chiefs are linked to land which was gifted to them on their arrival by the autochthonous population. This gifted land detained the chiefs in the area, embedding their wonderful ritual power – their *mana* – in the midst of the forest people and *bati*. When, today, the descendants of these same chiefs receive ceremonial gifts of baked pig and kava root from other clansmen, the primordial gift of land is repeated and the embeddedness of their *mana* is re-secured. Today, like all land in Serea, chiefly land has been legally transmuted into property. However, this bureaucratic transformation of the underlying mythical relation does not prevent the autochthonous 'possessors of the village site' from saying that the gift of land is reversible, and that the chiefs must remain 'true' (*vakadodonu*) to the people if they are to retain the unrestricted use of this land.

In fact, given all of this, it is vital to note that an important Serean counter-tradition cosmologically places the ancient forebears of the Waikalou chiefs inside the primordial forest rather than at the junction of sky, river and land. In fact, it was elders of the *bati* patriclan, Nadaloi, who after about 18 months of fieldwork, took me to see on their own land what they described as the mounds of installation of the *veli*. The *veli* were described as being the tiny primordial ancestors of the incumbent Waimaro chiefs, their powers being conceptualised as exactly contrary to those of the visible village chiefs. Nadaloi clansmen are termed *nai taukei ni veli* ('those who are together with the *veli*'), and they saw it as their duty (*itavi*) to ensure that I saw three largish rocks, resting on the banks of a small creek, one of which was known as the *veli's* turtle, another of which was called the *veli's* pig, and the other one of which was called the *veli's vale vo*, their latrine! The clansmen who showed me these rocks and mounds saw themselves as guardians of a site whose very location, deep within the primary forest, they knew archaeologically challenged the oceanic provenance of the village chiefs. These mysterious *veli* lands are today legally owned by the Nadaloi clan of *bati*. The chiefs, as it were, have practically nothing to do with these lands nor with the narrative that supports their potential ownership of them. It is clear that the chiefs cannot lay legal claim to these ungifted mythical lands without also completely repudiating the transcendental *mana* which is the charismatic basis of their chieftaincy.

What is clear of these histories and counter-histories is that, in addition to being narrated, they are also significantly inscribed in the land. Consequently, the earthworked lands to which Sereans today belong, invoke histories of being, arrival and ritual juxtaposition which are materially demonstrable through the tangibility of their landscaped effects. Indeed, these inscriptions seem to positively prove the oral histories which lend them meaning. However, as Hocart pointed out over half a century ago, the contrasts told by these histories are familiar to all Fijians because, shorn of their eventful detail, they recur in perhaps every village-chiefdom in Fiji (Hocart 1936, 1952). In fact, to the extent that each clan history is invisibly shaped in order to contrast with others or to mediate just such a contrast, these histories are considerably, if not totally, *mythical*. What does this 'mythical' mean? It means not that these narratives, these *itukutuku*, are completely false in contrast to an outsider's historical truth. Rather, the historical chronicles of the Serean patriclans are mythical because the events they narratively unfold are logically structured by features of opposition, complementarity and mediation, showing that these histories have profounder ritual affinities than discursive aspirations (Eliade 1954; Lévi-Strauss 1962/1989; Sahlins 1985). In a sense these chronicles deliver 'true' histories which make key ritual possible, rather than histories which enunciate 'truth' as a goal.

MYTHICAL HISTORIES AND RITUAL CONNECTIONS: *VANUA* AND
THEIR SACRED CENTRES

Ritually directed, these chronicles underwrite a definite kind of land division
and land association. Thus, *mataqali* lands in Serea cluster about a series of
points in the forest which act as terrestrial bases of the local patriclan
ancestors, the *vu*. These defining sites are earthworked and all but the chiefly
patriclans identify their earthworks as old villages (*koro makawa*). Patriclans
bury their dead in cemeteries situated right alongside or inside the site of
their old villages; so that, for most *mataqali* at Serea, old villages and
cemeteries comprise a single sacred site. However, for reasons just given, the
two chiefly patriclans know their sacred site only as a cemetery.

Insofar as the canopy envelops them, these sacred earthworks tend to
merge into the forest as an overgrown part of it. On the other hand, as living
'proof' that they were separate from the forest 'in the olden days' (*e gauna
makawa*) all of these sites – the chiefly cemetery included – incorporate old
yavu or house-foundations. This is because, as Sereans say, in the old days,
people were buried where they lived: in the foundations of their own houses.
Earthworked sites are also partially separated off from the surrounding
primary growth by stands of coconut-palms which, to Sereans, are always
a sign of deliberate cultivation. In fact, each palm is said to have grown from
a coconut, containing the umbilical cord of every male member of the clan.
In theory, at least, therefore, sacred sites of the forest host and encompass
the arboreal eternity of the individualised living as well as the decaying
bodies of the collective dead.

On the death of a clan member, a cortège of mourners transports the
corpse, wrapped up in barkcloth and pandanus mats, from the clan's big-
house in the new village, up to its cemetery and old village in the forest. In
fact, the making of a path between the big-house of a clan and its old village
re-activates the singular chronicle of the patriline by retracing its mythical
steps in reverse. Crucially, therefore, so long as funerals are witnessed re-
investing in the physical and mythical tangibility of the sacred earthworks,
the myths of the clans are kept alive and the upper forest is itself reproduced
as a forest of collectively identifiable separate parts. In a sense, burial re-
divides the forest. So that, whilst in festive mood, the membership of *mataqali*
look forward to the ceremonial greens to witness the culmination of their
historic convergence in the New Village of Serea, they look back mournfully
towards the Old Village of Soloira, to witness the unending return of separate
beings to a disjointed, fragmentary and essentially savage existence.

The Anatomical Embodiment of Vanua

Spencer (1941) observed that, when asked in English to say where they come
from, Fijians would always respond geographically in terms of the

whereabouts of their father's ancestor (*vu*) and its land. This would be true, and still is true, even if an informant has never resided in his or her ancestor's land. This strong affirmation of ancestral place is reproduced out of material interest and sentiment but also because Fijians sense that they transport their ancestor around with them, and with him, the essence of the *vanua* itself. So that, even abroad or in town, Fijians are always, in a sense, living *chez l'ancestor*! How is this cohabitation possible?

That the ancestor is always close by is evidenced by the heroism accorded to the *vu* in the latter-day war stories which Serean men delight in recounting. Thus, along with other men of the island interior, Sereans fought as jungle scouts in the rainforests of Guadalcanal in the Solomon Islands (during the Second World War), as scouts again in the forests of Malaya (in the anti-communist campaign led by the British in the late 1950s), and most recently as combatant peace-keepers for the United Nations in the Lebanon (Toren 1988). One old man told me that, whilst out tracking in the Malayan jungle for the British Army in the late 1950s, he was shot at, one day, by a sniper and felt that a bullet was about to strike him in the heart. However, at the last moment, he sensed the presence of the *vu* of his patriclan, who deflected the bullet towards his thigh, and he lived to tell the tale.

It might seem fair to surmise that, in such situations, the *vu* functions protectively as a kind of benevolent spirit. However, though Serean clansmen and women do *also* posit the mobility of their *vu* (the usual account being of a bright light, swishing through the air at night), they do not need recourse to this idea to explain ancestral guardianship. This is because, in addition to being rooted to the old village and its cemetery, and as well as being itinerant, the *vu* is corporeally constituted within the descendant's genital. Sereans most clearly articulate this thought in the stylised comedy of the standard joking relationships (especially with cross-cousins).[1]

Moreover, old villages, ancestors and descendants are also thought of as being herbaceously interconnected. As *vu*, the ancestors are thought of as 'origins', 'causes' and 'roots'. And, as *kawa*, descendants are thought of as enduring reproductive shoots or 'fertile stock' (Sahlins 1962). This means that patrilineally assembled descendants incorporate the ancestor as a plant does its roots: which is to say, intimately, organically and lastingly. Serean sorcerers (*dau drau ni kau*) are said to kill by lethally dissolving the organic connection between the roots, shoot and leaves of the clan.

In sum, patrilineal descendants are rooted to their ancestor in the land of the old village, a connection which is reproduced at funerals. However, they are also embodied by the ancestor as the somatic externalisation of his genital being. It is in this way that Fijian clansmen and women both embody and are simultaneously embodied by their ancestral clan land.

Land Alienation and Sickness of the Land

Since Sereans and other Fijians normally take for granted the organic connection between land, ancestor and descendants, the ethnographer learns more about the agnatic core through its pathologies – by being sociologically morbid – than through its ideals and harmonies. In the field, I first encountered land pathology when I shyly announced that my *raison d'être* for learning Serean language and customs was the completion of a doctorate from the University of London. I was surprised to see that several informants already knew what a doctorate from the University of London was. Unfortunately, their cultural construction of a doctorate stemmed from their belief that Russiate Nayacakalou, eminent Fijian ethnographer, student of Sir Raymond Firth and holder of an anthropology doctorate from the University of London, had given Fijian lands away to Fiji Indians whilst he was director of the Native Land Trust Board. Though Nayacakalou died prematurely of natural causes, Sereans say that he died because he helped alienate ethnic Fijian lands, affirming in their own minds, the direct link between the sale of lands, punishment by the *vu* and serious sickness. (And often they gave me the impression that all doctorates, including my own, were somehow bound up with this treachery.)

In his recent book on latter-day Fijian spirit healing, Katz writes of the illnesses suffered by members of four households in the village of Tavu in the easterly Lau Group of islands (Katz 1993: 251). One of the local traditional healers, in fact, diagnosed the problem in terms of the recent arrival of a new cross-island road which ran 'through a sacred area where the *Vu* are said to reside ... We always walk clear of them, staying away. Because the *Vu* live there and we respect the boundaries of their residence' (1993: 251). Villagers, engineers and healer alike made specially directed *yaqona* offerings – termed *nai madrali* – to appease the ancestral *vu*, and all but one of the afflicted recovered. In spite of this ritual offering, several elders were not happy that the road had not been diverted away from the sacred site, predicting rather that the 'sickness of the land' would inevitably return. This case mirrors the many similar cases of develement-related *imadrali* ritual, reported in the newspapers. Toren reports for Gau that, even after *kava* was poured on to ancestral land set aside for a local school, some of the children woke up with devils sitting on their chests 'trying to choke the life out of them' (1995: 166–7).

It is clear that, although for a while the pathologies of land alienation can be assuaged through the *imadrali*, there always remains the sense in Fiji that the ancestral *vu* rail against development much like the elfin *veli* at Serea work from their base in the forest to undermine the public role of the Waimaro chiefs. In this context, it falls to the new healers to put their finger on and invoke the putative land sales and abrogations of traditional alliances which all local developments seem retrospectively to involve. In fact, healers historicise personal illness not because they are political opportunists but because a whole category of illnesses seems necessarily to emerge from the sale of land, the over-long leasing of land, obstruction of access to ancestral land and the skewed distribution of rents. In short, modern land economy in Fiji damages the embodiment of the terrestrial ancestors by their descendants.

Absent Boundaries

Towards the end of the 19th century, chief Ratu Savenica Seniloli, who had been assisting in the attempt to record boundaries in nearby Tailevu province, momentarily resisted the jural terms of the conquering logic, remarking that: 'The recording of *mataqali* boundaries is in accordance with European custom only, and causes trouble and disputes ... it is not correct to write down the *mataqali* boundaries in accordance with European practice' (Macnaught 1974: 144). What of legal boundaries today? How is the separateness of distinctive clan lands *vanua* conceived today?

Most village chiefdoms (*koro*) are established with either a river or the sea on one side, so that sometimes barriers like the Wainimala River at Serea appear to create natural boundaries. For the most part, though, like the outward movement of ripples prompted by the dropping of a stone in still water, patriclan lands are thought of as having centres but no fixed circumference. *Vanua* are mentally mapped as emanations on either side of village-bound ancestral tracks, which are sometimes registered by special rocks or bluffs, or as the receding land, situated on either side of the line taken by the funeral cortège as it moves from the village to the particular clan burial ground. *Mataqali* lands are therefore spatially grasped (i) by way of the sacred earthworks which pinpoint their ancestral centres; and (ii) by centrifugal emanations, which become increasingly diffuse with distance. Except on their watery edges, their boundaries are entirely notional. This means that the topography of a particular *vanua* is unambiguously apprehended at its central site where it is periodically re-embodied in ritual, but only known locally further outwards with reference to the historic Land Commission maps stored in the offices of the Native Land Trust Board in Suva city.

At Serea, since the 1960s, the sharply focused euclidian model has once again been superimposed by developers in their efforts to initiate commercial logging and small-scale dairy farming. However, local models continue to blur the bureaucratic clarity of legally stipulated boundaries. Logging, for example, took place in the upper forest at Serea without enclosure. By contrast, though the lower slopes have been subdivided and enclosed by the clan dairy-men, fences have only crystallised under special *ritual* conditions. Thus, to thwart constant accusations of sorcery, as well to offset the threat of physical violence directed by their own agnates, independent farmers have had to make regular offerings (*leqa*) of cattle to boost the patriclan's regular contribution to village ritual. So much is this the case that the individual ownership of land and stock by farmers is regularly subverted by the material demands and symbolic efficacy of ceremonial distribution (Abramson 1999). As signs of privatisation, fences and boundaries are culturally ambiguous.

Other ethnographers have also alluded to the presence in Melanesia of land with centres but no boundaries. Speaking of 'the doctrine of first emergence', Malinowski wrote that the Trobriand matriclans were 'connected with a definite spot and, through this, with a village community and a territory' (Malinowski quoted in Young 1979: 144). He continued: 'all the descendants in the female line ... have acquired the right of citizenship in the territory surrounding the spot of her emergence' (1979: 145). 'Territory surrounding', 'definite spot', point of 'emergence': these are the parameters of the Trobriand land relation, not boundaries or areas.

The Ritual Totalisation of the Vanua

The temptation is to think that, in Serea and elsewhere in Fiji, *vanua* remain unbounded because those who 'belong with' the land cannot turn their own interiority inside-out to depict it geometrically. This would be to overlook the fact that plantation plots next to the New Village are bounded, and that the village chiefdom and its plantations are strictly marked off from the forest. Ontologically speaking, therefore, Sereans find boundaries perfectly thinkable. Rather, forest 'lands' *(vanua)* are unbounded for a specific reason: namely, that, in Fijian minds, they are regularly transformed in rituals which symbolically fuse forest ancestors, forest 'lands' and their particular clan descendants. Gardens, by contrast, are specifically bounded inside a very different ritual sphere in which primordial autochthony is overturned through the domestic imposition of civilising boundaries.

Thus, at the same time as burial processions up to the old villages reverse the historic convergence of patriclans by re-partitioning the forest, the rump of mourners left inside the New Village urgently drink to the fusion of lands, ancestors and descendants. Under the watchful eye of 'the possessor of the corpse' (*na itaukei ni mate*), and with the chief as their symbolic head (Ravuvu 1987), the male mourners emerge as the unified single 'flesh of the land' (*lewe ni vanua*). In these ubiquitous drinking rites *vanua* is symbolically transformed from a series of disparate bodies and estates into a *lomovata*: a union of all lands and peoples. (Symptomatically, the Serean rugby *union* team, being a body drawn from all patriclans, plays under the name *Lomovata*.) In this context, the ritual jointly transfigures ancestral lands and ancestored persons because the land is embodied. Being embodied, land is not only intensely experienced, it is also readily alterable through the ritual manipulation of bodies.

Consequently, whilst the official model of *mataqali* property registers ancestral land as a geometrically fixed and finite unit, changeable only by legal alterations in ownership, the ritual model of *mataqali* land relations renders ancestral land and belonging groups fluid: to be precise, fluid within mythical limits. On the ritual model, clan *vanua* unify, disaggregate and re-unify in a cyclical manner so culturally lessening the legal authority of boundaries.

RITUAL CENTRES AND INVENTED BOUNDARIES: A TALE OF TWO LANDS

The canopy of jural relations which were thrown over the Fijian landscape by the colonial power, and the network of legal boundaries which remain, have never been entirely realised inside the village-chiefdoms. In these spaces, land law has never really completed its mission. Instead, ritualised land relations continue to dominate culturally. This implies that juridically invented systems of traditional tenure have added to the complexity of pre-jural land relations, not replaced them. Precolonial land relations have been transformed but not reinvented. As a consequence, the efficacy of juridically invented models has been *within* the sphere of ancestral presences and relations. The major impact of land law has been to modulate the tenurial play of the ancestors, and in mainly unintended ways. This section looks at key features of this modulation.

Defensive Boundaries

In precolonial times, sacred earthworks existed for the Serean patriclans purely as points of existential articulation with their ancestor. With the intro-duction of property relations though, these earthworks have *also* become the defining centres of bounded estates. The ancestral *vanua* have been turned into potential economic resources. However, the present or future economi-sation of *vanua* is not the chief factor which underlies local investments in legal boundaries. Rather, boundaries now function primarily to defend the patriline (the *kawa*) from economic excess.

Thus, once upon a time, the fact that *vanua* overlapped on their indefinite margins would have been of little or no consequence. Most resources would have been readily available around residential centres and sacred sites. The limits of politico-ritual fealty would have been defined not by the fixed edges of territory but by both the violent and ritual encompassment of sacred centres of population. In effect, it is only certain economies which encounter land as a scarce resource and only certain cultural systems which protect scarcity with boundaries. Today, given the constant encroachment of development interests, patriclan assemblies know that they can enlist the support of the courts in defending the landed trunk of the patriclan from illegal seizure, providing, that is, they take on board the mutation of the patriclan into a jural corporation and the *vanua* into a legal estate.

The juralisation of mythical land in Fiji is therefore a substantial fact. However, 'on the ground', the legal model has not been adopted with all its cultural trappings. The local bounding of the *vanua* represents a pragmatic response to the categorical imperatives of the legal system rather than any systematic cultural borrowing of jural concepts. Certainly, the local investment of the *vanua* with legal boundaries does not signal any dilution of either the ancestor's potency or of his bodily possession of his land and his descendants' genitals.

Further Effects

Two key features illustrate the actual but weak impact of legal boundaries which are drawn bureaucratically around mythical centres. In the first place, though the *in situ* knowledge of boundaries remains extremely weak locally, the knowledge that there are boundaries remains strong. Sereans, for example, know that cartographic knowledge is stored up for them as a usable resource at the offices of the Native Land Trust Board (NLTB). On the other hand, day-to-day practices in the forest are not dependent upon having this sort of knowledge to hand. In fact, matters affecting the leasing of the land are left to the NLTB, whilst the local sale of the land is never contemplated. In effect, whilst Serean clansfolk live the continuous relation of embodiment and participation directly, they let the bureaucracy properly think the bounded relation of property. Whilst patriclan assemblies manage the ritual centres of *vanua*, the Native Land Trust Board manages their boundaries.

The second feature which reflects the fragile efficacy of boundaries is the skewing of the rent relation, once again administered by the NLTB. Because the ancestral centre of *vanua* can never be developed, and because even peripheral lands cannot be safely sold, the only commercial transfer of *vanua* possible has been its leasing. In fact, no matter how weak the subsequent power of boundaries, without the transformation of *vanua* into legal estates, neither Fiji-Indian nor ethnic Fijian farmers would have been able to take out secure leases. Generalised leasing depends upon the authority of land law.

However, the distribution of rent monies accruing from the transformation of *vanua* into leasehold is symbolically inflected by the logic of ritual, and inflected in a way that declares against the literal meaning of leasehold. This story has colonial beginnings. Thus, when the category of rent was explained to the Council of Chiefs in the early days of the colonial period, rent was mis-recognised by the chiefs as tribute (as *lala*). *Lala* were festive offerings, received by paramount chiefs (*tui*) from conquered villages, subsequently redistributed across a kingdom to connect subject lands and patrilines to the partible sacredness (*sau*) of the paramount's divinity (Mosko 1992). The

Colonial power inscribed this misrecognition in law. Consequently, and since
that time, Fijian rent monies have always been distributed not only to the
owning patriclan as officially designated but also, more widely, to (a) the
officially designated village chief (who sits on his Provincial Council); and
(b) the supposed head of the *yavusa* ('tribe') of which each *mataqali* is officially
said to be a part. Rent, to be precise, is collected by the NLTB and gifted to
the appropriate chiefs on the Provincial Council, for them, subsequently, to
redistribute the monies downwards and outwards, right across their ritual
domains. In sum, rent hatches economically on the basis of clearly
demarcated, separate property relations in land. However, once appended
to the ceremonial flow of feast and other prestige values, rent metamorphoses
symbolically in mid-cycle as a cascading flow of money which retroactively
unifies lands, clans and ancestors.

Under these conditions, informal rent agreements (Ward 1994) also
acquire ritual qualities. Thus, two Serean patriclans had, by the late 1970s,
informally leased a fraction of their land to local Fiji-Indian farmers. Cutting
out the managerial role of the NLTB (in what thus becomes a technically
illegal transaction), these Fiji-Indian farmers pay rent monies exclusively to
the leasing *mataqali*. However, these same farmers also feel obliged to
supplement their rents by making *ex gratia* gifts of sacrificial cows to other
patriclans in the chiefdom. In the process, these farmers acknowledge the
mingling of all Serean patrilines and their ancestors in each particular area
of land. Widening their alliances in the chiefdom by playing the symbolic
tune of the rent relation, these Fiji-Indian farmers make their own tenuous
economic position considerably more secure.

The Frozen Forest: the Unintended Efficacy of Boundaries

The ancestors hold sway over the political economy of forestland and their
descendants have helped turn legal boundaries into defences against
capitalist encroachment. So that, even where legal boundaries make rent
possible, the symbolics of its distribution react negatively on these
boundaries. It may appear consequently that the legal transformation of
mythical *vanua* is historically insignificant. However, in addition to making
legal defences and leasehold possible, the juralisation of *vanua* has had a
critical impact. It has intervened within, and affected, the cultural dynamics
of *mataqali* (patriclan) genesis.

Thus, though they feign to deny it, always stressing instead the eternity of
existing patrilines (*kawa*), Serean patriclans tend to split and divide under
stress. This locally understated process has been well documented ethno-
graphically for other areas of Fiji (Hocart 1952; Nayacakalou 1965).
Typically, lineal segments split off in the aftermath of a leadership contest,
leaving a vapour trail of rancorous dispute in their wake. In these circumstances, new *mataqali* appear, their secessionary elders discovering a new

true *vu* (terrestrial ancestor), a new true totemic species and a new true history of migration. The new *mataqali* post their presence within the village narratives of migration and convergence.

Today, new segments of *mataqali*, riven by discontent, coin distinctive names and begin to discover fragments of divergent histories. However, in spite of the fact that today this oral historical exploration of possibilities persists, the fissionary process has stalled. Even on the back of a newly enunciated history, aspirants to ritual autonomy fail to secure a *bure* (a big-house), fail to force their names into the herald's habitual ceremonial oratory and, crucially, fail to carve out for themselves a separate cemetery and a new land. (And, these groups are perhaps, not unsurprisingly, the most watchful guardians of the ethnographer's work, ensuring that at least in his discourse, if not in the herald's proclamations, their distinctiveness is historically inscribed someplace!)

Indeed, today, it is precisely the completed bifurcation of lands and patriclans which has been blocked by the legal registration of lands. So that, sitting inside old clans, many potentially new clans fail to force the issue in a manner that would, in pre-legal circumstances, have consummated their ritual existence. New fully fledged clanship, properly speaking, has now become wishful thinking because legality has made it impossible to put the finishing touch, as it were, to the discovery of new mythical lands in the forest. This finishing touch is registration. Registration confirms the authenticity of latter-day ancestors and their sacred centres, so that Sereans today do not eschew land bureacracy but use it to fix the existence of clans in the fluid ritual sphere. They deploy legal boundaries to set limits to the discovery of new ancestors and new lands. They appropriate one level of invention to constrain the inventive productivity of another.

In fact, it is the blockage on fission which turns out to be the most momentous implication at the organisational and ritual level of the legal freeze on territories. Before, where a new *vanua* could be carved out on the unbounded margins of other lands, agnatic fractions would break away and establish a newly autonomous clan assembly. Rooted in forest territory, organised for ritual and oratorically acknowledged there, the possessor of new land and new history would become a *real* agent within the chiefdom. Today, though, with nowhere to go, the denial of land-embodied agency has led to the spiralling of jealousy, serious violence and frequent sorcery accusations. In fact, the intensification of economic development in the 1970s, unleashed frightening levels of sorcery. By the end of the 1970s, indeed, the Methodist Church at Serea was working overtime, mobilising God on the front line against sorcery and social division.

CONCLUSION

Fijian land is categorically defined in law as property. However, Fijian land is not property like any other. This is because, as clan *vanua*, Fijian land continues to be ritually re-embodied by its descendants. As a result, *vanua* defines clan land primarily as a seat of being and only secondarily as property and estate. However, ethnic Fijian land *is* also property, so much so that it may be thought that the long-standing jural subsumption of Fijian lands might be a telling indicator of socio-economic incorporation and progress: indeed, that rational-legal culture might have corrosively penetrated downwards into the ritual realm.

The evidence presented shows that this is not so. In the village-chiefdoms of eastern Fiji, mythical narratives set up ritual mediations which, in turn, reincarnate olden times and powers: and it is these cycles which, even transformed, continue to govern local fields of land relations. This grassroots governance is expressed in the fact that jural culture and legal boundaries impact within the transforming sphere of the ancestors but neither on or in its own terms. The principal effects of land law have been relayed to a realm outside of the latters' jurisdiction.

Up to now, this account remains unacceptably one-sided. Any changes in the way mythical lands and legal boundaries are combined in the future will also invariably affect the well-being and security of the Fiji-Indian community. In this context, it is worth noting that the usual stereotypes are frequently trotted out to glibly cast this part of Fiji in the role of Mammon – as if Fiji-Indians see land only as property. This is not so. A Fiji-Indian party to the 1994 review of the Fijian constitution poignantly remarked:

We have been told of the very special – almost spiritual – ties of the Fijian with the land. For the Indo-Fijian, the tie is no less ... The ancestral tradition of the Indo-Fijian, still carried on in the rural areas is to give offerings and say prayers to the mountains, rivers, sky, the flora and the fauna of the village, for their continued supply of sustenance ... A symbiotic relationship of love and balance develops between the Indo-Fijian household and the land. For four generations of Indo-Fijians, that land has now acquired a very special sentimental and religious significance ... It is a myth to think that land is only a source of economic wealth for the Indo-Fijian. It is much more. (Datt 1994)

Quite so. If the political economy of land in modern Fiji is still a political economy of the ancestors – which it is – it is a political economy of *all* of the ancestors, regardless of the latters' ethnicity.

NOTES

1. The connection between plants, animals and genitals is made jokingly as Sereans (and other Fijians) pinch genitals and felicitously invoke ancestral nicknames. Such nicknames are often the *cavuti* (the forbidden plant and animal species of each different clan). Clans are called *mataqali* which is also the term for 'species'. Hence, clans are literally species. They are plant and animal species, connected to male origin ancestors of the land. Clan members are frequently called 'flesh of' their totem as in the cases of 'flesh of the corn' or 'flesh of the *kuka*' (the latter being a type of land-crab). Genitals are normally called by these same plant and animal names ... as they are irritatingly pinched!

REFERENCES

Abramson, A.L. 1999. 'Sacred cows of development', *Oceania* 69(4): 260–81.
Clammer, J. 1973. 'Colonialism and the perception of tradition in Fiji', in T. Asad (ed.) *Anthropology and the Colonial Encounter*. London: Ithaca Press.
de Coppet, D. 1985. '... land owns people', in R.H. Barnes, D. de Coppet and R.J. Parkin (eds) *Contexts and Levels: Anthropological Essays on Hierarchy*. Oxford: JASO.
Datt, K. 1994. 'Indo-Fijian concerns', in *Report on Consultations on Fiji's Constitutional Review*. Suva: International Alert and School of Social and Economic Development, University of Suva Press.
Derrick, R.A. 1950. *A History of Fiji*. Suva: The Government Printer.
Eliade, M. 1954. *The Myth of the Eternal Return, or Cosmos and History*. Princeton, NJ: Princeton University Press.
Fison, L. 1881. 'Land tenure in Fiji', *Journal of the Royal Anthropological Institute* 10: 332–52.
France, P. 1969. *The Charter of the Land*. Melbourne: Oxford University Press.
Geddes, W.H. 1959. 'Fijian social structure in a period of transition', in J.D. Freeman and W.R. Geddes (eds) *Anthropology in the South Pacific*. New Plymouth: Avery.
Hocart, A.M. 1936. *Kings and Councillers: An Essay in the Comparative Anatomy of Human Society*. R. Needham (ed.) Chicago: University of Chicago Press.
—— 1952. *The Northern States of Fiji*. Occasional Papers No. 11, Royal Anthropological Institute of Great Britain and Northern Ireland London: RAI.
Katz, R. 1993. *The Straight Path: A Story of Healing and Transformation in Fiji*. Reading, MA: Addison-Wesley.
Leenhardt, M. 1949/1979. *Do Kamo: Person and Myth in Melanesia*. Chicago: University of Chicago Press.
Lévi-Strauss, C. 1962/1989. *The Savage Mind*. London: Weidenfeld and Nicolson.
Lévy-Bruhl, L. 1985/1910. *How Natives Think*. Princeton, NJ: Princeton University Press.
MacNaught, T.J. 1974. 'Chiefly civil servants? Ambiguity in district administration and preservation of a Fijian way of life, 1896–1940', *Journal of Pacific History* 9: 3–20.
Mosko, M. 1992. 'Motherless sons: "Divine kings" and "partible persons" in Melanesia and Polynesia', *Man* 27: 697–718.
Nayacakalou, R.R. 1965. 'The bifurcation and amalgamation of Fijian lineages over a period of 50 years', *Proceedings of the Fiji Society 1961–2*.
Ravuvu, A.D. 1987. *The Fijian Ethos*. Suva: Institite of Pacific Studies.
—— 1988. *Development or Dependence? The Pattern of Change in a Fijian Village*. Suva: University of the South Pacific Press.
Sahlins, M.D. 1962. *Moala: Culture and Nature on a Fijian Island*. Ann Arbour: University of Michigan Press.
—— 1983. 'Raw women, cooked men and other great things of the Fiji Islands', in P. Brown and D. Tuzin (eds) *The Ethnography of Cannibalism*. Special Publication, The Society for Psychological Anthropology, Washington, DC.
—— 1985. *Islands of History*. Chicago: University of Chicago Press.
Spencer, D. 1941. *Disease, Religion and Society in the Fiji Islands*. Monographs of the American Ethnological Society No. 2. Seattle: University of Washington Press.
Suguta, A. 1986. 'The dilemma of tradition', in C. Griffin and M. Monsell-Davis (eds) *Fijians in Town*. Suva: Institute of Pacific Studies, USP.
Thomas, N. 1991. *Entangled Objects: Exchange, Material Culture, and Colonialism in the Pacific* Cambridge, MA: Harvard University Press.
—— 1992. 'Substantivisation and anthropological discourse: the transformation of practices into institutions in neotraditional Pacific societies', in J.G Carrier (ed.) *History and Tradition in Melanesian Anthropology*. Berkeley: University of California Press.
Thomson, B. 1908. *The Fijians: A Study in the Decay of Custom*. London: Macmillan.

Toren, C. 1988. 'Making the present, revealing the past: the mutability and continuity of tradition as process', *Man* 23(4): 696–717.

—— 1990. *Making Sense of Hierarchy: Cognition as Social Process in Fiji*. London: Athlone Press.

—— 1995. 'Seeing the ancestral sites: transformations in Fijian notions of land', in E. Hirsch and M. O'Hanlon (eds) *The Anthropology of Landscape*. Oxford: Clarendon Press.

Ward, R.G. 1994. 'Fijian villages: a questionable future?', in R. Crocombe and M. Meleisea (eds) *Land Issues in the Pacific*. Suva Macmillan Brown Centre for Pacific Studies, University of Canterbury and Institute of Pacific Studies.

Young, M. (ed.) 1979. *The Ethnography of Malinowski: The Trobriand Islands 1915–1918*. London: Routledge & Kegan Paul.

NOTES ON CONTRIBUTORS

Allen Abramson is a senior lecturer in Social Anthropology at University College London. He has carried out field research in the interior of eastern Fiji, focusing primarily upon the dialectics of gender, sexuality and the ritual context of land. He is currently carrying out field research in the UK into dangerous games and modern epic. He has also taught in the Universities of the South Pacific (Fiji), Glasgow and Edinburgh.

Jean Besson is a Senior Lecturer in Anthropology at Goldsmiths College, University of London. She studied Social Anthropology at Edinburgh University, and also taught at the Universities of Edinburgh and Aberdeen and the Johns Hopkins University. She has carried out fieldwork in Jamaica and the eastern Caribbean, and has published widely on Caribbean peasantries.

Philip Burnham is a professor in Social Anthropology at University College London. He has carried out field research in Cameroon, the Central African Republic and Trinidad. His research interests include the social ecology of shifting cultivators and pastoralists, inter-ethnic relations, cultural and institutional factors affecting development, and the interrelationship of education and social change. He has also taught in France and Nigeria.

Paul Durman is a postgraduate researcher in the Philosophy Department at Hull University. His research, 'Senses of Belonging and the Poverty of Ownership' – is concerned with the relationship(s) people have with the land as material (land, soil, property) and as an entity (Land, Nature, etc.). The principal sources are John Lock, Martin Heidegger and contemporary environmental thought.

Kusum Gopal is currently a senior research fellow at the Gender Institute, LSE. She has done three years gender-sensitive fieldwork in rural north India focusing primarily upon the dialectics of social justice and political protest with reference to land rights as well as connections between the environment, cosmological beliefs and ritual relationships to the land. Currently she is also carrying out research in India by looking at how public welfare categories are socially constructed, and, how gender roles and relationships define the politics of sexuality and reproduction.

Nathan Porath has conducted field research in South Thailand and East Sumatra, Indonesia on indigenous peoples. He is at present completing his PhD on the art of Sakai Shamanism at Leiden Univerity, the Netherlands.

Louise Perrotta undertook fieldwork in Russia in 1992–3 and completed her PhD on social aspects of political and economic change in the former Soviet Union at LSE in 1995. She has since worked as an independent consultant to the major international aid agencies, advising on the social, legal and political aspects of land reform and rural enterprise restructuring in Ukraine, Russia, Kazakhstan and Uzbekistan.

Veronica Strang is a Senior Lecturer at the University of Wales Lampeter and Director of the Centre for Australian Studies in Wales. Her book *Uncommon Ground: Concepts of Landscape and Human–Environmental Relations in Far North Queensland* was published by Berg in 1997. She also conducts research on environmental issues in the UK.

Dimitrios Theodossopoulos is a lecturer in the Anthropology Department at University of Wales Lampeter. In the early 1990s he carried out fieldwork on environmental politics and the indigenous perceptions of the environment in rural Greece. His more recent research and writing embrace diverse themes, such as gender and sexuality, the human–environmental relationship and the ethnography of Lower Central America.

INDEX

Compiled by Sue Carlton